RORY MACLEAN trained as a screenwriter. But during the premiere of his first feature film his mother fell asleep and his girlfriend ran off with the financier. Not surprisingly, he took a holiday. He returned with his future wife and *Stalin's Nose*, winner of the *Yorkshire Post* Best First Book Award. Among his other prizes is the *Independent* Travel Writing Award.

By the same author

STALIN'S NOSE

RORY MACLEAN

THE OATMEAL ARK

FROM THE WESTERN ISLES TO A PROMISED SEA

HarperCollins*Publishers*

HarperCollins*Publishers*
77–85 Fulham Palace Road,
Hammersmith, London W6 8JB

Published by HarperCollins*Publishers* 1997
Copyright © Rory MacLean 1997

Rory MacLean asserts the moral right to be
identified as the author of this work

A catalogue record for this book is
available from the British Library

ISBN 0 00 255216 7

Set in Monotype Bembo and Scotch Roman by
Rowland Phototypesetting Ltd,
Bury St Edmunds, Suffolk.

Printed and bound in Great Britain by
Caledonian International Book Manufacturing Ltd, Glasgow

to A & J

CONTENTS

CUILIDH MHOIRE

— ◆ —

Treasury of Mary

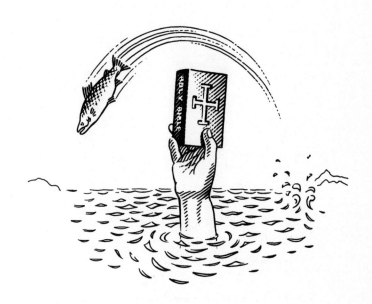

CHAPTER I

—◆—

UNDER GOD'S KILT

E MET, MY great-grandson and I, more than a century after my death. That is to say I met him; he would not have noticed me had I flapped my wings, danced a reel on his nose and blown Gabriel's trumpet in his ear. His ferry had been delayed by the storm and in his haste to get ashore he did not see me waiting on the pier nor did he recognise me in the Co-op where he bought a bottle of Old Mull to settle his stomach. The crossing from the mainland had been choppy and his face was as pale as a flounder's belly. He hadn't inherited his father's sea-legs, right enough, but the high forehead, grey-green eyes and gestures which rolled from his hands like waves up a beach confirmed that he was kin. There and then I, Hector Gillean, first son and last pastor of the parish of Gualachaolish, thought it would be fine to give him a name. So I called him *Beagan*, which properly means 'a small quantity' in the English, for the paltry boy had lost his moorings and been shipwrecked by death and life.

'WHERE THE HELL can I hire a God–damned cab?' raged Beagan, swaying in the pub doorway. 'Or better still a lifeboat?' A gust of wind howled in behind him and lifted the froth from the top of a dozen pints. Fergus Macaulay downed his dram before the glass was blown off the bar. Billy Munro the landlord blinked at

3

the stranger from under the hood of his anorak. 'Jesus, if I was any wetter I'd take root on this doorstep.'

Archie the Taxi lurched out into the gale, leaving a drink half-finished and a story part-told, while Isaac MacLeod, the harbour master, put on his cap to help carry the antique box trunk off the ship. The rusty Austin Marina sunk on her springs as they heaved it into the boot. Beagan dropped his second-hand copy of *Gaelic Made Easy* into a puddle, swore and kicked the car. Its wing mirror fell off and splashed into the slipway.

'These islands!' Archie enthused with a wave which embraced every kyle and cove. 'It's myself that is as fond of them as a mother of her baby-child.' Sheets of rain swept across russet and honey-coloured hills. Musselshell peaks vanished behind rolling banks of sodden cloud. 'But you'll not have come for the weather, you'll be here looking for your forefathers.'

'I've come to live at the old manse,' blustered Beagan. The twisting Hebridean seas had tied his insides into a double half-hitch knot. 'Unless I drown trying to reach it.' Visitors were a common sight on the island in high summer but come December they were as rare as the winter herring.

'My people went to Toronto,' Archie volunteered. Like everyone else in the bar, he had placed Beagan's accent. 'Maybe you'll be knowing them?'

'Sorry, no joy,' Beagan replied, feeling like hell. 'I grew up on the west coast near Vancouver.'

'Now that's a fine land, all right,' fancied Archie. 'Aye, a man can make good there.'

'Canada killed my father,' snapped Beagan and grimaced, remembering the child's nightmare of his fall, the clutched wounded heart, the brittle knees cracking on a hardwood floor. 'That's why I'm here.'

The taxi swayed into a passing place and gave way to an impatient red Post Office Land-Rover. John the Post was in a temper. He was late for supper and a gust of wind had blown half his letters out into the loch. Beyond the slapping windscreen wipers stood the ruined gables and walls of a dead village. Beagan knew that generations of islanders had left these waters for the backwoods of Ontario, the plantations of Jamaica and the sheep stations of Queensland. He knew too of their descendants returning on pilgrimages to buy tartan in gift shops and climb the earthworks to touch the castle walls. Clansmen from Kentucky were videoed in ancestral graveyards wearing baseball caps which read 'Genealogy is my line'. Whisky-soaked Australians sang 'The Bonnie Banks o' Loch Lomon'' at the Puffer Aground Inn. New Zealanders pinned their family tree to kilts at clan gatherings. To him the tribal tourists seemed ripe for ridicule, their twangs sounding discordant in the deserted hills. He understood that the local residents tolerated them, stuck on the single-track roads behind dawdling rental cars, slipping the dollars into their spurious sporrans, for they themselves were for the most part incomers. Even Archie had moved over from Kintyre. It was the tragedy of the islands; the place was no longer peopled by islanders. Beagan realised that the visitors came in search of a civilisation that had fought for its life and lost.

'Mark you, lad,' said Archie, glancing at the trunk in his rear-view mirror, 'not many bring as much luggage.'

'Those are the family papers,' explained Beagan. 'My inheritance,' he added with a bitter laugh. 'I come from a long line of hoarders. My forebears were too thrifty to throw anything away. Letters, diaries, old ferry tickets, notated napkins, anything of any importance they just dumped in the trunk.' Travel weariness and an aching head had eroded his reserve. 'They haven't been touched since my old man died,' he confided. 'See, he asked our housekeeper, sort of my surrogate grandmother, to give them to me on my twenty-first birthday, but she confused the dates and waited twenty-one years.' Beagan gulped angry breaths of the soft, wet air. 'So when the manse came up for rent at the same time I figured that it was here that the papers were to be read. Finally. This is where it began.'

'You'll be a Gillean, then,' guessed Archie.

His insight surprised Beagan. 'It was my great-grandfather who moved off the island.'

'Hunted off, more likely,' he flashed. History had honed a sharp edge to his tongue.

'I don't know much yet,' confessed Beagan, 'other than his name. The Reverend Hector Gillean. He was minister here about two hundred years ago. My father used to tell me and my brother stories about him, and this place.'

Beagan recalled his father, too big a man to balance on the edge of a child's cot, settling into the willow armchair in the Canadian house. Its weaving had creaked under his weight. Every night beneath pioneer woodcuts and nautical prints his stories had carried the two boys out over dusky waters to sail beside the gaff-rigged smack that had borne Hector out to the New World, away from his beloved Hebrides. The words had warmed them like the Gulf Stream and steered them towards a fine Peterborough lapstrake canoe from which had hailed their long-dead grand-father, the soft-hearted Jamie Gillean. His rag-taggle fleet of coal-burning tugs, leaky scows and puffing paddle-wheelers had once been the largest freshwater flotilla in North America. Their bossy great-uncle Zachary had waved from the first-class salon of the old Royal Mail Ship *Kipper*, tapped his fob-watch then tucked a galley proof of each of his thirty-seven trade newspapers under his arm. At a hundred bedtimes the tales had drawn the boys over black lagoons in a Ditchburn launch counting stars. Their father had switched off the lamp and in the half-light the engraving of the *Good Intent*, the etched palace steamers and water-coloured *canots du nord* had all seemed to break free of their aquatint moorings and sail out of their frames.

'I need to piece it all together,' bristled Beagan. Archie's driving and the winding road had conspired to turn him a bilious green. 'But hey, would you stop the car?' he added. 'I think I'm going to be sick.'

Along the shore the yews bowed to leeward, bruised by the winter wind, and a trawler took refuge in the bay. The taxi stopped and the sound of water was everywhere; beating on the heath, dripping off the gorse and streaming towards the sea which sur-rounded the headland on three sides. 'Mind your step there lad,' advised Archie. 'This place is like chicken wire laid over water. It's a wonder the whole island doesn't sink away.' Beagan stepped from the taxi and sank up to his knees in the wet bog.

'**F**ÀILTE!' I HAILED in welcome but he didn't glance up as I opened the door for him. '*Ceud mìle fàilte!*' I repeated but I should have saved my breath to cool my porridge. The boy didn't hear me. After such a wait he could have acknowledged my existence. His behaviour was not only a disappointment, it was discourteous, even in a melancholic man.

The manse felt colder than a forgotten cairn. Its thick stone walls were so damp that the death-watch beetles too had emigrated. The pages of *Oat Cuisine: Cooking in Scotland*, discarded by the summer's last tenant, had curled up on the stone floor like a *mille-feuille* scone. I considered leaving Beagan alone to fester in his rude discontent, respect for his elders appearing to be another virtue which he sadly lacked, but then he dragged the trunk in from the wet, slipped down on to his knees, turned the old key in the rusting lock and released the brass catches. When he pushed back its lid the spirits of the past darted out into the room like fish cut free from a net.

Other families might possess a patch of land, an old house or burial plot but Beagan's heirloom consisted of tracts of my hand-written sermons and caches of Gaelic verse, crudely printed Canadian news pages and packets of his father's lacquer recording disks. It was the trunk full of words that linked him back to a place where he, as one of us, belonged.

In a corner of the trunk under a bundle of ships' logbooks lay a battered leather box. Beagan opened it and eased out the old terrestrial globe. Its painted panels had faded with age. The Indian Ocean, once turquoise, was now a stained verdigris colour. Imperial Russia was dented and torn from Saint Petersburg to Tilsit. Great yellowed swathes of Cathay had rusted away altogether. At the time when my globe was made California's Pacific coast was not yet settled. Livingstone was still to map the African interior. The Arctic regions and much of North America, as yet uncrossed by a white man, were represented as an unbroken land mass and marked 'Unexplored Countries'. The world was portrayed not as it really was but as men then saw it, a place of promised lands awaiting discovery.

Beagan set the globe on the desk from which almost two centuries before I had removed it. He poured an immoderate whisky, raised his glass and addressed the building which he had never before seen. 'Home,' he fumed. 'God-damned home.' The anger startled me and, as I began to sense the measure of his distress, it took me back to my own aimless days.

I belong to the Hebrides, the sweep of islands formed when the Cailleach Bheur, the benevolent giantess of Celtic mythology, let stones fall from the creel carried on her back while wading off the Highlands' western shore. It is a place more of water than land, of wild seas and calm bays, amber burns and white desert sands which surface at the ebb-tide; islands among islands, pools within pools, the indigo skerry at Europe's edge. Ours was a family of mariners; a boatload of sailors and dreamers. The Gilleans had their own ark, or so my father often told me. When the rains came and Noah battened down the hatches against God's flood, the clan crowded into a cockleshell coracle and huddled under a tartan umbrella until the storm had passed. They were used to inclement weather. They were Scots. After forty damp days and nights their leather boat came to rest not on the mountains of Ararat, where the torrents had been stopped,

but on a soggy bed of peatmoss beside a silver Caledonian
firth. Our forefathers sent forth a curlew, for they had no
dove, and it returned with a sprig of heather. The men, their
wives, sons and sons' wives took each other in their arms
and rejoiced. They had found our home.

But my great-grandson, who seems not to hear that which
I tell him, was born in a land where everyone came from
somewhere else. Its people had been imported across the
sea on sailing ships and ocean liners. No family had lived
in his New World for more than seven, at most eight, generations, except the Native people who had been written out
of the newcomers' history. No one on his continent could
drink from a river that was part of himself or grasp a handful
of soil and say, 'I am of this earth.' Its settlers had been
washed across the surface of the land only to remain tied
to an old country by blood, keepsakes and dog-eared albums
of faded photographs.

It was I who, with the idealism of the living, had swept
the family from these waters. I had been a man of the
Enlightenment. I had believed that thought could renew
the life of the world and restore its original purity, energy
and justice. Two hundred years ago as an island minister
for a congregation of poor fisherwomen and trawlermen I
had taken ship west. In the loch below this manse I had
boarded my ark. The globe had been tucked under my arm.
My luggage was Testaments, Catechisms and the dream of
creating a nation of devout individuals bonded by a common
idea. The tool with which I hoped to help build this New
Jerusalem was neither the axe, plough nor theodolite; it was
the Word.

My sons, Beagan's grandfather James and great-uncle
Zachary, had inherited the vision. To preach it they had
moved from the Atlantic coast to the heart of the optimistic
young nation and formed the country's first national publisher. For them the Word was print. Print was the medium
of communication and through it they had propagated the

settler's belief in a better life, trusting that it would fuse the new land's disparate peoples into a just society.

Beagan's father Sandy had also grown up looking forward towards one ocean and back across another, washed west by the flow yet drawn east to the stream's source. He had pursued his hopes to the Pacific coast. For him words, precious words, had to edify. Canada would be united by radio waves and reason. Sandy had never waited for the world to improve; instead he had set about trying to change it. Like us all he had put his faith in a dream.

'What delivers a man from poverty of Spirit?' asked Beagan aloud, squinting at my copperplate script. I thought for a moment that he was striking up a conversation. That was fine, right enough. The boy seemed to have turned over a new leaf.

'The Word is revelation of Truth for the Salvation of men, also for the Duty of men,' I answered, settling myself down across the desk from him. 'And do you know what Paul tells us of the treasures of wisdom?'

'In the beginning was the Word, and the Word was with God, and the Word was God,' Beagan answered, incorrectly, then turned the page, and I realised that he was only trying to will the words back to life. 'Christ,' he cursed, staring at a detailed homily I'd written on *John*, 'I'll need a bloody microscope to decipher this writing.'

'Hear me,' I commanded, angered by both his incomprehension and his insolence. 'I'll have no blasphemers in this house.' But the boy heard me not.

Beagan continued his disconcerting habit of reading my sermons aloud as he unpacked the Bibles and albums and sorted ribbon-wrapped love letters from dusty broadcast scripts. 'The zeal for preaching God's sacred Word must not slack or go backward,' he stormed while arranging our books in the shelves, 'otherwise we fall into ignorance and darkness.' There were two complete sets of North Atlantic Admiralty charts, a dozen canoe route-maps and the patent papers for thirteen marine inventions. The die of *Red Herring*'s propeller was unearthed from the trunk and placed in a corner. He stacked glass negatives on the kitchen table and bellowed out a psalm: 'I remember the days of old; I meditate on all thy works; I muse on the work of thy hands.'

I paid him little heed, still smarting from his coarseness, but then, it shames me to admit, he flattered my vanity. The silver daguerreotype which he unwrapped remembered a well-made man of fair complexion and steady green eye, bearded, bald and standing some five foot ten in a long black preacher's coat. Beside my photographic likeness he set a snapshot of his father as a boy on the Muskoka Lakes, spanner in hand and tie stained by *Primary*'s greasy bilges. In the distance James's old steamer *Kipper* puffed and wheezed her way around Wigwassan Point.

Beagan laid out the journals, pamphlets and packs of correspondence tied with frayed twine. There was an unused receipt for an Atlantic crossing and a rough sheet of parchment postmarked Nova Scotia and covered with a stranger's hand. 'Thank God,' the forgotten migrant had written three lifetimes ago, 'I am well pleased for coming to this new country.'

Every day he delved deeper into the trunk, perusing our jottings, wading through my writings, until I had to confess that he did possess one virtue, right enough: a passion for memory. He read with a desperate, instinctual hunger that drew the past inside himself. But no matter how much he studied, my clearly articulated principles of right and wrong did not seem to anchor him. It was as if the years of anger and confusion since his father's death had blown him too far off-course and now only the indulgence in ardent spirits could numb him to their winds.

'We are all partial to a dram, but a little temperance

would do you no harm,' I advised, yet Beagan finished the Glenlivet anyway, spun the globe on its axis and stumbled, his face blazing with liquor, out into the night.

'Where the hell am I?' he shouted into the blackness and heard no response. It would have been more useful for him to have asked *who* he might be. The woven folds of the northern lights rustled above our heads. Shooting stars fell from the heavens. The tartan hem of God's kilt blazed a luminous arc across the sky.

BEAGAN BROKE THE surface with a cry, climbed out of the sea, up on to the rocks and ran. He seemed to be on fire, his skin steamed and vapour trailed in his wake, like some primeval amphibian hell-bent on rushing evolution. The blizzard swirled out of his path and he heaved, as the ocean after a high wind, around the sweep of the wild loch, across the rusty waves of heather, towards the blue mist of distance. An icy squall washed him against the manse, into the bathroom, under the shower of scalding needles. He gasped at the humid air, grasped the showerhead in his hands and wept. In his dreams he had again heard his father's stories, sailed once more down the rivers that flowed and carried him on the current. 'It flows far away into the distance and you can never quite see the end,' he had remembered him tell. Beyond an open window the ocean had sighed with the incoming tide. 'And do you hear the water slapping under the bow?' The bedroom had smelt of pine pitch and brine. 'Do you hear it?' Beagan had shaken himself out of the haunted sleep. The freezing swim had flushed away the night's shadows but it could not still the havoc in his heart, the whirlwind of days that had been scattered by the white wings of death. On the earth outside, beneath the wintry clouds, all that remained to recall his passing was the trail of moss footprints across the dusting of snow.

The evening before I had drifted in to him on the wave

of a dream. I had whispered in his ear but he had awoken with a start and struck out at the darkness crying his father's name in fear. The rest of his night had passed uneasily, every gust of wind and creak of stair worrying him, and I had realised that if he could hear us, how easily his growing curiosity might be frightened from him. It became apparent that I needed to take care, to nurture us in him like the cloudberry in the lee of the croft. I decided then to dress up guidance as fate, coming to him as coincidence and telling our story through his imagination. My sons James and Zachary would help me, in time his father Sandy too, joining us as needed, mapping out his past, his country's pasts, remaking our worlds in him.

So I stayed there by his side through that first year while he pored over the brittle volumes. I guided his hand from Memorandum to Nautical Almanac and when his back was turned, even leafed on to entries of particular interest. I showed him that the trunk itself had been passed down from father to son for three generations. My initials were carved into its lid. The brass corners and fine-tooled lock had been added by Zachary. Jamie had restitched the worn leather handles and Sandy had painted it with a left-over tin of seashell-blue enamel. Beagan saw that each of us had in turn worked both to preserve the trunk and to make it his own. He did not resist my interference, if indeed he sensed it at all, and my presence no longer seemed to frighten him for he took less often to intemperate drink.

IT WAS LATE the following January that Beagan noticed the innocuous brown envelope. It lay sandwiched between a luncheon menu from the SS *Campana* and a swatch of wedding-dress silk. More than twenty-one years before, the letter had been shoved unread into the bulging trunk and forgotten. He opened it and found it to be a bill. This came as a surprise. It stated that the

13

family owed back-taxes on land in British Columbia. His father Sandy had once owned a short stretch of Canadian coastline but it had been sold at a loss soon after his death. No property had been mentioned in the will and the deeds, if any, were lost. But bureaucrats never forget and here, in black and white with a red maple leaf in the corner, was confirmation of ownership of a small island off the Pacific coast.

Beagan made some calls. From the manse beside the Atlantic he spoke to his brother in a television studio overlooking the Pacific. The sailboats, Alex said, were out in Vancouver Harbour. 'A whole island? Hey, that's great. It must be in the bay off the old house somewhere.'

'Can you look into it?' asked Beagan.

'You bet, but it's pretty crazy round here.' Hollow voices and ringing telephones echoed down the line. 'It looks like I got my break with the network.'

'That's good news.'

'So why don't you quit travelling and come check it out yourself?' risked Alex. Once every year he tried to persuade Beagan to join his film production company. 'It's nuts that you don't come home.'

Beagan hadn't been back in almost two decades. The New World was the place where a man's dreams were meant to come true but the betrayal of his father's hopes had led him to see the country as a failed nation. It had made an exile of him, travelling without reflection, living as if in a fog, and he had drifted through a miscellany of jobs, letting the current carry him where it pleased like a sailor adrift without a sail.

'There's a real opportunity here now,' added Alex.

'Give me a break, OK?' Beagan told his brother. 'I have to finish going through the papers first.'

'You going through your savings too?'

'They're almost gone, so thanks for sorting out the manse's rent. But I may have an island in the end.'

'What's in the papers? Anything that could make a movie?'

'You know, it's weird,' Beagan admitted. 'These last months

14

the stories have sort of come alive. With all this reading I don't feel so alone.'

But Alex was distracted by his assistant before Beagan could continue. 'Hey, bro, I've got to go. It's L.A. on the other line.'

'Can you make a few enquiries?'

'No worries,' he said and hung up.

Property in Canada is not sold by name, as Bramble Cottage or the Dunrobin Estate would be, but by number. Newly-weds might set their hearts on picturesque Lot 43 Concession B. A retired couple could pool their lifetimes' savings to buy Island 161A, Township of Georgian Bay.

It was the family lawyer who called Beagan back. There had been a bit of a mix-up, he explained. The problem was with the original transfer document. It seemed that when transcribing the long list of lot and concession numbers his typist, possibly wishing she too was sailing in Vancouver Harbour, had missed one out. A simple mistake, but the lawyers and purchaser had failed to spot it, the transfer had been effected and the sale completed. Until the discovery of the brown envelope no one had known that his father's name had remained on the property rolls attached to the overlooked island. But it had and now it belonged to Beagan, if he cared to settle the matter of two decades' outstanding property tax.

Beagan put down the receiver. On the desk the diaries and half-read letters were piled at wild angles like something washed in by the tide, the jetsam of genealogy. He sensed that his salvation was written between their lines but rather than read the papers he now decided to relive them. He chose to claim his chance inheritance. He would retrace the family's voyage from Scotland, across Canada and through three generations of family history to his promised island. The bulging old trunk would go with him.

The manse was closed, the globe boxed up and the trunk repacked. There was no fatted calf to kill but frozen New Zealand lamb from the Co-op made a rich farewell stew. Archie the Taxi dropped by with a bottle as he had on occasion over the year and, in keeping with tradition, threw the cap into the hearth. It bounced off the Calorgas heater.

'Some days I wouldn't thank you for a dram, but if the crack's good then a bottle won't do,' he confessed, holding his glass of Talisker against the light. 'That trunk of yours looks awful heavy,' he added in jest. 'Are you sure you won't be wanting me to drive you?'

'I'm not travelling by land,' answered Beagan.

'Aye, then it'll be dear to fly with it. There's no way that will fit under an aircraft seat.'

'My father once told me that to understand a country you have to know its waterways,' Beagan said, reaching for the bottle. 'The first fishermen and explorers, map-makers and settlers all travelled to Canada by sea, then went on over it by its lakes and rivers. Did you know that there are more lakes in that country than in the rest of the world put together? Well, that's how I want to cross it, by water, along the channels which connect, communicate and link.'

Archie lowered his glass without draining it, an unusual event in itself. 'I hate to spoil your plans, lad, but you do know that most people go by road nowadays? A Chevrolet's considerably faster than a kayak.'

'I don't know if the water route still exists,' Beagan admitted, 'but I need to try to find out.' He knew that to reach across the country and back into his history, to try to make sense of that which had made him, it was the only way to travel. 'It may sound mad but this feels like the first true decision I've made for a very long time. In any event I've already bought two dozen packs of Kwells seasickness pills.'

'Two dozen packs?' repeated Archie, taking a deep breath and refilling Beagan's glass. 'Well then, that's an investment. So it's ourselves that had better get a move on. You can't go away to the ships until the whisky's finished.'

*   *   *

S SURE AS death Beagan still drinks too much and I would twist his nose were I able. He and that Archie stayed up half the night talking, like two bedevilled soaks, about women and pleasure boats, schooners and malts. It did not please me well.

It was a fine morning with only a wee bit of drizzle and Beagan wore a new shirt as parents of my time would have dressed their children in their first pair of shoes. In his hand he clasped the diary-book which I had held at the same parting all those years ago. I was reluctant to join him on the journey. No one should have to live their life twice. Yet none of us travels alone, there is always an angel by our side, and it seemed only natural that I should be his guardian. In any case the other figments of himself would be with us along the way, right enough, and it was myself who wanted to watch over him at the outset of our second emigration.

My great-grandson and I left the rainy island as black burns drew winter's shroud from the mountain's shoulders. The lonely blue-shadowed hills were wet with tears for absent sons. Above the departing Cal Mac ferry the clouds parted, as they had done when the refugee had been myself, and I half-expected to see my own father at the end of the dabbled beam of sunlight bidding farewell in his soft rhythmic Gaelic.

'Slàn leat, Beagan,' I heard him call. 'Blessings be with you.' And I remembered the hole that my own parting had made in my heart. Then a squall obscured the view and it began to rain so hard that I imagined the mountain to dissolve, the land to break apart and my island to be washed away into the sea.

CHAPTER II

THE GOOD INTENT

I HECTOR GILLEAN, was born the son of a ship-wright, a builder of skiffs and yawls, the maids-of-all-work in the nineteenth century. My mother was a , saillery woman, stitching on her knee the tawny canvas which gave life to her husband's boats. I grew up with the scent of wood and resin, to the laying of keel and sighting of line. At three years old I crawled into the places too small for my father to caulk seams and pick out curly shavings. Aged twelve I built my own *bàta* from off-cuts and flotsam. We called the Atlantic Ocean *Cuilidh Mhoire*, Treasury of Mary, and I rode her swells on shifting decks as if boat and boy and water were one. 'This boat can sail the world,' I imagined and saw myself on the seven seas, steering for Siam and running towards the Carolinas. At night, home from the lobsters in clothes sea-wet, our family ate tatties or kippers cooked in oak ash and listened to tales of Red Rufus of the Minch and the cold green angels that meet drowning fishers who cry, 'I am no more.' My father's story-telling was fine, right enough, and it sustained us when food was scarce but no yarn could ease the hunger that had began to gnaw at our hearts.

My sisters were Una, Meg and Annie, my brothers Iain and Finn. The girls had married crofters and warmed their husbands' hearths in the embrace of the ocean's arms. Una died in childbirth. Meg and Annie raised their bairns, burnt red ware and prickly tang for the kelp trade, grazed their black cattle on the common land until the factor cleared

them out and pulled down their roof and they had to emi-
grate to New South Wales. My father and I stood dumb on
the sands and watched them go, mouths agape like fish fresh
pulled from the loch, little understanding the change being
thrust upon us. Then Finn, a handy seamen, went to sea on
a China-clipper and was never seen again. There had been
no work to keep him at home. Iain, so his story went, fought
at Trafalgar and for his bravery was granted the right to
produce his sword at any time. When the laird's men tried
to evict him he drew his blade and was arrested. The sheriff
demanded an explanation. Iain pulled the King's permission
from his pocket, the sabre from its scabbard and declared,
'If you can no read your head's the first to come off.' I held
fast to his coat-tail as they dragged him to the boat and let
go only when the bailiff bit my fingers.

Scotland in the early nineteenth century was a nation in
ferment. The English sword had butchered the clans and
crushed the Highlanders' spirit. 'I do swear,' my father had
been forced to vow, 'that I shall never use tartan, plaid or
any part of the Highland garb; and if I do so, may I be
cursed, may I never see my wife and children, father, mother
or relations, and lie without Christian burial in a strange
land, far from the graves of my forefathers and my kindred.'
To refuse to submit risked transportation. A thousand years
of tradition were uprooted by Acts of Parliament and the
advance of commerce. The value of an estate was no longer
measured by the number of men that it could raise but by
the profit its land created. Sheep produced more wealth
than crofters so rent was racked from five to twenty pounds
a year and families, unable to pay a figure equivalent to
twice a labourer's annual income, were cast adrift from their
homes.

My heart would sink as one by one the yawls left our bay.
I knew each boat, had helped lay the keels of most, and
held the familiar bows in the water as downcast men spread
their patch of sail above their weeping women. The water

was cold and I wished for shoes. Only one optimistic soul ventured, 'We will be back before the lifting of the peats,' but I knew that none would ever see the island again. Above the broad green landing girls no longer sang on the shielings and bracken crept into the fields. Iron bedheads rusted in a tangle of gorse.

The Reverend Hugh McKay McKenzie, a stickit minister marooned on the island without patron, watched the boats leave too. In the slate-roofed manse he resolved to give me the chance that others had been denied. He drilled my English and favoured me with extra Latin and Greek. From him I learnt that language could structure the wild spirit of man, that discipline was essential to survive in the uncertain world. He turned my love of family into compassion for men, my passion for stories into a respect for the Word.

McKenzie also taught me the use of globes. There may have been no other pair in the Highlands, certainly his were the only ones on the island, and they helped me to see beyond our sad shore.

'West! West!' he enthused curving his hand from Asia, across Europe and over the Atlantic. The elbows of his jacket were worn through and his breath smelt of turnips. 'Listen now, *a bhalaich*.' My boy. 'It was to this fringe that Caesar pushed the Celts, across these waters that Saint Columba brought Christianity, along this route west that Brendan the Navigator sailed his leather boat.' He placed our sorrows in the tide of history. 'And here,' he jabbed a broken fingernail at the sketchy New World shore. Its jagged edge scratched Nova Scotia. 'This is where our people are now going.'

'YOU KNOW,' SHOUTED Beagan across the bustling terminal, 'one in four of the emigrant boats that made this crossing early last century was lost.' A monstrous orange hull rusting into lobster-red stripes loomed above him. 'But I would have felt one hell of a lot safer on one of them than I do right now.'

Davey, the tall and wiry Glaswegian first officer, stopped whistling 'For Those in Peril on the Sea' to sidestep a demonic Valmet mobile crane. 'Did you forget your bathing costume then?' he yelled. It was noisy enough on the Felixstowe pier to wake the dead. 'It's my suggestion that when this oary boat starts to sink, you drink a bottle of voddy and let her go down around you. Bugger the survival suit.'

The *Global Trader* was the world's largest baked-bean can, a floating warehouse that shipped twenty-four thousand tons of white beans across the Atlantic to Heinz every month. On her return journey her two thousand containers held a mixed cargo: twelve thousand litres of vodka, eighteen tons of frogs' legs, Chanel perfume, powdered cyanide and a gross of Range-Rovers. A crewman hung from the raked bow slapping anti-corrosion paint on to the hull.

Beagan paused to get a better grip on his trunk. Lugging the papers halfway around the world could prove inconvenient, though he understood that no ship sets sail without its anchor. Except maybe the *Global Trader*.

'Good thinking to bring along something to read,' bellowed Davey, ''cause there'll be no brilliant conversation onboard unless you can natter in Hindi.' His shout brought to mind the cry of a snared animal. 'Apart from the skipper and me, all the officers are Sri Lankan. The company's not training Western masters any more, and the crew is Indian.'

Midshipman Pereira, the Goan steward, helped lift the box trunk over a guard-rail. His smile was pegged on to his face by a solitary tooth. 'Here very good,' he boasted. 'I work on ships ten years. Brother work on ships. Father work on ships. Grandfather, he shoreside working.'

'Pereira, you're a pure waste of space.' Davey led Beagan around a cairn-like stack of containers. 'We've been through the whole jing-bang of cheap labour: Irish navvies steaming on poteen, Red Chinese jigging about the deck doing T'ai chi to Mao's little book, fairy Filipinos and now the bloody industrious Indians. Off-duty Pereira here knocks his pan making toty wee model ships in bottles. He even sent one to the Queen.'

Davey stopped at the foot of the gangway in the middle of a rail line and stabbed a bony finger at Beagan. 'You'll not be a journalist, will you?' His tortoise-like neck extended up from his shoulders and his head twisted as if on a stalk. 'A bloody journalist cost me my job in the navy.'

'Hey, keep your shirt on.' Beagan glanced up and down the track. 'My great-grandfather emigrated to Canada and I'm trying to retrace his route, that's all.' As they climbed up towards the smell of diesel oil he explained about claiming his inheritance – both Pacific island and family history – but Davey couldn't hear above the scream of the gantry cranes. The trunk banged on every step and Beagan tried to remember where the Kwells were packed.

Passage aboard a container ship along the fixed route between Britain and Montreal was not the voyage of a lifetime. Of the great fleets which had once carried passengers and freight across the North Atlantic only the *Global Trader* remained. Romance for the sea had been displaced by the cynicism of routine. The ship would be back from the New World and her crew drinking in the bar of the Hope and Anchor two weeks from Friday. Its monotonous shuttle reminded Beagan of his own drifting years, the dreary round which had eked out a living but wasted half his days, before he had unlocked the trunk and released the spirits of the past.

The owner's cabin had twin beds and a dayroom with two defunct televisions. The drawers were lined with old Admiralty charts. A tub large enough to double as a lifeboat was moored in the *en suite* bathroom. On top of the mini-bar Pereira had placed a model of a square-rigged Indiaman. 'To remember by,' he suggested with a mixture of embarrassment and pride. Beagan set the old globe beside it.

The thump-thump of darts missing a bull's eye drew Beagan to the officers' mess. The officers sat in a long row, left to right in descending order of rank, slouched over the bar, each nursing a bottle of beer. Jagjit, Vijitha and Lakshman were all bearded with hair meticulously groomed and their skin mahogany beneath short-sleeved white uniform shirts.

'Not much in the way of glittering company, I'm afraid,' apologised the captain by way of introduction. He was a soft-spoken and diligent man from Hornsea.

'If he'd wanted glitter he'd have caught a jumbo jet,' crowed Davey, snapping the top off a Beck's and offering it to Beagan. 'This one's on me.'

'I'd accept it,' advised the captain. 'Davey won't offer again.'

'It's the only entertainment you'll get this side of America.'

Beagan looked around the stale, weary mess and wished that he had a boat of his own. 'I've got a lot of papers to go through.'

'Good, because there's no ballroom onboard so dancing is out too,' continued Davey. 'But there is a video. And the wee fairy lights.'

The bar was framed by a string of flashing decorations and flanked by the only two women on board. To the left hung a portrait of Queen Elizabeth II, to the right an under-clad blonde on a Grolsch calendar. 'My officers like them up year round,' explained the captain. The men barely looked up from their beers. Routine seemed to have so dulled them that Beagan almost ran his hand across their faces to sweep the cobwebs from their eyes. 'Jagjit bought them the same Christmas that the Seaman's Mission gave everyone onboard a Montreal Expos baseball cap.'

'I tell you, mate, life at sea is a barrel of laughs.'

Beyond the slouching Sri Lankans three rectangular portholes hung ninety feet above the cavernous hull into which the containers were being swung. To stow the cargo by hand would have taken six weeks. The Valmets took less than twenty-four hours to unload and refill the ship. The *Global Trader* would cast off before midnight. 'Aren't there any other passengers?' asked Beagan.

The captain gestured out into the hold. 'Your only other company might be our uninvited guests.' Since the collapse of communism a stream of frustrated migrants had poured out of

eastern Europe to the Atlantic coast. 'Romanians have been breaking into the terminal at Antwerp and hiding in any container
marked for Canada. One crossing last year we had eight
stowaways.'

'If this was a Greek ship they'd be fed to the sharks,' said Davey.
'Clever buggers those Greeks.'

'The immigration authorities fine the company $5,000 for every
stowaway found on board,' explained the captain.

'How do you catch them?' asked Beagan.

'We don't. They jump overboard in the Saint Lawrence and
the longshoremen find bedding and charred crates where they lit
fires. It gets a little cool at the bottom of the hold in January.'

'Sometimes we just find their bodies,' reported Davey. 'Bit like
your old emigrant boats, eh mate?'

'There was a lot of death then,' confirmed Beagan as his
thoughts reached back to the Reverend's copperplate diary. 'And
hope.'

'The next line of dreamers off to the promised land,' said the
captain in a droll, solemn way. 'Let us know if you hear any
voices.'

I T IS THE waves which I remember. They dipped and
strained and drove us over a pewter sea. I can still
hear their jagged breakers rip along the hull, see curl-
ing billows froth at their crest, ride the deep furrows
which bore the ferry-boat down between monstrous grey
rollers. Each swell wrenched us off our heading. Any wave
taken at the wrong moment could end our days. Yet I loved
to ride them, to taste the salt spray, to feel the surge and
ebb beneath my feet as the ferrymen pulled their round
bonnets low over their eyes and dug their oars into the wild
waters.

My father had sent me away from Gualachaolish. There
was not the money to feed me, let alone to pay for my

studies. He had locked in the cupboard my Almanac and
copy of Bunyan and I had left to live with a cousin on the
mainland. In the twelve months there I did not read a single
book, not even the Scriptures, and lost all scruples about
Sabbath-breaking. My free hours were squandered on drink
and cards. I had earned my crust and fed my stomach but
starved my soul.

Then one Sunday evening with friends I had fallen into
conversation of religious matters and sins from which I
could not free myself. All of a sudden a terrible fear and
trembling had seized me. I saw that evil had come upon me
disguised as dissolute days. My life had been wasting away,
labour serving no purpose but the spawning of selfish satisfaction. I had to hide myself away, weeping alone and praying. I did not know what had brought on these thoughts.
It may have been conscience or the common strivings of the
spirit or even Satan but whatever the reason my distress
made me see the one field of usefulness which it was in the
providence of God to set before me.

Men since Abraham had left their father's house to live
in foreign lands and spread the Word of God. I had identified with the tradition and followed across the globe's
painted oceans the journeys of missionaries exiled for the
sake of Christ. With McKenzie's introduction I had applied
for a scholarship at Edinburgh University and studied for
the ministry. I had had no wish to be parted from the
beloved people whose society was dear to me but there lay
overseas opportunities that were denied us at home. I had
answered an advertisement for a missionary 'with health
and strength of body, the entire possession of the five senses
and a vigorous exertion of locomotive powers'. My fluency
in both English and the Gaelic had secured an appointment in
the province of British North America. I had been preparing
to leave Scotland when my father's letter arrived begging
me to return home.

The wind tore at our backs and the ferry-boat chased the

whitecaps into our bay. Its oars twisted in the trough of lofty waves and kind hands seized the bow. A shaft of silver light shot through the low leaden clouds and illuminated a great white skeleton lying on the shingle like a beached whale. An ox dragged logs down from the steading. Sawyers cut timber into planks. The whale's bleached ribs were larch moulds. Its spine was an oak keel. The bony frame was the shell of a ship.

'We are going to find our fortune,' laughed gorbellied Little Donald, taking my arm. The smith, a man of ample size and optimism, was unaffected by the stormy air that whipped the island. On a sinking boat he would have looked forward to the swim.

'Aye, and the streets of America are paved with gold.' Duncan, the brogue maker, stood on a stone so as not to muddy his shoes. His sport was baiting Donald's enthusiasms. 'All men wear silver buttons and buckles too.'

'I have heard tell of it.' Duncan's barbs never snared the smith. 'And that there are trees which give both soap and sugar.'

My father lay down his adze and shook my hand. 'We have been told to leave, Hector,' he said with a dull gesture along the beach.

'In the name of Providence, not all of you?'

'Aye, one and all right enough.' His eyes had the shade of the grave. 'It is for this that we are building the *Good Intent*.' I looked across to the boat.

'Come warm yourself and we will read you the letter.'

The last of my people, hardly twenty souls, left their labours and followed Donald's stout piggin-jar girth up the path. Smoke rose from but half the black houses and rotting barley thatch lay where it had been scattered by the gale. The laird's sheep grazed on the common ground.

'The factor came ashore this last month and gave us summons to quit,' Duncan explained, treading on the dry heather verge. His fine footwear contrasted with a lean face, dried and cracked like a shrivelled old boot. 'He even denied us the right to fish after Easter Eve.'

'As if any landlord owns the sea,' said my father.

'A cur every inch of him.'

'He is a man who levies tribute on the fish landed.' Ewan Cameron was snouted like a dogfish with pointed nose and a swirling determination to swim free of any net. 'And he cares not a straw for ourselves.'

There had been no burning roofs or dousing of hearths on the island. Bedridden grandmothers had not been thrown out into the rain as they had in Sutherland and on Skye. Estate officers had not hooked up potatoes or dammed mill streams as on Lewis. The crofters had simply been told to go. 'The land is not yours,' the factor had said. It mattered not that their families had lived in the place for a dozen generations. The laird had offered the islanders a stark choice: settle in a remote glen on a bare neck of turf or be transported to the New World.

'That *croit* will not even grow bracken,' snorted Cameron.

'Then your father told him, "We have need of neither charity nor another man's ship, Mr Munro."' Donald recounted the incident with pardonable pride. My father did not lift his head. '"The Gilleans have always had a boat of their own."'

The factor had laughed and turned away but the laird, when he learnt of the plan, had given leave to fell timber in his hills. It was his ox which dragged the logs down to the shore.

'I am certain that he wants to support the wisdom of our decision.' Donald's frank, generous nature had a fine simplicity.

'Or save the cost of our passage,' suggested Duncan.

Inside, the croft was dusky and smoke-dried. The women, hair plaited under white mutches, sheltered children out of the rain. A hook hung from the middle beam with a pot pendent over a grateless fire. Cameron's eldest, the spinster

Kirstie, poured hot water on a handful of oats to make me a brose. She apologised for the lack of butter but it mattered not. I ate with a keen appetite, hunger being the better sauce.

The men gathered around the kettle, sat on stools and waited for the creased letter from a cousin in Nova Scotia to be reopened.

'He writes that there is good land nearby him.' Jewels of raindrops glistened in Donald's eyebrows. He read aloud, 'Thank God I am well pleased for coming to this new country as I find myself quite easy, having occupied land called my own free from all burdens whatsoever. I go out and in my house at my pleasure, no soul living forces me to do a turn against my will, no laird, no factor, nor any toilsome work but I do myself.' Every man and woman present knew the words by heart. The letter had been read a dozen times that month. 'Each man and wife who settles here is granted 150 acres at a cost of one shilling sterling per acre.'

'One hundred and fifty acres.' Duncan stooped to flick a spot of dirt from his shoe buckle. 'See that now, in America we will all be lairds.' An industrious cobbler could make four hundred pairs of shoes in a year. He hadn't sold fifty in the last eighteen months.

'Wait you now, it is certain that the voyage will be hazardous and the life not easy,' I ventured. 'The land must be cleared and I believe the winters are hard.'

'But no winter can be colder than one in a land with tacksmen.' Donald made much of his little knowledge of the New World. His uncle had served with the 78th Highlanders under Wolfe at the capture of Quebec. 'We are sailing ourselves to the Nova Scotia, Hector.'

'God willing, liberty and posterity will reward honest industry.'

'Aye, and it is you that we want to join us.'

The spontaneous agreement of the others embarrassed me. Only my father remained silent.

'It's myself that is for it,' stated Cameron. 'As long as the people are driven from their homes there will be none to buy my fish. I cannot even feed my own.' His daughters no longer followed the herring with their father but were bound instead to work as fisher girls on the mainland.

'I know it as a fact that the waters there are so full of fish that a man might catch one in his hand,' enthused Donald. 'A woman too, sure enough,' he added for Kirstie's sake.

I made my excuses and told them about my appointment. My passage had been arranged and I was to sail from the Clyde at the end of the month. There was urgent work that needed to be done in my new parish.

'But our destinations are not a day's fair wind apart,' rushed Donald. 'I have seen it on McKenzie's globe. Your Cape Breton Island lies hard by Nova Scotia.'

I tried to interrupt but Cameron began to speak. 'Hector, we are too few in number. The ship is wanting of men.'

'We need both a navigator and a pastor,' insisted Donald.

I flushed under their gaze. Even Kirstie met my eyes. 'Guide the *Good Intent* to the New Scotland,' said her father.

As winter turned to spring the ship took shape on the shore. We took from the hills the last tall trees with few branches, for branches mean knots in the wood, and cut them into boards. The men fitted the strakes fore and aft, working from one side of the hull to the other, and ran the line of planking along her length. Grown oak frames were sawn to shape then set into ribs. Extra strength was built into the bow and the hull shaped before laying in the deck. As we were so few there was to be but one cabin below with partitions of canvas dividing bachelor from spinster, family from family. Rough boards would serve as bunks. I did my share of carpentry, setting the garboard strake, hollowing out the rabbet and bending over the wooden plane until it seemed to take on the shape of the timber. My father over-saw the building, the laying of keel and sighting of line, but the eviction had changed him. There were no longer stories on his lips.

In measured steps the children, thin and querulous as hungry birds, moved among us trying to calculate the boat's length from rudder to high curved stem. Amidships they quibbled, lost count and returned to the stern to start again.

'Sixty-two *slat*,' shouted the youngest, his corduroy knickerbockers unfastened at the knee.

'Sixty-two feet,' said Neill Ruadh, who had paid more attention to lessons. Each child ran his hands down the hull, touching the boat as if in blessing, and spoke of it as if about part of Creation.

I made it my duty to instruct them and after they had collected crabs and gulls' eggs from the crag we sat together to read. The curious ones wondered about the journey and Donald would desert his forge to excite them with stories of wild Indians and coconut palms, blue-feathered jays and white polar bears. After our lessons they caulked the seams with thin cedar wedges or clenched the copper nails in the cramped hold, all that is but Neill Ruadh who could never bear to be inside a closed space. In a locked room he would plead for the door to be opened.

The mast that we chose stood on the headland. It was an old Scots pine, not too tall but one which had grown in the wind and storms and so had tension in its wood. We shaved the bark and squared the trunk, then planed its sides to eighths, to sixteenths, to thirty-seconds until the edges curved into an even shaft. The men wedged it up, eased the supports and launched the modest trading smack, a boat far smaller than other emigrant ships, but one made for our people by our own hands.

Sail canvas was stitched across a dozen knees, hemp ropes were spun and oats baked into thin, hard cakes. There was

herring to clean, a little salt beef to lay in and whisky
enough stowed. The scars on Kirstie Cameron's fingers
recalled the tired slip of gutting-knives. Her slow chanting
song set the rhythm for the other women milling grain in
the quern, turning the upper whinstone with a stick. As
she sang I wrote to my sponsor to make my excuses. Any
disappointment that the Edinburgh Ladies' Society had felt
over my delay in taking up the post was offset by their joy
in having more funds to buy Bibles.

We took the Books every morning and nightfall and I led
the people in worship. Heads were bowed and hearts raised.
We prayed for God to guide us over the ocean, for Jesus to
be beside us at the helm, for the Spirit to be with us in
every weather and current, each lying down, each rising up,
in the trough of the waves, on the crest of the billows, on
every step of the journey that we were about to undertake.

On a cold spring morning in my thirtieth year I stood on
the wet shingle hearing the cries of children and the screams
of birds. Gannets plunged into the water like white hands
around the rowing boats which ferried the islanders, their
sacks and kists out to the ship. Under my arm I cradled a
new diary-book, its crisp pages unmarked by a single pen-
stroke, and the terrestrial globe. In the manse the evening
before I had sat for the last time beside the Reverend
McKenzie. He had decided to remain behind with those few
who had chosen not to join the ship. When I had stood to
leave him he had given me the globe and the Improved
Metallic Memorandum 'found to be of great advantage to
Travellers and all persons who wish to preserve their
Writing'.

'I won't be coming with you either, Hector,' my father
said. He held the oars of my own *bàta* and had neither sack
nor kist.

'But there is no life for you here.' I imagined him sitting
by the peat fire in a turf bothy with only a scattering of
hens and a handkerchief of land. His adze and chisel would

rust, his muscles weaken and his eyes grow dim. There would be no sweet flummery of oatmeal. His lot would be the winding-sheet.

'This is my father's island.' His knuckles swelled like great barnacles as he held the oars. 'These waters are part of me, it's their voice which calls to me.' I would have gladly remained for one hundred years if I could have helped save him but he said, 'The voice which you hear calls you away. We have no choice in this matter.' The shingle crunched as we pushed away from shore.

The *Good Intent* had a fine heart in her. Her lines were pleasing and she had a lively keel. The tide was with us and the ship seemed anxious to be underway. Ewan Cameron, who had been elected to take her helm, was in high feather. As the wind freshened he gave the word and we pulled up the anchor, forged by Little Donald from Duncan's metal bedframe, and settled the throat of the mainsail to ease her helm. Our ark shuddered for a moment then lay over and dipped in salute to the sea, rose up and gathered her way. All those around me lay down on the deck and wept knowing that they would never again see their kindred. Their wails swelled my cowardice and I sank to my knees to pray for His guidance and protection 'that Thou wouldst keep my feet from sliding and my eyes from tears and prevent me being a spot on Thy cause'. It was a parting unlike any that we had ever experienced, the start of a journey from which there would be no return in this life, and every one of our number, some fifteen exiles, waved and cried as the familiar isle slipped away to stern.

'*Slàn leat*,' I heard my father call in his soft rhythmic Gaelic. 'Blessings be with you.'

The ship glided on the silver wings of its wake, swept forward by wind and will, barely touching the water, the

nearest thing to dreams that hands had ever made. I stood
on the bow and flew from trough to crest like a figurehead
gone prematurely bald, cloak blown back, arms outstretched, reaching, rising, falling, twisting, wallowing west.
There had never been a more promising prospect; astern lay
the sins of man, forward soared his hopes.

In the first fair days no one stayed long below deck. A
man named Rankin put on the forbidden kilt as soon as we
were out of sight of land. He had brought the pipes too and
let their music carry out over the sea, which attracted the
attention of a pod of bottle-nosed whales. Donald carried a
bag of oats, his pillow at sea and seed for his plot, and
entertained us with his fanciful stories.

From the first afternoon each child stared forward hoping
to be the first to catch sight of Novia Scotia. 'You can be
sure that we will arrive on a sunny day,' argued Neill Ruadh,
holding court at the bow. The boy never went down into
the hold and even took to sleeping on deck. 'For Little
Donald tells me that it is a land of perpetual daylight.'

Each morning I sat with them in the sun beneath the
headsail and tried to answer their questions.

'Ah well, *a bhalaich*, this is the way of it,' I explained and
we traced our route on the familiar face of the globe, across
the curve of ocean, from old home to New World and tried
to link past and present with stories. 'We will not be the
first to pass this way.'

In the old days, I told them, sometime after Moses had
led the Israelites out of slavery to search for honeyed
Canaan, our islands had been the repository of Christian
learning on the edge of medieval Europe. In the monastery
libraries the monks had read Virgil and Solinus. Celtic
missionaries, who from Ptolemy had understood the world
to be round like a well-formed apple, had come to see it as
their duty to spread their knowledge. They had been borne
out in small boats alone on the sea, trusting in God to carry
them to lands where they could best serve Him.

'But listen now,' I told the children. 'The greatest of these men was Brendan of Clonfert, the navigator saint.' Early in the sixth century God sighed and His breath had blown a currach of oak, ash and leather far into the North Atlantic towards the summer solstice. 'Aboard it were Brendan and his fourteen sailor-monks searching for the Promised Land of the Saints. They visited the Island of Sheep, saw Judas Iscariot cast upon a barren rock and alighted in a paradise where the birds sang Latin hymns and chanted verses at vespers. It is even said that a Gaelic-speaking whale allowed the monks to land on his back to say Mass.'

'But how did they know the route?' asked one child.

'Angels lit candles in the windows of heaven to guide their way,' answered Neill Ruadh. 'Just as they do for us.' He had seen me take our bearings from the stars at night.

'For seven years the exiles suffered great deprivation and maelstroms but they placed their faith in God and survived to penetrate a mighty bank of fog and reach their promised destination. They found the New World, and mark you this, it was four hundred years before the Vikings and almost a thousand years before Columbus.'

The children were quiet. 'And will it take the *Good Intent* seven years to reach the promised land, Mr Gillean?'

'No, Neill Ruadh.' His young friends laughed in relief. 'It will take us four weeks only.' The ship sheered the kind waters in a hissing sound. 'Or maybe three if the wind is good to us.'

'CAN YOU IMAGINE having the faith to cross it alone?' asked Beagan, following the *Global Trader*'s plot across the chart, over the bow, towards his great-grandfather's horizon. He felt the weight of Hector's Memorandum in his jacket pocket. 'You've got radar and gyrocompasses and GPS which can fix our position to within fifty metres but still I'm filled with doubt. Where the hell are we?'

Davey paced back and forth, his trainers squeaking on the rubber flooring of the long, light, glass bridge that swept across the ship's beam. 'This is our certainty,' he said patting the Decca Navigator. 'Sod the rest.' On its screen there were no other vessels, neither brigantines nor oil tankers, only the first growlers and icebergs away to the north-west. No calls crackled from the radio.

'We won't see land for a few days,' the captain volunteered, offering Beagan a mug of stewed tea. 'And if we do we're in trouble.'

The ocean had spread her skirt of seas and the steel ship which at anchor had seemed like a beer-bellied leviathan had shrunk to the size of Pereira's dainty model. Her bulk, so ungainly in port, had found lost grace out on the cold grey waters. Beagan had filled the first morning poring over the contents of the trunk and strolling around the deck, his ear cocked for the cry of a freezing emigrant. Instead of Romanian voices however it was odd snatches of Gaelic which he had heard whispering in the wind. He worried that he had taken too many Kwells.

'I read somewhere that the sea is no friend of man, only an accomplice in his restlessness,' said Beagan, scalding his mouth on the hot tea.

'No one leaves their wife, their children, their home if they don't feel a need,' the captain explained. He had been a sailor all his life. Both his father and grandfather had run away to sea. His family had pleaded with him to become a railway engineer or an airline pilot but it wasn't in the blood. He had joined the merchant marine and earned his Master's Certificate steering ships through the Malacca Straits, around the Cape and for almost three decades across the North Atlantic. 'Things at sea are understood,' he added.

'It's a job, that's what understood,' retorted Davey, lowering the binoculars. 'The romance went out with the ark.'

The *Global Trader* had a reputation for serving the best curries on the North Atlantic. Chief Cook Fernandes was a Catholic from Goa. His assistant, the *bandari*, was Hindu. Colonial history and Empire echoed through their menus: Scotch broth, Bombay curry, China chow chow, Irish stew, roast chicken, cold cuts. Other traditions lingered. Sri Lankan and British officers dined at separate tables. The Indian crew ate on a different deck.

In the galley Davey dished out two double servings of prawn vindaloo and handed the larger one to Beagan. 'I could snaffle this to a band playing.' Jagjit and Lakshman ate in silence at the far end of the airless room. 'Three or four poppadoms?' he asked.

'Better make it three,' hazarded Beagan. 'I'm taking it easy because of the swells.'

'You should eat now before it gets really rough,' Davey advised. 'Later you'll only throw it up.' He lead the way to their table. The linen was stained dapple-grey. The tarnished cutlery had seen service on an Empress liner.

Beagan was reluctant to eat. The motion had unsettled him. 'I suppose it's better than auk.'

'Auk tandoori? Can't say I've tried it.' Davey crumbled the poppadoms over his plate and reached for a tray of condiments.

'In the sixteenth century Spanish whalers came this way to hunt humpbacks and belugas. Their crews lived off freshly slaughtered auk.'

'Have a word with the cook. I don't know how the Hindus will take it, but I'm game to try anything once.'

'The auk is extinct.'

'Then they must have been dead tasty. Mango chutney?'

Beagan dabbed a spoonful beside the ocean of vindaloo. 'I read too that Basque and Breton caravels sailed this route to fish for cod on the Grand Banks.' He picked at a prawn then lay down his fork. 'It's said that the fish were so thick they'd flick the water white like a shower of hailstones. Did you know that European armies lived off salt cod for centuries? The poor too. And every year those whalers shipped home twenty thousand barrels of oil to light the lamps of Europe.'

'You've got a head for facts,' said Davey. His eyes narrowed in suspicion. 'You sure you're no journalist?'

Beagan shook his head. 'It's just history; you know, learning from past mistakes. My mistakes, maybe my family's too. It's why I'm going back to Canada,' he added with a spark of nervous animation. 'The boats that crossed the Atlantic, for example. Do you know what those people all shared? The search for something better.'

'Not on this boat, mate.' Davey poured half a tub of yoghurt on to his plate. 'This is where you end up when you can't get nothing better.'

Beagan swallowed his excitement with a mouthful of curry. 'Did you end up here because of what happened in the navy?'

Davey's expression darkened. 'I told you that we'd get on just fine if you didn't ask questions.'

'Hey, I'm not prying,' Beagan said.

'Just shut it.' Davey ate on in silence. Jagjit and Lakshman finished their meals and discreetly left the galley. Beagan slipped a book from his pocket. The ship had begun to roll. He watched the water rock and shiver in his glass and started to feel queasy. He had decided that it would be best to lie down in his cabin when Davey put down his fork and said, 'I'm telling you this for free.'

Beagan had only little trust in himself but there could be no doubting the effect which he had begun to have on others. His nature seemed now to put people at ease and they confided in him. But as his stomach performed a double somersault he wished for better timing, or a Kwell.

'I joined the navy right out of school, practically before I could tie my own shoelaces.' Davey used a chapati to clean the sauce off his plate. 'I worked my way up above decks and was promoted to officer. I was not too far off having my own command when this mate of mine . . .' He paused to find the right word. 'Let's just say something happened to him.' A jab of the chapati stifled Beagan's question. 'Something bad, all right? Call it a tradition; a little bit of history. Well, the press got hold of it and this journalist came down to Portsmouth, told me that the public had a right to know and convinced me to patter. He said it was my responsibility. The story made headlines. They sold a bundle of newspapers. My mate was pardoned.' He wiped his mouth with the threadbare napkin and dropped it on the plate. 'But me? I got booted off the bloody bridge and out of the service. The journalist misquoted me you see, which was nothing for him, but the navy wouldn't have me. Nobody would have me. It condemned me to a life sentence on this rusty old tug. So don't talk to me about betterment. If you ask me history is best forgot.'

Beagan's glass slid across the table. Davey caught it with a practised hand. 'I'd suggest you get yourself around that curry. Didn't the captain tell you we're heading into bad weather?'

The swells, churned turquoise by the ship's passing, surged deeper, longer, stronger. In mid-Atlantic the wind lifted plumes of spray over the deck that dashed the windows and bent the bulkheads. The *Global Trader* pitched into furrows, bucked through fifteen-metre swells and plunged into the eye of a winter gale. Beagan sat out the storm astern in the accommodation block, watching the reflection of the waves flash across his cabin ceiling, clutching the diary to his churning stomach. The trunk had been lashed to his bedstead. Hector's globe spun on its axis with every roll of the ship.

After Saint Brendan, the Vikings, the Basques and Bretons, explorers and traders had followed along the North Atlantic route, sailing west to reach the east, looking for lands of cinnamon and cloves, greedy for the riches of the Indies. Their charts recorded mountains of gold and fantasy islands named Antiglia and *isola de braçill*. They had mistaken Greenland for Asia and quartz for diamonds. The miserable emigrant hulks that came after them, crammed with the victims of both promise and pogrom, also failed to find that for which they searched.

It wasn't difficult for Beagan to conjure up their memory, to spot a currach or windjammer riding a distant swell. He squinted at the far white horses and fancied catching a glimpse of the *Good Intent*'s sail. Beyond sight of land and without points of reference all sense of time and place was lost. Each day was an echo of the one that preceded it. Admiralty charts showed banks, basins and trenches, a whole world below the surface, but no rock or island above it. The only measure of human scale was provided by the plot. Decca waves and SatNav had replaced the sextant, bearings were now taken from satellites not stars, but the thread of their sightings remained all that strung man across the vastness of the sea. So it was with history, the plot of every individual life marking a moment in time as a navigator's bearings set a position on the globe. Beagan traced the ship's route in the same way that he followed the family's track, each point indicating a course across the ocean, looking at the path of those who had gone before in the faith that it would guide his way.

The *Global Trader* surged over the Celtic Deep, crossed the Porcupine Sea-Bight and rounded King Arthur Canyon as ten thousand vessels had before her. She shuddered in the cross-current. Rollers whipped her amidships. A freak wave, which might have lost her the deck and swept the containers overboard, lunged out of the ferment and crashed astern. Beagan held open the account of Reverend Hector's voyage and read aloud.

'Without,' his great-grandfather had written three lifetimes earlier at about these bearings, 'the expanse of water and sky is our only prospect, unvaried by any object save the distant outline of some vessel at the verge of the horizon, a speck in the immensity of space. Within, as the weather turns against us, an evil wind stirs below decks. We grow sulky and even savage in our privations.'

As the ship rolled in the rude waste of sea Beagan took another Kwell and thought of Davey pacing back and forth in his tiny cabin, caged like an animal, locked in his anger, accepting poor fortune and not acting to change it.

'Last evening three men, armed with sticks and foaming at the mouth, rushed up the hatchway and without a note of warning attacked a group cooking at the sandbox. By chance Ewan Cameron and Little Donald were on deck. They laid about them lustily with their fists and speedily drove the poor souls back down below.'

He imagined the captain watching astern wearing dark glasses and an air of lonely detachment. His vista was empty but for the curl of the exhaust trail.

'As the storms delay our progress the stores become depleted. The prospect of hunger threatens and we are as helpless as infants under suffering. Hope flies beyond the far horizon like the speck of those distant vessels.'

T HE SNARED SHROUD unwound fast and the corpse, instead of falling, shot forward into the sea and spun across the swells like a dolphin racing the ship. It skimmed the black waters, dawdled beneath the waves then dived into the deep, the stiff and naked young flesh luminous on its journey from the seen to the unseen world. The mother, with the spume of her child's departure slapped across her raw cheeks, wailed all the louder and tore at my boots. Rankin, the unfortunate piper and poxy himself, was at pains not to swallow his chanter.

'Be to me as a star, be to me as a helm, from my lying down in peace to my rising anew.' Most days, between the tears of the congregation and the rain from heaven, the communion cup was never empty. But that day the cup froze over and the service did not proceed as planned. Little Donald, more for propriety than charity for the bereaved, broke free the frozen end of the winding-sheet from under my foot.

I closed the Book as the assembly swelled about the woman, drowned her solitary sorrow in shared tears and washed her out of the cold in the embrace of a dozen arms. A week before Neill Ruadh had been to all appearances strong and healthy. Now by a stroke of God's justice he was forever released from the fear of confinement.

'Thirty days out of Scotland our frail cargo of hopes and fears lies dying,' I recorded in my diary-book that bitter night. 'The sweet breezes of spring have chilled into wild gusts of winter and stolen the prosperous voyage. The mainsail has been reefed and lashed down and the ship makes no progress against the violent westerlies. Cholera rages among the emigrants and the *Good Intent* has become a floating charnel-house. Our mean rations are all but exhausted and weevils have spoilt the bread.'

The rasp of a raw cough disturbed my writing. I could see little by the dim green flicker of the fish-oil lamp but it sounded like Duncan the cobbler. The air below deck reeked of pitch and urine and I prayed for dawn. Until his fit passed the minutes hung upon me. Then Neill Ruadh's mother cried out in her sleep. I picked up my pen. It had clogged again.

'Yet even worse than the paucity of food is the lack of fresh water. The great Atlantic Ocean, which swirls to the horizon in every direction, holds not one glass to slake a man's thirst. The liquid carried aboard has turned putrid and is palatable only with drops of vinegar. Many refuse to drink it and instead lay canvas sheets on the deck in the hope of catching rain. One family has even turned to whisky. Father and son, mother and daughter mix it into porridge and swill it down after their last husks of oatcake. They laugh and rage, cry and sleep dreaming of the crystal clear stream that will run through their Grant only to awake with throats more parched and burning than ever.'

BEAGAN STARED AND strained but he could not make out the next sentence. The Reverend's pen had started to run dry, scratched a snail's trail across the parchment, then released a blob of viscous ink which had spoiled half a paragraph. It was the inkblot as much as the words which helped Beagan picture his great-grandfather wrapped under a fold of sail in a cold corner of the hold, the diary on his knee, his forefinger stained black. He imagined that it was past midnight. The day of Neill Ruadh's burial had exhausted him. Hector had buoyed the emigrants with his spirit and then in the dark solitude of the night had prayed for strength, attempted to sleep, and when it had not come begun to write with great care on the clean white paper. 'Justice,' he had noted, 'is in all things rigid, inflexible and beyond human comprehension but if for offences committed against God it would better have been me, not the child, whose life . . .' Then there was the blot. The sudden spill from his poor, faulty pen almost made Beagan weep. Hector had bought it at considerable expense not six months before in Edinburgh.

Beagan shivered, even with his thermostat turned to its highest setting, and knew it was improbable that he would die aboard the *Global Trader*, except possibly of gluttony. He was warm and well-fed where his great-grandfather had suffered starvation in a frozen, stinking hold. Yet in the journal there was no word of complaint, no doubt of his duty to keep hope afloat. It made Beagan feel as if his own time had been lived as an observer and not a participant in life. As he rubbed a smudge from its cover he saw himself adrift on the vast and furious ocean, unable to communicate beyond the wave-tossed baked-bean boat, seeking to convey the treasures of his heart yet unable to find the words to express them.

A voice had called out and Hector had laid down his diary, leaving an inky fingerprint on its cover, crossed the heaving cabin and found another young soul dead. A handful of soil clawed from the graveside of his kindred was locked in the stiffened little fist. The hull had groaned in the angry billows of the raging sea. Out on deck the rigging had sung and Ewan Cameron feared that another gust might snap the mast. Beagan read the dull, tired pen-strokes which had concluded the night's entry. 'God in His wisdom has taken three from us this week, called to His side to do higher service. The track of our ship is strewn with dead and the living spend the days watching a shark follow in our wake with great constancy. The gales murder curiosity and the questions of the bairns come no longer. The globe remains in its box.'

THE WEATHER WAS no better by dawn nor by the next. In the creak of the wooden ship women wailed. The men sat on coils of hemp and sang. The tin cup had made its rounds, the grog done its office. Little Donald had told a tale, another story of kind fortune and Indian warriors, and Duncan, who was in his cups, coughed and hawked as he polished the precious shoe buckles that he kept secured in a small cotton sack. Rankin the piper, the most taciturn of them, had let the drink go to his head and song carry him beyond the evil-smelling hold.

Gu ma slan do na fearaibh
Chaidh thairis an cuan.
Gu talamh a' gheallaidh
Far nach fairich iad fuachd;
Gu ma slan do na fearaibh
Chaidh thairis an cuan.

Here's good health to the heroes
Who sail o'er the sea.
To the land of promise
Where they'll not feel the cold.
Here's good health to the heroes
Who sail o'er the sea.

A child had been born to us and I was desirous of baptising him. I passed by the men, ducked into the low byre of the hold and in the gloom struck my head hard on a beam. I felt the wet warmth on my crown and reaching out to steady myself grasped soft locks of hair and a woman's shoulder.

'So you are still flesh and blood,' teased the voice. I could not see her face. She inspected the graze. 'Come into the light, Hector.' I was guided back to the foot of the gangway and felt the sting of whisky clean the wound. 'You wouldn't wish our minister an infection for want of your dram, would you Duncan?' the voice jested. Duncan, no longer dreaming of Nova Scotia, received the now empty cup back in his hand. I thanked him for his trouble.

'It's no the trouble, it's the expense.'

I turned to behold my rescuer and, as my sight adjusted to the shadow, recognised Kirstie. Four decades of toil had fastened in her a fearless and patient faith that had knit her face perhaps too severely, for she smiled little now, though when she did the years were washed away. 'You will have come to see our Mairi,' she said.

In a cubicle of sagging grey canvas on a bed of pine boards lay her sister. 'New sons for a new world, Mr Gillean,' said Mairi and held the baby to her breast.

For two more weary weeks the *Good Intent*, first tossed by storms and then becalmed for a windless eternity, tacked across the Atlantic. Some emigrants begged Cameron to put about and run for home but he showed them no courtesy and bade them to swim back to Scotland if they so wished. My journal remained closed throughout those joyless days. There was no pleasure in recording the ship's suffering. I spent long hours trying to encourage our company and when I could stole short moments to talk with Kirstie and Mairi. But malnutrition and monotony had set in us a deadening lethargy and I prayed most zealously for our aching spirits.

'YOU BELIEVING IN ghosts?' Pereira asked in his elaborate, sing-song English. The Goan steward was silhouetted against the soft green glow of the instruments. 'When I am here at night sometimes I thinking there is someone right behind me.' Weird celestial music haunted the dark bridge. A closet of wire coat-hangers tinkled as they rocked with the swells. 'When I turning around there is nobody at all there. Except young Jagjit.' The second officer stood apart from them keeping a silent watch on the empty sea lanes.

'Maybe it's a stowaway?' said Beagan even though the voices that he had heard did not speak Romanian. 'Or someone who has died.'

'No speak of such things.' Pereira seemed shocked. 'If you do they maybe coming true.'

The storm had abated an hour earlier and Beagan had laid down the diary. Lamb korma was on the evening's menu, but the reading had dulled his appetite and instead of descending to the galley he had thrown on an anorak and slipped outside into the night. The air temperature had dropped and fog, thick as the bank which had enveloped Saint Brendan's leather currach, denser than that which had bewildered Beagan's wasted years, clung to a black pearl sea. He had made his way forward, put the noise of steam and steel behind him and paused to listen to the hiss of the ocean seething under the bow. In a matter of days the *Global Trader* would reach Canada and the prospect filled him with trepidation. The ship, Davey had told him over lunch, was on schedule. Nothing unusual was anticipated along the rest of the route. There would be no more bad weather and little other marine traffic, surprises that might upset the smooth operation of the machine and her crew. But neither the high-tech certainties nor the mindless, ping-pong routine had comforted Beagan. The sea through which they plied had absorbed too much suffering; the tears of the tens of thousands who died before reaching the far shore, the most recent tragedy of Vietnamese boat people drowned over the Grand Banks, possibly even now the perished hopes of a frozen stowaway. Maybe there was too much history, as Davey had said, but after years of running from his own past Beagan had begun to prepare to meet old ghosts. The thought of it scared him speechless.

On the bridge Pereira listened to the drone of the engines then glanced over his shoulder. 'On last crossing retired master's ashes burying at sea. Captain order engines stop, say quick prayer and, while *Serang* make photographs, throwing ashes overboard. Old master had designing urn himself, thick and busy in holes so it might fill with water and sink very fast. But lid flying off in a big way and ashes scatter over the new, damp paintwork.' He listened to the night. 'Are you thinking it is maybe him?'

'It could be Vijitha's party,' suggested Beagan.

'Maybe,' nodded Pereira with little certainty. 'Maybe. We going later?'

At the end of the watch Pereira led Beagan down four flights, deep into the bowels of the ship towards the sound of singing. The smell of incense hung in the air. Plastic sandals stood on mats by each cabin door. On the walls hung garish prints of Brahma and Bombay movie stars. Small studio portraits of sons and daughters were tacked to the head of every bunk. Beagan had met the Indian crew only when they had emerged from behind watertight doors or vanished down gangways, their overalls stained with oil, beaming broad smiles and sharing with him the faulty valve or pump in their care. Among them only Pereira spoke English. The others relied on the vast bo'sun, a grinning brown Buddah in bleached white boilersuit, both to translate and dictate. He was their *serang*, or boss, and presided over them like a queen bee over her hive. On his word the crew swabbed and scrubbed and slapped on another tin of the six thousand gallons of paint applied to the ship every year.

The crewmen, each with a litre bottle and a shy grin, greeted Beagan's arrival with applause. Space was made for him on the front bench. Vijitha from Colombo was celebrating his promotion to electrical officer and two dozen tired, excited men clustered around a table laden with duty-free gin and Four Bells rum. Three trays of onion and hot chilli bhajis were raised on a bed of Coke tins and beer cases.

'It a lonely life at sea,' Pereira told Beagan. 'We trying to be cheerful and diligent in our work, doing the needful, but it ten months long that we being away from our families.' As he paused to applaud the arrival of a latecomer Beagan recalled Hector's kindred left behind in the Hebrides. 'I have a little girl. She two years old. In this life I seeing her once only.'

There was little conversation between the lonely, respectful, soft-spoken men. Words were not spoken but sung. The Hindu ballads were about missing home. Every crewman knew the lyrics and all joined in for the chorus. The bo'sun sang a wistful solo. The radio operator tapped out a Morse code rhythm with the fingers of one hand, drummed with a lighter and the heel of the other. Pereira's melancholy lifted and he flashed his single tooth. 'Here very good,' he said.

Away from the cynical huddle of officers Beagan sensed something of the precious hope which sustained life on both ships, but then Davey and the captain arrived, out of uniform, and the crew rose to their feet. Spontaneity drained out of the proceedings. Vijitha made a speech thanking them for their support then sang off-key Elton John's 'Sacrifice', his only English song.

'Not again,' droned Davey and slunk off to the officers' mess to watch a video.

N O MATTER HOW fervent my prayers, no matter how hard I struggled to bring comfort, the islanders took to lying in their bunks for days, awake but unmoving, not caring if they next heard the rasp of keel on shingle or the voice that calls them home. At first I tried to cajole and encourage them but when gentle efforts failed I drove them from their beds with the fear of hell-fire and damnation. Every morning I urged them together and pressed Duncan, 'What is the Chief End of Man?'

The brogue maker's face was thin and anaemic. He had lost a second tooth in the night. 'Man's chief end is to glorify God and enjoy Him forever.'

'What,' I demanded of Kirstie, 'is God?'

She answered with eyes lowered. 'God is a Spirit, infinite, eternal and unchangeable, in His being, wisdom, power, holiness, justice, goodness and truth.'

I prodded them through the Questions and Answers of the Shorter Catechism, the Ten Commandments, the Six

Petitions. My call was for them to be ever more diligent. I bade them to kneel with me. Our psalms filled the hold, drifted out over the becalmed sea and wrapped the body of the ship in an embrace of prayer.

The daily discipline focused tired minds and anchored the drifting hours. But faith alone will not forever hold together body and soul. A man must eat and there was no food. Then Duncan surprised us all by announcing that he would catch fish. The cobbler had never in his life hauled a net yet he began bending his precious leather needles to form hooks and setting them on to laces. His bright buckles were fashioned into lures. He stood on the deck in his stockinged feet and cast the glittering line over the side. The sight of him raised the first laugh heard on board in over a month and before it had died down the cord went taut. Hand over hand he pulled in the laces, the buckles and a great cod. It was the largest that Ewan Cameron had ever seen. But no sooner was the line back in the water than another was caught. The fish were unable to resist his gaudy lures. Duncan hopped from foot to foot and began to land cod by the dozen. The children hung his trophies from the rigging and we gorged ourselves until we could eat no more. Not one to be shy of coming forward Little Donald then turned his hand to making a more efficient rain-gathering system. That evening our parched throats drank the sweet water which fell from heaven.

Later the cats' paws rippled the still surface and the sails filled with a fair south-easterly. I took up again writing my diary at dusk. Astern under a starless sky the piper played a lament, *Cha till mi tuille*. I will not return.

'Our spirits have lifted,' I recorded in good heart, 'with the knowledge that we have drifted over the New-found-land fishing banks. A plentiful catch sustains us as does the certainty that land cannot be too . . .' The pen spluttered and clogged. I shook the wretched instrument and sprayed a trail of clotted ink down my trousers, along the deck and over the piper's left shoe. He failed to notice the offending blot and it seemed churlish to interrupt the music. As I began to clean the nib with a well-stained handkerchief a voice whispered in my ear.

'At your books again?' Kirstie stood at my back smiling. The incident had not escaped her attention.

'One day in New Scotland,' I said while rising to my feet, 'I will buy myself a reliable pen.'

'There are many who will be thankful for that.' She glanced at Rankin, blushed and looked away to sea. If modesty is the ornament of women Kirstie wore hers with a confidence. 'Any sign?' she added.

'No.' We peered forward into the darkness. 'Your father thinks that it will be at least another day.'

Kirstie's cheeks were raw from the winters of wind, and barrels of brine had salted away her lightness of heart, but as she pulled the heavy shawl about her shoulders I noticed the nape of her neck, its skin as fair as cotton grass in the moss. We walked together to the bow of the ship. Patches of sea salt, which had dried on the deck, crunched beneath our feet. 'Tell me about your ministry,' she asked.

I had to admit that I knew very little. 'Cape Breton is, I understand, an island of small settlements divided from one another by inlets of the sea, large lakes and forests. The pioneers there are chiefly from the Western Isles and Hebrides but exist in very poor circumstances. Of the town of Promise itself I know only that many have grown up unbaptised.'

'Can that be true?'

'Aye, I believe that it is so. The country is vast and there are few pastors to spread God's Word.' I lowered my voice. 'In places the Bible is a sealed book.'

'Do these settlers not have their letters?'

'Some of them can neither read nor write,' I confirmed. 'The want for education and religious instruction is so urgent that when a teacher or clergyman comes among the people they flock with great eagerness and in large numbers to hear the Gospel preached to them in their native tongue.'

'Then your services will be in great demand. More even maybe than our own need.'

'I pray that my life may be of some use there.'

Alongside the mast, just beyond the illumination of the ship's lamp, petrels and skuas glided like angels at the edge of man's vision. The sails had been dipped and the night air was cold. Kirstie shivered and we turned to retire below when there appeared in the void, off to port, a single light. In the seven weeks at sea we had seen no other ship at close quarters. Kirstie's excitement, as my own, could not be checked.

'Can you see what she is?' she asked. It was too dark to discern any detail. 'Maybe . . . maybe it's a clipper filled with furs making to Europe,' she guessed. 'Or another emigrant ship? There, do you see its mizzen?' I could see no sails.

It was then that another light appeared. Two ships sailing in such proximity was an unusual sight. But when the third and fourth lamp appeared we realised that the lights were not being carried by vessels. A voice called out and Kirstie began to cry yet I heard neither her weeping nor the shouting about our ears. I did not feel the bodies pressed around me. My soul at that moment was alone with God and to Him the only homage I could offer was my own tears. The dozens of lights on the shore glowed as a constellation of stars. The flashing white manes of waves broke on the rocks of the New World.

FIVE DAYS OUT of Felixstowe the radar reached over the horizon and echoed back the coast of Newfoundland. Across the blackness Jerry's Nose peeked above the western shore and Clarke's Head overlooked Gander Bay. A secluded hamlet called Joe Blatt's Arm beckoned from the spot where an English sailor had jumped ship and broken his wrist. Fishing harbours named Leading Tickles and Witless Bay, Come by Chance and Great Paradise clung to the rough, wild shore. The first island of the New World had been made at the end of Creation. God had dumped on it all the refuse of His material: the spare granite from Ur and a job-lot of lava from Harran, the deep inlets, barren plateaux and stunted spruce not wanted in the Garden of Eden.

By daybreak the wind-swept, sea-washed tail of the Appalachians had fallen astern and ice lay about the *Global Trader* like an archipelago of ten thousand silver islands. A blizzard came and went. The harp seals were calving and the captain picked his way through the snow-sheets, passing the vast ship so close to the females that their cries could be heard from the bridge. He steered to avoid the packs of nursing mothers, the ice around them splattered with blood and afterbirth. In the thicker fields the ship lost her momentum. She slowed, shuddered then crunched to a stop. The captain eased astern, back down his track, then ran full ahead into the barrier to punch his way upstream.

As the Gulf narrowed and the banks of the Saint Lawrence drew together the ship regained the proportions of a leviathan. The coast was steep and deeply indented. Red-roofed, white-walled lighthouse hamlets perched on escarpments at the edge of dense forests. A timber-framed summer cottage, wrapped in dawn's mist, gripped on to a rocky ledge. At the foot of the cliffs clapboard villages clustered around the gleaming lead spires of Catholic churches. A serpentine freight train skirted the river's north shore at Point-au-Pic. Its engineer sounded his horn, a long wail of the Prairies, and the ship answered with its whistle.

The long Canadian winter still clung to the late spring and an icebreaker had to clear a channel at Les Escoumins. A jaunty launch darted between the floes and slipped alongside the *Global Trader*. Jean-Louis le Bois, the Saint Lawrence pilot, filled the bridge with the scent of spruce woods and *Eau Sauvage*. His clothes were crisp and stylish. He smoked heavily, ate Fernandes's hearty bacon aŋd samosa breakfast and twanged in nasal Québécois over the VHF radio-telephone.

'This river, she has a long *histoire*,' he told Beagan. Story and history. 'I am a member of *l'Administration de pilotage des Lauren-tides*, the oldest *corporation* in North America. We know the river before the English, almost before the Indian.'

'It was the French who first found the Saint Lawrence,' acknowledged Beagan. He had unearthed from the depths of the trunk a tattered school history book embossed with proud emi-grant ships and puffed sails. 'The English missed the turn-off.'

Five years after Columbus had stumbled on to the West Indies the merchants of Bristol, miffed by the Spanish success and anxious to cut out Moslem middlemen, had sped John Cabot west to buy the goods and spices of the East. They had fancied that he would reach China by sailing around the world. It had not been appreci-ated that a continent blocked the way. Cabot sighted Baffin Island, the frozen wasteland lying well within the Arctic Circle, and thinking that he had come upon northern Asia headed south to find Japan. But instead of Kyoto he found Newfoundland.

'It didn't much resemble the Orient,' added Beagan. 'Cabot overlooked the mouth of the river and sailed on maybe as far as Florida, reaching the mainland of America before Columbus, the holds of his ships filled with goods for trade, his eyes searching the shore for the golden cities of Cathay.'

A generation passed before Jacques Cartier, a navigator from Saint Malo, became the first European to see the Saint Lawrence. Unlike Cabot, Cartier had come looking for more than just a passage to the East. He had hungered to substantiate the dream of his age: that the discovery of promised lands was rewarded by the possession of their riches. The Native people, whom he called Indians because of Columbus's geographical mistake, had obliged him. They had 'fed and caressed him', even looked upon him as a god and asked him to perform miracles in healing the sick. They had also assured him that, 'A moon distant there is a land producing cinnamon and cloves,' and he decided to follow the river west-ward. He had anchored his ships below the Charlevoix cliffs and pushed upstream in bark canoes and longboats searching for a paradise 'rich and wealthy in precious stones'. But he had found neither China nor a mythical northern Eldorado; the gold which he discovered was iron pyrites and the so-called diamonds were quartz. Cartier like Cabot had failed to achieve his goal. He is best remembered for his misunderstanding. On reaching a Native settlement at the confluence of the Saint Charles river he had heard his guides call the place Canada and erroneously applied the name to the land. In fact *cannada* is the Huron-Iroquois word for a village.

'No gold. No diamond. *Rien. Alors*, what use is Canada?' asked le Bois and dismissed the country with a Gallic shrug. 'For sixty year nobody care, nobody come, until – *paf!* – Europe fall in love with the beaver hat.'

The first permanent white settlement in Canada was a trading post named *Kebec*, an Algonquin word which meant 'where the river narrows'. The second outpost was established upriver at the foot of an extinct volcano called Mont-Royal.

'Each year one ship come from France,' le Bois explained. 'The first Saint Laurent pilot, *le Pilote du Roi*, was a Breton called Abraham Martin. He row out from Pointe-au-Père – across the river from Les Escoumins – and guide the ship 328 mile to Montréal.' His expansive gestures suggested a thousand miles of frosty wilderness. 'The voyage upriver took maybe four month so the ship, she spend the winter in Montréal. There was not time to reach the sea before the river freeze up, eh? But Martin, he return to Pointe-au-Père by horse to wait for spring and the next ship.'

'It must have been a lonely life.'

'*Ah non.*' Le Bois drew deeply on his Rothman. 'They say he had two wife: in town *une belle française* for summer – someone *propre* and *parfumée* – and at home *une Indienne* – dark and a little smoky – to keep him warm through the winter. *Pas mal*, eh?'

'So the Plains of Abraham,' observed Beagan, recalling the field where in 1759 the French dream of an American empire had died, 'were named after a bigamous river pilot.'

Le Bois gave him a long sideways look. 'It's all that bloody reading he does,' said Davey. 'It gets up my nose too.'

Martin's sons had become pilots as had their sons after them. His family had remained the river's navigators for generations, even after the British had defeated the French and renamed the *corporation* Trinity House, until traffic on the river had multiplied faster than his offspring and new blood had to be recruited. Le Bois was one of the seventy-three pilots who each led 120 ships along the Saint Lawrence every year. The journey which had once lasted four months now took eighteen hours.

'All the *histoire* is in Québec,' laughed le Bois. '*Et le future aussi. Maîtres chez-nous.*' That morning the *Global Trader* passed a dozen ships: snub-nosed American Lakers, scruffy Egyptian freighters, a Russian cruise liner. The commerce of nations rode out to the sea from the continent's heart. The Seaway linked the Atlantic to the Great Lakes and made ocean ports of cities 2,600 miles inland.

The Charlevoix cliffs levelled into pretty hills with strip fields running up from the shore. Barns crowned the heights and the older farmhouses, with the steep pitched roofs and overhanging eaves of Normandy, betrayed the first settlers' origins. Poplars lined the roads as they might in the Loire. Out of the mists rose the snow-capped turrets of Québec City, flanked by the industrial cranes of Levis and Beauport. The ship, which only days before had been in the emptiness of the ocean, was downtown, with ferries and *bateaux-pilotes* scuttling about her. The copper-peaked Château Frontenac dominated the stern skyline as surely as the battlements above Carcassonne. Beneath the grey rock Citadel, whose ramparts had challenged the power of Britain for control of the continent, nestled a place more European than American. Its narrow streets echoed with the solemn psalms of Mass and the smell of fresh *brioche*. Horse-drawn *calèches* rattled over uneven cobblestones, past zinc-bar bistros and snug cafés where students mapped out their lives on paper table napkins.

It was night when the *Global Trader* slipped beneath the cantilevered *Pont de Québec*, an Eiffel Tower laid on its side and the first bridge west of Europe. On the south shore, high on a lofty point called Cap Charles, a Union Jack was run up a spotlit mast and the river boomed with a chorus of 'God Save the Queen'.

For twenty-five years Delphis Duhamel had followed the Marine Traffic List, listened to Coast Guard radio and hailed every passing ship by raising its national flag and playing its anthem. Two vast loudspeakers built into the cliff and powered by a 1300-watt amplifier broadcast his welcome. His collection of 140 flags included the colours of the Czech Republic, Togo and Vanuatu.

'North Korea was the most difficult one for him to get, eh?' le Bois told Beagan. Davey seemed to ignore them and studied the river charts. 'He ask the Embassy but they think maybe he is a spy and send nothing. So he find a nun who go there to work in a mission. She bring him back the flag.'

Beagan speculated aloud that Duhamel must be a retired mariner who missed the life at sea. Davey looked up from the map and rolled his eyes. 'Mate, did you come up the Clyde on a bicycle?'

'*Pas du tout*,' corrected le Bois. 'He is a furniture salesman. He do it for his children, so they grow up to know the world from the ships passing their garden. They stick pins in a big map in the living room. But now his children leave home and he cannot stop. Night and day he is out there with his Labrador, blowing each ship to blazes.'

'At least he looks further than his own backyard,' said Beagan. Along the waterway he had noticed far more blue *fleurs-de-lys* than red maple leafs and the observation had rattled him.

'This is an important year for us. In October we Québécois vote for the right to run our own country.'

'You mean Québec, or Canada?' asked Beagan, perplexed by the flush of emotion.

'The old Canada, she is a lost cause. *Tout a changé.*' Le Bois turned to Davey. 'Duhamel tell me there was a time when he play "God Save the Queen" – *les deux versions, vocal et instrumental* – three or four time a day. Now he only play it once a week.'

'Gie the horn a wee pamp,' ordered Davey. The *Global Trader* blew her whistle and dipped her red ensign.

*   *   *

Beagan awoke when the movement stopped. The ship no longer swayed. The fans and boilers were silent. Instead of the roar of high-pressure air and the thump of diesel engines, electric gantry cranes whirred overhead. They jerked the containers off their hasps and lowered them on to waiting flatbeds. A freight train shunted in a siding. Tractor trailers idled on the tarmac outside the Racine Terminal, anxious to collect their loads and move on west.

In the mess the officers sat in a long row, left to right in descending order of rank, drinking beer. Beagan's bar bill dangled from a fairy light. The captain had kept a meticulous record. Neither the Queen nor the Grolsch calendar girl waved goodbye. But below decks Pereira's single-tooth smile flashed beneath the cowl of his parka. 'Cheerio, young man,' he said, giving him a handmade model of a Scottish yawl. 'Good shoreside luck.' In twenty-four hours the travelling warehouse would be back on the sea lanes. In a week Davey might wonder, over a plate of chicken tikka masala and chips, if Beagan had ever been aboard.

Beagan packed the globe and books back into his trunk. He slipped the bottled model in between the loose diary pages and a leather-bound address book. Outside the air was freezing. There was not a Romanian in sight. Beagan clambered down the gangway to find no saluting Mountie or welcoming brass band. He hesitated on the last rung, took a deep breath then stepped on to the concrete pier. No thunderbolt struck him down. The earth did not open up and swallow him. 'So far so good,' he thought. He decided that it would be a fine idea not to kiss the ground and went to call a cab.

CHAPTER III

PROMISED LAND

WE CAME IN with the tide, to the chuckle and snigger of pebbles in the swells. The mantle of rainclouds muffled the cold April dawn. The silent forest soared above us, looming so close to the water as to offer only a mean edge to which to cling. I fell to my knees to thank God for our deliverance but before the words were formed my prayers were interrupted by shrill cries ringing through the dark groves of pine.

'Savages,' guessed Little Donald and raised his fists to fight. But the strangers who fell upon us brandished handshakes not tomahawks. One fair-skinned ruffian, his tattered greatcoat concealing want of other garments, embraced Duncan like a brother. In the ensuing scuffle he lost a shoe in the mire. Another slapped me so hard on the back that the globe flew from my hands. The fall dented the Iberian peninsula. A third man shook Kirstie Cameron's hand with an enthusiasm which threatened to dislocate her shoulder. Then the scallywag tried to kiss her.

'Gather your tail,' barked Cameron, sweeping them back with his dogfish snout. 'Was there ever a more brazen welcome?'

'What is the name of this place?' I asked but their yells were more bestial than human and I did not comprehend the answer. 'The light shines in the dark and the dark understands it not,' I added.

'It might be that we *have* landed in China,' suggested Duncan.

The ruffians bade us follow them from the strip of beach, through the curtain of trees, deep into the hushed woods. They ran ahead leaving us trailing alone beneath a dense canopy. The frowning trees, black and ominous, closed in and shut out the sky. The sun did not penetrate the narrow passage. No light dispelled the sombre gloom. No sound disturbed the vast silence. The women whispered in small voices and held hands. The men fell quiet treading on the unfamiliar pine-needle earth. Nothing had prepared us for either the great loneliness of the forest or the unholy din towards which we were then drawn.

In a clearing a wild woman with loose red hair danced barefoot on a stump and wailed. Grimy children whirled about her, howling like young wolves, stretching their limbs, testing their new-found freedom. A knot of young men clad in tartan trousers lurched forward, seized the siren and carried her off. Their empty bottle was trampled underfoot. Packs of boys kicked a bundle of books until, to cries of disappointment, the spines cracked and the pages took flight like swallows along the shore. A hundred women, with petticoats tucked above their knees, cackled as they trampled clean their bedding in tidal rockholes. Beyond them close-packed sailing boats, their masts like a great forest stripped of limbs, ferried more emigrants ashore. The newcomers fell on to the beach, spilt into the shallows, flung sand into their faces and squealed. 'What is this Babel?' asked Little Donald in disbelief.

Cameron seized an agitated juvenile by the arm. 'Friend, what is the name of this place?' he asked in the Gaelic.

'The books are mine! Mine!' he shouted and struggled to break from his grip.

'In the name of Providence where are we?' I repeated in English.

'Where are you?' he replied shaking himself free. 'The

gateway to the promised land, sirrah.' He ran off laughing so loud that I thought he must be deaf. 'They call this place Ship Harbour.'

We bunched together around the globe, turned it in our hands and scoured the unfamiliar seaboard. 'There it is. Here,' said Kirstie curving her finger along the coast. Ship Harbour was a port on the southern shore of Cape Breton Island, separated from mainland Nova Scotia by the narrow Gut of Canso. We had missed the harbour's mouth and anchored the *Good Intent* over the lonely headland.

The thin blue smoke of wood fires rose from log cabins set in stump-cluttered yards. We skirted the compound, trying not to step on the crisp white pages alighting in the muck and went in search of an authority. A stevedore stopped Little Donald to offer him work and a tavern-keeper hailed us from an open door. Stray whelps sniffed at our heels. A milch cow watched us pass. At the centre of a cluster of painted frame houses, next to the wooden stores, stood the clapboard inn. The sounds of argument assailed us from within.

'Damn your blood, you bounder.'

'Then clear off out of here. I am pig-sick and tired of your hum-ha tongue-tied talk.'

Inside two men faced each other from opposite sides of the table, leaning forward so their noses touched yet yelling for all British North America to hear.

'May I remind you that it is only through my efforts that you secured this position?'

'Only through the sweat of my brow, toady. I owe no man nothin.'

At our entrance they broke off and I asked for directions to the Emigrant Office. The Englishman, the shorter of the two combatants and dressed in the fashion of years long past, bowed then sneezed. His once fine clothes were worn so thin that he kept warm only by wrapping a blanket around his shoulders. 'Sir, I am at your service.' Duncan noticed that his shoes needed new soles.

'This ain't'no office and he's fixin to leave,' interrupted the American, dispensing with pleasantries. 'And if you're friends of his then you boys can git too.' He shooed us away with a shapeless palmetto hat as if we were chickens.

The emigrant officer took the opportunity to explain the nature of the disagreement. 'It has been the custom, long before the arrival of this Vermonter, for this establishment to serve as my bureau.' He fussed with his whiskers. 'Now Goodenough here, as the new landlord, has doubled the fee.'

Goodenough took a different view of tradition. 'Your customs ain't worth shucks. I told you my price. Pay up or make tracks.'

'Sir, you bite the hand which has fed you. My teeth are on edge.' The officer again addressed our party. 'This Yankee drank up a good farm in the United States then thought he could do no better than to turn loyal and get one here for nothing.' At the end of the War of Independence one in every five Americans had remained true to the Crown. The price of allegiance for many was exile. But among the fifty thousand Loyalists who had fled the United States were some not drawn north by patriotism alone. Canada had given free land to all comers.

'And I don't give a red cent for your King of England,' he laughed, hitching up his leather leggings and pointing at his feet. 'I'd kick him, his queen and all you Englishers out of my house. Now I said git.' A violent gesture flipped off his deer moccasin which hit Duncan in the eye. Little Donald raised his fists and cursed in Gaelic for the second time that morning. He was not a man to let an insult go unanswered.

'I can out-holler you too,' challenged the American and let loose a tirade of profanities.

The officer held up his sheaf of papers as a shield and retreated shouting, 'God's blood.'

I ended the contretemps by asking where we might obtain

provisions. 'You got money?' came the swift reply. I confirmed that we had limited resources. 'Then why didn't you
say so, Reverend?' Goodenough called for his wife and ush-
ered us back over the threshold. 'We'll fix you up.' Then
he added, 'You're Scottish, ain't you?' He slapped Donald
on the shoulder. 'My grandma was Scots so no hard feelings.'
Donald, not understanding the English, did not respond.
Goodenough chuckled and whispered, 'And don't tell a soul
but my pa was an Englishman.'

As the others carried the over-priced supplies back to
the ship Cameron and I rejoined the hapless officer. He
crouched on a log surrounded by a band of emigrants. In
the bay beyond, the brigs were being fitted out for the more
profitable return voyage. Their ballast was jettisoned,
bunks cast aside and cargoes of white pine timber for the
home market dragged on board.

'Faugh, how this place stinks,' the officer said, turning
from the babble. He tried to fasten his waistcoat but finding
an absence of buttons instead pulled the blanket around
him. 'I've had my fill of New Worlds.' He was the third son
of a landed family, forced to seek his fortune in the colonies
when their estate in Rutland was seized for gambling debts.
His first destination had been Australia but an attempt to
domesticate the kangaroo had failed and his convict servants
had robbed him. India too had proved to be unsuitable. While
there he had contracted a sinus complaint and lost the
remains of his fortune in the jute trade. His most recent plan
to homestead in Upper Canada foundered when, having
insufficient money to complete the journey, he was thrown
off the ship in Cape Breton. A sinecure saved him from starvation but the maritime damp irritated his joints and after a
lifetime away from England he dreamt of going home, even
though no home remained to which he might return.

Yet in spite of his misfortune he was generous to us. I
translated Little Donald's letter for him and he directed
Cameron to the location of the settlement, a few hours'

sailing down the coast. 'But my destination, the town called Promise, doesn't seem to be marked on the globe,' I observed, showing him the sphere.

'Nor will it be for a long time, sir.' He explained to me that my congregation lay two days' walk north on the shore of saltwater Bras d'Or Lake, the golden arm of the sea which cleaved the island. 'But may I advise you to delay your journey for a fortnight and ride with the mail? The road is rascally beyond any conception.'

Although I agreed that my baggage could travel in such a manner, I was determined to leave the following morning.

'Odsooks, sir,' the officer warned, 'this land is so intersected by water that in many places you would be better advised to travel by turtle than on foot.'

'But today is only Wednesday,' I insisted, not wishing to appear ungrateful. 'Please understand that it is my ardent desire to reach by this coming Sabbath those who have waited so long for my arrival.'

Goodenough offered to accompany me 'a piece of the way' but the charge for the pleasure of his company was exorbitant. We took our leave of him, and Ship Harbour, to return to the *Good Intent*.

At dawn a cold silver moon rose out of the sea and hung above the melancholy forests. To sustain me on my walk I had a small loaf, some cheese and the Shorter Catechism. Under my arm I carried the globe. As Cameron made ready to sail I rowed ashore and waved the last farewell. I turned inland and entered a verdant corridor cut between the deep woods. The earth was wet underfoot and the logs, where laid over gullies and streams to make a corduroy road, were covered in thick moss. I slipped and only through the fortuitous position of a stump saved the globe from spinning off into a mudhole. I was on the road to Promise.

*   *   *

'WELCOME TO YESTERYEAR.' The sodden banner drooped over the parking lot. 'There are no trash cans in Pioneer Village.' Beagan dropped his Fillet o' Fish wrapper in the bin and hurried out of the Atlantic sleet into the Interpretation Centre. 'Follow the Fish' signs directed him to a shoal of spring tourists swathed in luminous wet-weather gear. The children and cameras were wrapped in plastic. 'Let's take a walk back into history,' shivered a freckle-faced, red-haired Dalhousie student in long tartan skirt and windcheater. 'Let's see how our forefathers lived and discover old Scotland in New Scotland.'

'Hey, do you sell those cute bagpipe-shaped air fresheners here?' asked a holiday-maker from Ohio.

In Montreal the day before, the immigration officer hadn't understood why Beagan had stayed away from Canada for so long. 'You are no longer a resident,' he had declared in a crisp German accent. 'You are a visitor.' The passport had been stamped 'Admission valid for six months' and his sense of belonging had been replaced by the curiosity of an outsider.

Beagan had rented a car from a woman wearing a sari and driven back east towards Nova Scotia. Along the *autoroute* pine-needles had lain browning on the hard shoulder, their white covering of frost blown away by passing trucks, and the smell of skunk hung in the air. Headlights had played across the faces of diners eating blueberry pancakes in roadside restaurants. A lone jogger ran up a suburban strip of Burger Kings and Japanese car dealerships, past billboards which assured '*VOUS êtes important.*' A few miles further, across the border in the Maritimes, the same poster read 'We appreciate *YOU.*' There were no signs in Gaelic.

In Halifax faded grand hotels waited to receive the Queens and Empresses which sailed no more. Beagan, like the trans-Atlantic jets passing overhead, had skirted the city and headed up the coast along highways as straight as Roman roads, through marshlands of stunted pine, into the glens of Antigonish County. The lush orchards and ploughlands of the mainland had fallen away behind him and he had driven across the Canso Causeway straight to Cape Breton's Yesteryear Pioneer Village. 'Make a day of it . . .

fantasy fun for all the family.' The site was his starting point, not so he could watch the multi-screen Highland Pioneer Experience or eat Ma McIntosh's Real Down Home Baked Apple Pie but because it was to this place that the Reverend Hector's church had been moved. The old building had become a relic in a museum.

The waterlogged tourists waddled past empty drying racks and the sail-loft exhibition. They watched nets being tanned and photographed the cooper fashioning barrels. Children helped churn butter in cottage kitchens as their parents asked for directions to the nearest McDonald's. Wannabe actors spun sea-dog yarns at the dockside between video shows. From beneath her umbrella the guide spoke in a quiet Canadian way, so anxious not to offend that she seemed to swallow her words. 'Pioneer Village is a living museum to the maritime heritage of Nova Scotia,' she recited, 'a one-of-a-kind seaside treasure in Canada's Ocean Playground.' But there were no boats in the water. Grass had grown over the gunwales of dories beached on the shore. The schooners along the wharf were no longer seaworthy and survived only to house the fish-filleting display. Over-fishing, predatory seals and a change in water temperature had all but eliminated cod from the Grand Banks and the two-year fishing ban announced by the government had been extended. Some mariners feared that the flounder and haddock might never return.

Few of the visitors bothered to look at the church as it boasted no 'rural heritage' demonstration. Their passing interest was limited to the building's relocation. They glanced at the photographs of the timbers being dismantled, the numbered logs being stacked on low-loaders and driven halfway across the province. As the tourists swam on to the souvenir shop Beagan paused at the door of the church. His coat dripped water over the threshold. He slipped up the aisle, stroked the worn pews and stood by the pulpit. There lay a Bible which fell open at *John* and on a whim he read aloud, 'I am the voice of one crying in the wilderness, make straight the way of the Lord.' Beagan stood and waited. He seemed to want something dramatic to happen. He half-expected to hear a blast of Gabriel's trumpet and to see Hector appear before him saying, 'It's good of you to come laddie, but could you no have wiped your boots at the door?' But instead of a heavenly fanfare the only sound which he heard was the patter of rain on the roof.

'Damn it,' he sighed and turned away.

At The Pedlar's Curios Shop the lurid crowd bought salt cod imported from Spain and Olde English beeswax candles. Garish plastic lobsters with spring-loaded claws were the most popular item. An American paid in US dollars and argued over the exchange rate. In the cafeteria young families huddled over steamy bowls of Crofter's Highland Soup. 'What do we do next?' an eager tourist asked her tour guide. 'The Ceilidh Trail or the Great Hall of the Clans?' Beagan nursed a cup of tea beneath the pickled pouting alewives and stuffed silver eels. He wiped the condensation from the window and watched a solitary wooden canoe slide through the shallows towards the village. It didn't surprise him that the church had felt empty. The dislocated building was like a body after death, a shell. The move had separated it from the Reverend's spirit. To find it he needed to go to the place where the church had stood, to where his great-grandfather had lived, to where Hector's sons Zachary and Jamie had been born. He spread the road map on the table to look for Promise and noticed that the canoeist had vanished from the bay.

'FATHER!' CRIED JAMIE laying his paddle across the thwarts and catching the pier. 'Hello, F-F-Father.'

I stood up and struck my head on the overhanging church eave. '*Ist!*' My first day back in the New World with Beagan had left me a little overwrought. 'And botheration.' The modern felicity of phrase had its attraction but little else had met with my approval. 'Mark you this, James,' I shouted, clutching my bald pate and pointing at the wall. 'They have used nails. Nails.' I waved him

forward. 'Dear God, as if we had the resources to buy nails.'
Jamie pulled his Peterborough lapstrake ashore and joined
me by the church. New steel bolts had been hammered into
the old logs to secure the dovetailed corners. 'I tell you,
James, this is worse than inaccurate, it is wasteful.'

'Maybe the Lord's Will alone no longer holds the building
together,' suggested Jamie.

I straightened my long black preacher's coat and struck
my head again. 'I'll tolerate no impiety; one desecrator in
the family is terrible enough.' Beagan may have begun to
engage my affections during the crossing, yet the boy
remained soft and cowardly like a crab after casting its shell.

'It's simply a modern precaution, Father,' explained
Jamie. 'People today are very concerned for ph-ph-physical
safety.'

'It is their spiritual well-being that should concern them.'
I tried to pry free a nail with my fingers. 'When I first
arrived in Cape Breton I expected some parishioners to be
destitute of the ordinances of the Gospel. I did not expect
to find it so three generations later.' My fingernail split.
'And where is your brother? Is he not with you?'

Jamie shook his head. 'He who made time made plenty
of it, you used to say; but still not enough for Zachary.'

'He agreed to meet us here. I am disappointed.' My dis-
pleasure mounted as I inspected my second son. 'And what
on earth is that costume you are wearing?'

Jamie was dressed in britches and a worn striped cap. His
suspenders were frayed and tatty. 'It's my sporting outfit,
Father. After your death I became an avid recreational
canoeist.'

'In my day there was little time for recreation,' I recalled.
'He that will not sow on a cold day will not reap on a warm
one. But from what I have seen here it is apparent that I
took too much leisure. Much too much. At what are you
smiling, James?'

Tireless principles can at times be exhausting but the

crusty, dour tenets warmed Jamie's heart. 'It is very good to see you again, Father.'

I too saw the humour in it and spread both my arms and wings. 'My boy, forgive your ungrateful progenitor.' We embraced, which for spirits is something between mortal laughter and a blending of gases, then I added, 'Is it not fine to see our old kirk again?'

'Yes,' hesitated Jamie. 'Yes, because it was here that I always remember you, standing at our head like the captain of a ship, with me quaking in f-f-fear of the Questions.'

'Zachary learnt his Shorter Catechism but the mischief was always coming over you. As I recall you never studied hard enough,' I admonished as we slipped into the building. 'And you will have forgotten your Gaelic too, but *crannag* means both a ship and the pulpit.'

Jamie dawdled at the door. The mention of his elder brother's name unnerved him and his stutter grew worse. 'The ch-ch-church was to have been built in Promise in time f-f-for your arrival,' he said.

'And soon thereafter the schoolhouse.' I laughed at the memory. 'Aye, as I walked through the forest I saw a wide, important and most useful field of labour awaiting me. I looked forward too to the handsome stipend of eighty pounds per annum. Eighty pounds, *a bhalaich*. In those days a man could live a comfortable life on that.' I took my place behind the pulpit. 'Was it not old McKinlay who sat there in the front pew?'

'You always sat us next to him,' Jamie nodded. 'I wanted to hide here at the back with Fisher MacFie.'

'Mark you, it was many years before I was paid anything at all. Not that it mattered, no one had any money, but I hadn't known that at the outset. As for the building of the church itself . . . oh but wait you now. This just will not do.' I had turned the pages of the Book. 'Is this not in English? Where is the Gaelic Bible?' Together we looked under the pulpit and in the cupboard but found only a pornographic magazine and a stash of empty beer bottles. 'Carnality and sin,' I hissed with indignation. 'Carnality and sin.'

'Maybe it's in the old trunk?' suggested Jamie. 'That's the last place I saw it.'

'Right enough. Good, then the blasphemous Beagan will bring it along with him. Well, come you now, I will show you my route to Promise.'

'But what about Beagan?'

'The boy is still swilling tea in the cafeteria,' which I had to admit was preferable to frequenting a tavern. 'He will not be too far behind us when he begins to look at his own map. It and the globe are in the trunk too.' I stood at the door and pointed northwards. 'If I recollect aright this was the direction.' My memory reached out beyond the litter bins and The Pedlar's Curios Shop. The parking lot turned into a rough mail road and the sodden banner became the evergreen cloak which wrapped grey granite hills. 'There had never been a forest the like of it, James. You cannot imagine it.'

I walked through great pine cathedrals and intimate beech chapels where finches and blackbirds celebrated their praises in song. The frosty spring light flicked the tips of trees and filtered down to the forest floor. Wild meadows embraced the track of ice-blue lakes which stepped away to the horizon like footprints left by God. I paused for lunch, a communion of bread and water, and watched a doe drink by the shining stream. But my progress was slower than I had anticipated and not long into the afternoon the corridor sank back into shadow. It narrowed then split and, as advised by Goodenough, I took the right fork to follow a trail of uncertain blazes. The air cooled and I began to wonder where I might lay my head when from behind a confused mass of felled timber a log cabin came into view.

The quick stroke of an axe echoed in the clearing. I climbed over the bush-fence and tried to hail its inhabitant. The axe chopped on and a vicious dog bounded forward. I retreated up a nearby maple tree, lodged the globe on a broad bough and clung to the trunk. It was not a pleasant reception. The hound growled and snapped at my heels. My attempt to calm the animal with kind words only incensed it further and I was forced to scramble to a higher perch. But the racket did flush out the woodsman who, when the dog failed to obey his orders, resorted to a cuff across the ear to silence it.

'For sure yous'll be looking for a place to sleep,' he said, his Irish brogue pinched by an American twang. 'I's keeping the tavern here.' He gestured at the shanty. 'Yous welcome to stop over.'

The so-called tavern was dark, dirty and cramped. Its floor was made of loose split logs and the chimney was a simple square hole in the roof. Snowshoes hung on the wall. The only light came from a hearth burning on bare soil. Its flames flared up as the wind stole through chinks in the walls.

'Yous'll be heading for Promise, I calculate,' guessed my host. His face, rosy and plump, was impressed with a lattice of scars and lines from fifty fights and as many years. As there was no chair he offered me a stool. There was no table either. The only other furniture in the house was a finely inlaid oak closet inside which was an old-fashioned couch-bed. 'Theys'll be right pleased to see your face, Father.'

'You know the town then?' I asked, anxious to learn something of my destination. 'I have heard very little about it.'

'For sure it's a grand place. Good land. Honourable folk. Yes siree, theys always pay their bills on the nail.'

'And the church? Is it a fine building?'

'Well now, Father, that I cannot say for certain. I'd be lying to yous if I said that it was and that wouldn't do. Nope, not you being a parson. Truth is it's been a fair old spell since I was there. But I knows for sure that theys expecting yous. In fact I heard tell theys were expecting yous last month.'

His knowledge of my arrival intrigued me. 'And how in this great wilderness did you come by such intelligence?'

'I like to be at the centre of things.' I could imagine no place less near a centre. 'That's how come I built the inn here.' The Irishman leaned forward, eyes wide with excitement, and stabbed the floor with a crooked finger. 'Here, right here, yous be exactly halfway 'tween Ship Harbour and Promise.' A boy's optimism bubbled through the veins of an old man. 'Any idiot sees that everything is going forward in this country. It's not possible for trade, agriculture and manufactures to get set back. The whole caboodle keeps advancing. So I calculate that this road will get mighty busy. Folks will pass along, see the inn and say, "Hell," sorry Father I mean theys'll say, "Hurrah, we's halfway there. Let's stop for tea and grits or sandwiches and potatoes." We'll feed them up good so that theys'll spend the night and eat breakfast too and pay us well and I'll be as rich as Midas. That's for sure what's to happen.' He leaned back on his haunches proud of his plan. 'Wasn't it a grand thought Columbus had to find out America?'

Over coffee made of dried roasted dandelion roots he talked of his years in Virginia and the family feud which drove him north. 'I've no axe to grind. Here a man can do good. Any settler can reckon in one year having potatoes enough and in the next twelve month grain aplenty. In the third year theys'll see food to spare.' He shook his head in wonder. 'No man goes hungry here. For sure this'll be *tír na nóg*.' The Irish promised land of eternal youth. I asked him how long he had been at the halfway inn. 'Going on five year,' he replied.

Once the fire had burnt low we retired as there were no candles. My host, fully clad, made a nest of odd rugs in the couch-bed. I lay down on blankets by the dying embers.

'This is my first night here in the New World,' I told him.

'God willing it won't be your last, Father.'

I tried to sleep but the cries of unknown animals disturbed me. The bush rustled and mysterious feet padded across the pine shingles. I awoke dreaming that a bear had broken into the cabin. The night was so black and starless that I could not make out the window frame and groped in the darkness for the door. Then the beast belched and I recognised the grizzly snores as those of the Irishman.

We rose before dawn and broke our fast with scarcely palatable milk fresh from the cow which fed on wild garlic. The Irishman, the globe nestled in the crook of his arm, guided me back to the trail, all but invisible in the dim glimmer of morning, and readily accepted payment for his hospitality. 'Yes siree, one day this here spot will be marked on your globe,' he said handing it back to me. 'But 'til then yous won't be needing it, Father. Yous'll be in Promise by dinnertime.' He then vanished into the woods with his axe. The sound of chopping chased me away down the path.

All day I followed the dark line of lofty pines expecting at every turn to see a cluster of houses or catch sight of the silhouette of the church but by nightfall I had still not reached my destination. As twilight descended on the land the forest dressed in crêpe. A chaos of dead timber was cast like matchsticks on the forest floor. The old firs fell, rotted and fed the saplings which sprouted on their corpses. Wind and worms reduced the great trunks to dust. The cycle had not changed since the waters of Noah's flood had receded. The wilderness remained untracked, unmapped and virtu-ally untouched by the mark of man. Like Adam cast from the Garden I too was afraid. At the base of grey granite

71

cliffs I lit a fire. The flames shrugged off the cowl of night by raising above me a gilded green canopy embellished here and there with jewels of stars. Within the dome of light I ate my cheese and bread but the sound of a nearby stream forever rolling by filled my heart with a strange melancholy.

By the end of the next day I knew that I was lost. The blazes, which had been few and far between at best, had now vanished altogether. Tangled undergrowth obscured the path. Roots snatched at my feet. I took my bearing from the sun and tried to steer a straight course but at every step a dozen possible tracks snaked off between the beeches and spring-green hemlocks. My food was finished and, as it was too early in the year for berries, I lay down hungry but with faith that the morning would bring me to my destination.

It was not until late afternoon on the sixth day that I smelt the wood ash. The forest, through which I had imagined that no man had before walked, revealed the suggestion of a path. Fearful of missing a fellow traveller I hurried along the trail, marked by now with fresh footprints, and slipped in my excitement, cutting my lip. My shouts startled a grouse which flew across the path. I ran on, pushed through a stand of sugar maples and crashed into the clearing. But instead of a man with hand raised in greeting there waited by the melancholy stream only the smothered fire which I recognised as my own. My route had described a circle. I slumped against the grey granite cliffs and wept, famished and sickened by my weakness.

The next morning, as I tried to retrace my steps back to the halfway inn, I realised that the angel Raphael walked beside me. He carried a pilgrim's staff and accompanied me as he had Tobias on the road into Media. He was a talkative soul, well versed on the manner of driving away wicked spirits, and I enjoyed his company. After we had travelled some miles together he said, 'You will agree then that you are lost.' I could not fault his observation. 'Well, you can navigate. Why not turn back into the forest and head north?'

'Into the unknown?' I asked. Raphael nodded. I had comforted myself with thoughts of platefuls of fried Irish flat cakes. 'But do you have a map to guide my way?'

'Go out into the wilderness and put your hand in the Hand of God,' he replied. 'That shall be better than a known way.'

Some days later I lost track of time. I had not slept. The long cold nights passed like inky sacks of infinite weight dragged across the sky by a weary old man. Strange visions kept me awake. In the shadows I saw faces. I imagined conversations in the sigh of the wind. The fancies infuriated me and I tried to focus my tired and confused mind. I came on a river swollen by the spring run-off and, though my hunger had waned, tried to scoop a trout from the water. The undertaking succeeded only in dampening both my spirit and my clothes. A single speckled egg, stolen from a grassy bank, tasted so bitter that I retched it up.

At night racoons scavenged about my camp, their black masks giving them the look of highwaymen, and a flying squirrel chattered as it leapt from spruce to larch. I lit a fire and raised the golden dome into the trees. Sleep came with bad grace and brought dreams. The woods fell quiet and I thought, 'An angel must be passing overhead.' I opened my eyes and beheld her standing over me, her long white robes billowing in the night breeze. Above her the canopy had become a giltwood library ringed with pine-needle books. The angel took my hand and led me up a spiral stair. Below, my body slept beside the fire. We paused at a shelf to select a volume and I read about riding the swells in clothes sea-wet and coming home from the lobsters. A pamphlet remembered the *Good Intent*, the laying of keel and sighting of line. There were volumes about my childhood, tomes on my father, a worn French grammar and a leaf from the *Christian Instructor Advertiser* which called for 'a missionary with Evangelical zeal, a love for souls and good health equal to the requirements of the calling. Free passage and outfit provided'. Every book in the library touched on my life, on past, present and future. I climbed further up the steps reading, spiralling upwards, until my head pressed against the apex of the dome, the boughs parted and the dark shroud of the night sky rose over me and encompassed me. I started and reached out for the angel's hand but clutched only leaves. I tried to speak aloud but the words stuck in my throat. Then I remembered that even in the deepest forest the Lord was with me and saw that the north star glittered above me. It changed into the angel who glowed and burnt as the fire at my feet. I laughed with the joy of recognition.

'*Slàn leat*,' she called in the Gaelic. 'Blessings be with you.'

I awoke laughing, blinded by the sun, with a stranger standing above me. In the glare I discerned deep mica eyes, a broad nose and face. His skin glistened with bear grease beneath a simple blue cloth garment tied at the waist by a root belt. He held a hatchet in his hand. The Indian pointed with his weapon and spoke in an unknown tongue. My end had come. I rose to my knees and prepared to meet my maker.

'*Seul?*' he asked in French.

'I am not alone. My Master is here with me,' I replied, breaking off my prayers.

He laid down his hatchet, pointed at the globe and said, '*Écossais, jouez pìob.*' Play the pipes. *Pìob* was the Gaelic word for bagpipe. His request took me by surprise. My life appeared not to be in danger. I stood up. '*Jouez pìob,*' the Indian repeated in his mélange of languages and pranced back and forth, his long black hair swaying, blowing into an imaginary bagpipe and bellowing an awful wail. I picked up the globe. '*Oui, oui.*' His smile revealed remarkably white teeth. '*Maintenant,*' he said and again mewed like a love-sick cat. When I failed to act he took the globe from my hand and blew at Greenland. No sound emerged. He looked disappointed and said, '*Cassé.*' Broken. '*C'est dommage.*' He picked up his weapon and turned to go.

'Please,' I managed to say. '*S'il vous plaît, où est Promise?*' '*Comment?*'

'*Je suis perdu.*' I am not alone but I am lost. '*Où est le village de Promise?*'

'*Ah, village Écossais? Pas loin.*' He pointed away to the north-west and flashed an affable smile as if I had overlooked an obvious signpost. '*Un jour.*' A day's travel.

'*Et j'ai faim.*' I am hungry. '*Beaucoup faim.*'

He made me nettle soup. The exquisite hot liquid scorched my throat. As I ate, the Indian sat on a carpet of moss and examined the globe's printed panels. He was of yellow complexion, stout and well-made, and I guessed that he was Micmac, a nomadic tribe of the coast which had allied itself with the French in the eighteenth century. '*Belle, mais cassée,*' he sighed after blowing at the subcontinent.

'*C'est le monde.*' I tried to explain by pointing at the eastern seaboard of America. '*Nous sommes ici.*' He did not understand. '*Il est comme une carte.*'

'*Une carte?*' He nodded and scratched a map in the sand: a forest, a line of hills, inlets of the sea. '*Voilà; c'est facile.*' But I could not picture the route.

'*Est-ce qu'il y a un chemin?*' Is there a path?

The man laughed easily and shook his head. It was difficult to relate my gentle rescuer to Little Donald's stories of brutal savages. '*Vous venez avec moi.*' You'd better come with me. '*En canôt.*'

His canoe was ingeniously made without nails, leather or hemp. The birchbark had been sewn together with the dried roots of trees and sealed with pitch. The Micmac, who called himself Gogo, taught me to kneel in the bow and to hold a paddle. At first I found the vessel, which is sharp at each end, unstable but I gained confidence as we followed the black curve of a river. It moved with good speed and grace, riding through the fast rapids and skirting the innumerable fallen trees.

On the water I began again to appreciate the beauty of my surroundings. The oppressive pines fell away and my lungs filled with the salt smell of an inland sea. Pools and lagoons, brooks and burns etched the banks of golden Bras d'Or Lake. Channels reached far into the bush and clear springs splashed out into the bays where young loons preened and fished. A turtle sunning itself on a deadhead watched our passing. A flash of black ducks took flight. Gogo set the course, cast a disappointed look at the mute globe and began to sing in his Algonquin dialect. Deep glens gouged down between the highlands to the water. The mists rose up from bogs and meadows, curled through the dark aisles of forest and wrapped the shore.

I didn't notice the town. It was the movement of a fisherman in a dugout which caught my eye. As we neared the headland he drew up beside our canoe, doffed his cap and sneezed. 'Thanks to God you have come,' he said in Gaelic then wiped his nose with a sleeve. As we cleaved the saltgrass shallows grazing cattle stirred in the bush. A Highlander hobbled across a stumpy field with his *cas chrom*, lay down the turfing spade to help his wife reach the beach. Two scruffy ginger urchins scrambled down the bank. Eager hands grasped the gunwales. McKinlay, the elder and storekeeper, strode into the water with arm outstretched and shook my hand.

'We feared for your life, sir. Your baggage arrived two days ago.'

'I feel as if I have walked from Dan to Beersheba.' I gestured to the Indian. 'And I would still be lost were it not for this good Samaritan.'

McKinlay spoke to Gogo in Algonquin but his thanks was drowned out by the wail of the pipes. Red McNeil, clad in a tattered kilt, sounded the welcome. His wife led him forward followed by their freckle-faced twin daughters. Gogo tapped my shoulder and nodded at Red. '*Ça c'est bon.*' He was content to be relieved of the globe.

The cluster of mean timber huts was all but indistinguishable from the trees. 'Where is the town?' I asked.

'There's no town but what you see,' replied McKinlay. 'This is Promise.'

A swirl of duckdown wafted over the path out of the wood. Anne McNeil wailed and chased through the flurry of feathers into the clearing of spruce-thatched tents. Children as wild as bear-cubs took refuge in the hovels. Their faces pressed against attic windows as their mothers bagged the birds left part-plucked in the excitement. Other women ran after the pinions which floated through doors, settled on stretched deer hides and sailed over split-pine shingle roofs, then stuffed them into homespun pillowcases. One plume settled on the nose of a cow observing the commotion. Others landed on the cod fillers which dried on clotheslines. 'There are those among us,' confessed McKinlay as a way of explanation, 'who never before saw the face of a clergyman.'

'The Good Lord has blessed us this day,' exulted Anne then gave her husband a look which left him no choice but to agree.

The few young people gathered in from the fields so that they might obtain the rare exhibition of a stranger, turning their backs on Gogo as if he were not there. They scanned my appearance with such eagerness that I blushed and with head down strode across the town. In under a minute I had walked through its centre and out the other side. Promise consisted of more salmon-curing racks than houses. 'I understood that well on one hundred families resided here.'

'Aye, that they do, but spread over the country not in the town,' said McKinlay.

'Some folk, sir, live on the backland and come to Promise only to buy flour and rum,' volunteered McNeil, then added with a hint of envy, 'One of them has two wives.'

'It's law that is needed to keep them in order and gospel to give them some better ideas than they have now,' dictated his wife. Her jaw jutted out with every word spoken.

'They say that they cannot meet you for want of clothes but I fear it is more for a want of heart,' lamented McKinlay. 'This stubborn forest has driven many men to despair.'

'And the church?' I asked, my voice strained. 'Where is the church?'

Red McNeil's twins, as headstrong as their mother, each took a hand to lead me up the brow of a hill. Our small group stopped within a thicket of larch. Underfoot was black granite and through the tangle of brush I glimpsed the sparkle of water but there was no church to be seen.

'We chose this spot,' said McKinlay. 'For certain it's the finest on Cape Breton.'

'It's ourselves that had intended to erect the building in time for your arrival,' said McNeil at his wife's insistence. 'But, well, sir, we had a terrible winter.'

'That's right enough,' she added.

It might have been because of the exhaustion of the journey or perhaps as a reaction to the arrival but standing on the hill I felt a great wave of sadness wash over me. I had left my home and family, travelled for months, lost dear friends and arrived in a poor, lonely place to find no manse, no school, no church. The work demanded by my calling did not daunt me nor did the absence of physical comforts depress me. The warmth of the welcome was not lacking for I could see that the settlers were gladdened by my coming. They were resolute, cheerful and diligent in a situation that was both difficult and novel. But even as I resolved to give myself heart and soul to them and the place, there swelled within me a nagging, nebulous sensation that something had been lost.

'We shall build a church here, on this spot, where we will worship together.' I turned to include in prayer all those gathered in the forest and saw that my Micmac rescuer had vanished. 'By faith,' I quoted from *Hebrews*, 'Abraham, when he was called, obeyed to go out unto a place which he was to receive for an inheritance; and he went out not knowing whither he went. He became a sojourner in the land of promise, as in a land not his own: for he looked for a city which hath foundations, whose builder and maker is God.'

THERE WAS NO Promise marked on the new Nova Scotia highways map so Beagan dug deep into the box trunk and unearthed an original, hand-drawn Township Plan. 'Scale: 40 Chains to an Inch,' read the legend. 'Mining Rights Forfeited.' A rigid, right-angled grid pattern had been imposed on the irregular shore. Concession lines struck through the bush unimpeded by rivers or hills, subjugating nature to the plan. His great-grandfather's wilderness had been tamed by tape measures, the unknown banished with the stroke of a surveyor's pen. In each boxy lot the Crown Land Officer had recorded a settler's name: McNeil, Red; McKinlay, Isaac; MacFie, Hamish. In one corner plot a clerk had written, 'Site reserved for Promise Presbyterian Church.'

Beagan drove north away from Pioneer Village and the Highlands of the New World rose across his path. He had made no attempt to walk the Reverend's circuitous trek through the bush. That trail had been followed through the diary's pages. Instead he sped up Highway 105 past deserted farms and tried to imagine the unbroken forests that had confronted the first Scottish settlers. His back began to ache, not from the rental car's uncomfortable seats, but from thinking of the labour needed to wrestle a single field from the bush.

The once wild land had for a single generation lain smooth with meadows ditched and pastures cleared but it was now being reclaimed by nature. The trees pressed in on derelict homesteads. Powder-blue paint peeled from rotting walls. On the car radio listeners rang a phone-in programme for advice on tracing their ancestors from Lewis, Uist and Eigg. Beagan heard in their voices something so plaintive that he had to stop and check the road map for fear of losing his way.

Above a town named Dunvegan stormclouds rumbled across the steel sky. A tear in the firmament released a gleam of vermilion dusk. The first drops of cold rain turned the earth iron red. At Glencoe a sorry herd of cattle sauntered under cover around a beaver-dam lake. Plastic ducks paid no heed, petrified mid-waddle on verdant lawns, but the sleet drove the locals indoors. Apart from the disembodied radio voices there seemed to be no one on Cape Breton. The few other cars on the road drifted out of the haze, lifting waves of slush over Beagan's windshield, but he saw no faces behind the wheels.

He pulled into a neon-lit pizzeria to order a take-away. 'Hawaiian Crab-Meat Special' cheered a poster but the oven hadn't been switched on so he settled for spaghetti and tinned meatballs. The black and white television on the counter played a government Prosperity Initiative commercial. 'Can Canada compete?' demanded the announcer. 'Yes we can,' enthused the orchestrated reply, 'here at the centre of things.'

As his supper warmed in the microwave the owner ground his teeth. 'It's not worth my while heating up the oven, eh? Just for one pizza.'

Beagan sat on a stool shivering and wondered what Hector would have made of it, this New Jerusalem which left him feeling cheated, even deceived. 'Where is everyone?' he asked. He was the first customer that night and the owner had no change.

'Gone away.' The owner gestured out the window at the weather. 'Wouldn't you?'

A damp Canadian flag washed into view. The Clansman Motel was a horseshoe of pale mint clapboard cabins curved around a dirt track on the edge of Bras d'Or. The single picnic table turned its back on a barbecue fashioned from a wheel hub. 'Cabin 11 empty. Pay tomorrow' read the scribbled notice stuck to the office window. The screen door creaked open on to a room of fern-green plasterboard walls and an air of transience. The sagging double bed brought to mind travelling salesmen, nights of foamy beer and roughly fondled breasts. On the coffee table lay the previous month's *Inverness Oran*. It advertised jobs in Australia. 'A fantastic challenge is waiting for you on a farm overseas.'

Beagan dragged the trunk in from the wet and ate a mouthful of tepid spaghetti. He leafed through the sermons and Sustentation Fund accounts. In an envelope lay an edge of sail canvas. He picked up Hector's Memorandum, turned its onion-skin yellow pages and read, 'We laid the foundations of our church. With axe and scythe we cut away the bush, spiralling round and round the centre, pushing back the wild wood. Stumps were burnt or torn from their roots by oxen, boulders split and levered aside. Our foothold on the brow of the hill was enlarged, a plateau cleared where a man could stand and look out, his sight not hemmed in by a barrier of trees but open to the broad vista of water.'

Beagan paused to finish the last meatball. It was cool in the cabin and he wrapped a blanket around his shoulders. The rain blowing off the lake bubbled through the cracked panes and formed a puddle beneath the window sill. He felt his great-grandfather's isolation, a man forever separated from home and family, then with a little less gravity began to wonder if there were any single women alone and cold in an adjoining cabin. He would have enjoyed the company. They could share the warmth of his blow-heater. But when he plugged it in the fuse blew out and he turned with a sigh back to the diary.

'We beat trails like animals between town and quarry and our legs were torn by underbrush and brambles,' the journal continued. 'Isaac McKinlay and MacFie the fisher built two of the corners. To make the others the shore farmers assembled in a bee, as is the custom here when clearing land or raising barns. They felled the spruce and cut the lumber by whip-saw, then rolled the logs over a pit where, with one man above and another below, a drag-saw sliced them from end to end. The logs were mortised or notched so that they locked at the corners of the building. Shingles of cedar were fashioned with an axe and pine planks cut for the floor. Around the rising walls another acre of ground has been cleared to be the sacred resting place of the departed dead.'

A small lead Communion token slipped out from between the leaves and fell into Beagan's lap. He felt its weight in his hand then pulled back the brown cloth drapes and gazed out at the headland. The view promptly vanished behind a curtain of mist. Promise lay beyond the clouds.

'NO ONE WHO ever dwelt in a body worked so hard as did they.' I sat bolt upright, collar tightly fastened and Bible in hand. Jamie perched beside me on the bedstead looking over Beagan's shoulder. 'It was every board that had to be cut by hand. There was not a sawmill in fifty miles. Even the children helped by filling the chinks between the logs with moss and wet clay.' As Beagan lay down on the bed I nodded at the memory. 'Aye, and those good men worked still in the fields and at their nets.'

'Beagan read somewhere,' said Jamie, 'that a naked man standing outside in winter would have f-f-frostbite in twenty seconds and in summer be sucked dry of blood by mosquitoes in six minutes.'

'That may well be, James, but we did not uncase ourselves outdoors,' I reminded my son. 'Except when we bathed. It was the one physical pleasure of those days, swimming in Bras d'Or. The men washed at the foot of the cliff path most evenings. I remember the pale white skin of the tired bodies seemed luminous against the dark green wood.' I held out my hands. The callused tip of my forefinger was smudged ink black. 'We were building something where there had been nothing, right enough.'

'It was the labour that brought you together.'

'It was faith, James. As hard as oak, as lasting as pine.'

In the plasterboard room Beagan's eyes drooped, his head fell and the diary dropped on to the pillow. I spread my cape and raised above us an evergreen cathedral. The sagging bed stood in the glade which was the nave. Around it McKinlay and MacFie, the McNeils and their twins bowed their heads in extempore prayer.

'Before the church was completed our services were held out in the open.' I stretched out further and conjured up old Promise around Beagan's sleeping head. Unshod children sat on the motel coffee table. Men dressed in best black fingered the pages of their Bibles with earth-stained hands. The women wore clean muslin handkerchiefs knotted under their chins. Anne McNeil flaunted a bonnet as a personal extravagance. 'It is myself that would have no kneeling or genuflexion, no candles or crucifixes, no pomp or trappings to stand between man and God,' I recalled. The precentor stepped in front of the broken television set and intoned a psalm. It was sung by the congregation. 'Our words of praise rose into the air and He came among us and blessed us with His presence.'

The town looked as it had before Jamie's birth, the spruce-thatched tents, salmon-curing racks and McKinlay's store. 'Gosh, how clever,' he said, laughing at the trick. It was still Sunday. Families settled under the pines at the end of the first service to eat lunches of squirrel pie, cheese and bread. The men drank from jugs of West India rum, which they had traded for fish, before assembling for the second sermon. 'Can I learn to do that?' asked Jamie.

'It is simply a matter of concentration,' I explained as we walked among the worshippers. 'Now pay attention.' Before our eyes dormant plants came into bud, fruit trees flowered and birds called for their mates. 'In that first difficult year,' I continued, 'the blessings of spring were spoilt by a bedevilled summer. The mosquitoes descended on us like a plague of locust and, worse still, the potatoes rotted in the field. Aye well, the farms on the shore could cope with the blight, their rich soil produced a good variety of crops, but the disease ravaged the families on the backlands. Their poor, rocky plots could grow little else and to fend

off starvation the men were forced away from home to dig
coal at Sydney Mines. Some took work as gutters on American saltbankers fishing in the Gulf.'

Beyond the cracked window panes and far across the
island Jamie saw the paupers frequent the wharves at Ship
Harbour. They begged for handouts of Indian meal and
flour from every trading schooner.

'Would you be remembering the old canoe?' I asked.
Jamie nodded. It was in the canoe that MacFie had found
my body. 'It took me out to those who could not come to
our tabernacle in the wilderness. In log hovels I preached
to congregations of broken men and suspicious neighbours.
I read them the Word of the Gospel by the light of my
own candle, which I carried so as not to tax their meagre
resources. In the presence of God I married couples who
had lived as man and wife for decades and baptised their
middle-aged children. They wept afterwards over suppers
of sooty porridge.' Jamie winced at an unpalatable memory,
unable to forget the practice of burning the head of grain
before winnowing.

I wore my shepherd's tartan plaid and knelt back in my
birchbark canoe. The motel bed drifted alongside me, its
counterpane inflated like a hovercraft's skirt. Jamie
perched on the headboard. When Beagan began to snore I
reached over to turn out the bedside lamp.

'Aye but there was a fearful intransigence too. It was
myself that attributed much of it to the excess of tea drinking,' I said. 'They drank slushes of that boiled black liquid.
It dulled the appetite, right enough.' Beagan mumbled in
his dreams and I lowered my voice. 'So instead of wallowing
in paucity I enjoined them to improve their material condition. The Shorter Catechism makes a bold virtue of getting
along in the world. A man with an empty stomach worries
little about feeding his soul so the duties of my station were
not only to nurture neglected spirits.'

'Mother told us that you mediated in quarrels, prescribed

and provided medicine, even advised on crop rotation and drainage.' A summer breeze caught the bedhead and Jamie grabbed hold of the canoe's thwart. 'And there were always widows to be consoled.'

'It was hard on the women, James. A horse's work was taken out of them. They were made to harrow, gather and carry crop, knit and spin with distaff and spindle as they walked, even when with child. There was butter to churn and bread to bake. In any spare moment they turned their hands to the loom to weave blankets or cloth. For most a bit of gay ribbon was a luxury beyond their purse. And when the women lost their brothers or husbands there were never any savings. It is hard to keep a house with empty cupboards.'

Beneath leg-o'-mutton sails a trap skiff rode up to Saint George's Channel and hauled aboard a swelling, silvery catch. Between the spreading and lifting of the nets its crew hailed other passing fishers: Acadian French, Newfoundland Irish and the ubiquitous American Loyalist. Men who had taken their rent from the sea in Scotland continued here to live from the point of the hook.

'We collected alms to help buy seed for the less fortunate and provide books for those in need. Some settlers had bartered their Bibles for cheap spirits but many who were before abandoned found purpose in the true Word. It brought them knowledge, and without knowledge people can be neither good Christians nor good citizens. They began to toil with strength renewed, to spend as little as possible, to live on the commonest fare until a sum of money was saved either to buy an adjoining tract or to send a child away to be schooled.'

With a sleight of wing another season slipped away before our eyes. The waters of Bras d'Or were burnished crimson and gold. Skeins of geese flew south as cold white fingers etched the autumn leaves. They floated on the wind and landed on Beagan's bed. A gentle rain began to fall and he shivered in his sleep. As Jamie tucked the blanket around him the sound of praying reached our ears.

'I recollect standing in the nave of the church, watching the last beams and ribs rise above me, seeing that the roof resembled an upturned boat. Sure enough, its ridge was the keel, its apse curved like a stern, its gable cloven as the bow.' I nodded towards the headland in approval. 'It was a fine *bàta*, a finer ark than any I had built. The ship of the Lord, James.'

In a moment Jamie stood beside me inside the newly completed church. 'It would be a Sabbath-day in October that the long table was run from prow to stern and decked in white cloths for the first Holy Communion. I preached in the Gaelic then in English. We sang from the Psalms of David, the communicants sat at the table and the elders passed among them the goblet of spruce beer – it was not wine that we had – and great chunks of bread which they took and broke and ate and said, "This do in remembrance of me." God's faithful gave thanks for their blessings and worshipped Him in sincerity and in truth. "Glory to Thee forever, Thou bright moon this night. There is no speech nor language where Thy voice is not heard."'

We gazed at my old congregation then I folded my cape and the fern-green cabin walls of the motel closed in around us. The church and its brethren vanished. A passing car's headlights flashed across the brown cloth curtains. Jamie perched beside me again on the bedstead. I turned towards him and said, 'It was a time when there was no doubt.' Then our eyes fell on Beagan who groaned, his rest disturbed by the journey, and together we wrapped gentle dreams around him to soothe the uneasy sleep.

BY DAWN THE rain had lifted. A cool breeze blew off the water, over the yard of sycamore shade and through the screen door.

The motel sat on a wide grassy strip between dark pine cliffs and the shore. Beagan awoke strangely refreshed. His head was so full of images of the land as it had been in his great-grandfather's day that he decided to walk the last mile to Promise and crossed a clover field to reach Bras d'Or. He strode over rocks wrapped in linguine seaweed, past tomato-red fishermen's shacks and around green gunwaled dories with high van Gogh prows. Seagulls squatted on the shingled roofs and crabs scuttled away into the swells. In his pocket was the old Township Plan and the Memorandum.

As he walked it was easy for him to picture the past. Little seemed to have changed around the bay. In his imagination the emaciated settler set foot on the virgin shore. He could see Gogo's canoe slipping through the saltgrass shallows to deliver both Reverend and globe to the parish. He heard the chop of axes and hymn of voices sparkle over the water. Hector's head bobbed above the surface, bathing at the foot of the cliff path, then before his eyes it sprouted a seal's whiskers and dived out of sight. As he rounded the point he conjured up a vision of trap skiffs and Cape boats tacking home ahead of the first blizzard.

'Frost clings to the morning and makes rigid armour of long johns hanging from the line,' his great-grandfather had written during the long, cold December. 'Winter proclaims her arrival with gale winds and horizontal snow. I enter the pulpit in heavy coat, woollen mittens and skull cap carrying a bucket of live coals to warm my feet. No trousers do any good without two pairs of stockings.' Beagan imagined the still waters frozen into sheet ice and felt the bitter wind wail down from the Arctic. 'The men busy themselves cutting wood and hunting moose. They drive the beasts into deep snow then butcher them. Their wives make moccasins from the legs and wear the hide, hair and all, stripped straight from the carcass. The gamy smell lingers about them in church.' The writing became scratchy and indistinct. The pen had run dry and Beagan pictured Hector refilling it while blowing on cold blue fingers.

'Those who do not remain active are sped to higher service above. During Christmas week Alistair MacQuarie lost his arthritic cow, lame horse and wife. I found him weeping before his five children and reading the Gaelic Bible. "This," he said, stroking the Testament, "is my sole comfort." But the dead cannot be buried as the ground is too hard to dig. They are placed on a handsleigh and hauled to the village by relays of mourners wearing snowshoes. Their tears freeze on their beards. The coffins are laid in a cellar, sealed so squirrels can not steal in to bite off ears and nose, until the thaw.'

Beagan pictured a cabin fall vacant, its owner having died or moved on to Upper Canada, and the Reverend take up residence. Anne McNeil brought him steaming dishes of salt pork and *colcannon*, boiled cabbage and potatoes pounded with milk. As he waited to eat, his stomach growling with hunger, she complained about a neighbour's overindulgence in ardent spirits. Her twin daughters cleaned for him, whispering and giggling with every polish and sweep. MacFie stopped by with a few fresh smelt or gaspereaux caught through an ice hole. His nose dripped from the cold which he could not throw off. He never accepted the offer of a chair but turned his beaver hat in his hands and apologised after a few brief minutes, 'Would you forgive me, Mr Gillean, for so overstaying my welcome?' Hector was forever writing, making notes, accounting for the alms, but all too soon the lonely winter evenings closed in and the fire burnt low. No warmth remained in the empty house. Beagan felt his blood run cold as he read that the ink in Hector's vest pocket had frozen during February's bitter nights.

His heart thawed with a diary entry scribbled in late April. 'All winter the woods have remained without voice. A great coldness has silenced the earth. But this last month the murmur of water under the thinning ice whispered of spring. The frozen bay groaned and strained then snapped. Now children clatter between the hissing floes before their mothers, hands wringing, scold them back. Icicles drip from the eaves then drop into muddy drifts. Snowbanks tumble down shingles, slide off roofs and thud on to doorsteps. On the beach the fishers talk of full nets and bellies while sorting their killicks, grapples and buoys.'

Beagan listened to hear the newcomers curse and crash their way through the bush from Ship Harbour. They laughed as they embraced old friends and cried for those lost to the cold. Their axes bit into the virgin forest and seeds were sown between the hemlock stumps and girdled pines. Logs were chopped and heaved and dovetailed into cabins. The whole village seemed to moan with growing pains. Song echoed from the new tavern and the blacksmith's anvil rang under the hammer. The congregation swelled and the fresh voices filled the settlement with prayer.

Beagan's fancies were deafened by a great Mack truck thundering past, 'Snap! Crackle! Pop!' scrolled down its trailer. The driver of a camper van dribbled bits of Big Mac down his Toronto Maple Leafs hockey shirt. A police car screamed after a speeding scarlet Pontiac. The old shore had met a modern wall of crushed stone. Beagan scrambled up the incline and on to a new highway. According to his dated map Promise lay beneath it.

He could not spot the foundations of the church from the hard shoulder and followed a rough path into the bush in search of them. Away from the asphalt ribbon, around the place where McKinlay's store had once stood, he lost his way among the chestnuts. Saplings sprung from the husks of old oaks. Wild spring iris pushed up through the blanket of autumn leaves. Instead of the jighooks and communion tokens which he had hoped to discover he found Coke cans and disposed nappies. There was no manse, no walls, no commemorative plaque. The plots had been reclaimed by the wilderness. The houses had rotted back into the earth. Beagan realised that the town was gone, buried by time and hidden by progress, and the heavy fog of despair closed in around him again.

Guided by the drone of traffic Beagan turned back towards the road, tripped on a moss-covered float and fell against a rusty Studebaker. He stood up and bruised his shin on a sheared propeller. A startled chicken flapped off its fish-flake roost and scuttled away into the undergrowth. In place of fields of golden corn and laden squid racks Beagan had stumbled upon acres of old bathtubs, rotten hulls and decrepit threshers. He picked his way across the yard of cast-offs, through a wall with a holed rowing boat as its gate, towards a building. Beagan knocked at the door and, when no answer came, stepped over the threshold and on to the forecourt of a petrol station. 'Old Church Texaco' read the sign. 'Last Gas for 50 miles.' The red-haired attendant, who was filling up an ancient Newfoundland-registered station wagon, was undisturbed by Beagan's unorthodox entrance. 'How's she going?' he asked, scratching the downy growth of his first beard.

'I'm looking for Promise,' said Beagan.

'Excuse me?'

'The old town. The map says it should be around here.'

'Sorry, mister. Don't know any place by that name.' The dated gas pump chimed like a clock with every litre delivered. 'Except the ghost town, eh?'

'A pioneer town?'

'Search me.' The attendant began to clean the windscreen, pausing to itch his chin with the rubber end of the squeegee, confident that his past was not worth knowing. 'It was history even before I was a kid.'

An Acadian Lines coach whistled past the station. Beagan examined his Plan. 'This road doesn't seem to be marked on here.'

'Hey, it's new,' counselled the boy, his tone deepening to emphasise the importance of the development. 'Three hours to Halifax. Eighteen hours to Toronto.' He threw his arm westward with a gesture to illustrate speed. 'Man, that's moving.'

'You going down the road too, bud?' asked the driver of the station wagon. He, his pregnant wife and two quibbling kids carried cardboard mugs of complimentary coffee and jam-filled doughnuts back to their car.

'Yes,' replied Beagan. 'Sort of passing through.'

'We're heading for Ontario,' he volunteered. Newfoundlanders have the gift of the gab; they can talk a lobster into its pot. 'My brother says there's jobs going at General Motors.' He untucked a pack of Camels from his T-shirt sleeve. 'I'd offer you a lift but we're kinda full up.' The car sank on its springs as the family clambered aboard. 'You hit your sister again I'll belt you good,' he told his son as the woman counted the notes twice before paying for the fuel. 'At home it's real bad now, eh?' he told Beagan. 'The wife got laid off from the fishplant. The two of us gotta work to make a go of it so we're going west.' The engine roared·into life, spitting a thin slick of oil over the asphalt. 'Hey listen bud, don't stay around here too long. You know what they call a Cape Bretoner? A Newfie who ran out of money on the way to Toronto.'

The station wagon shuddered into gear and lurched on to the highway, its muffler scraping the pavement with a shower of sparks. The attendant pocketed the dollars. 'Stupid Newfies.' His curse betrayed a touch of envy, as if he felt himself dislocated without ever having left home. He slunk off towards the office then turned to direct Beagan up the road. 'You could try talking to my granddad. His hearing's none too good but his memory's okay.'

The shack had once commanded an uninterrupted view of the water but the highway had cut it off from Bras d'Or. Its windows rattled with every passing truck. A dog on a chain barked as Beagan approached. The front door opened and a voice yelled, 'What day is it today?'

'Saturday,' replied Beagan.

'Can't hear you.'

'Today is Saturday.'

'Hallelujah,' declared the obese old man. 'Pension day.' His hearing may have ebbed away with the years but his eyes, which settled on Beagan, gleamed like quicksilver. 'I knows ya,' he hollered. 'I knows your father.' It seemed unlikely. Neither Beagan nor his father had ever been to the east coast. 'I never forget a face and you and your father looked as alike as two cod in a salt bucket.' He leaned his head to one side, eased a fat finger into a bushy ear and talked as if to himself. 'I remember the day Jamie left. He done good in Toronto, your dad.' His chins wobbled as he raised his voice. 'Yes sir, he done good. Now where's me cap?'

'James was my grandfather,' clarified Beagan. He had often been told that the Gilleans had a strong family resemblance.

'I would have gone with your dad but I had Mother to look after.' He found his cap in the electric cooker. It was a gift from relatives and he had left it on the porch to rust. He preferred his old cast-iron stove.

'My grandfather,' repeated Beagan a little louder. Another truck roared past, all but shaking him off the doorstep.

'You looks good for your age, I'll say that. Must be the easy city life. What you doing back here anyways?'

'I've been looking for Promise,' sighed Beagan, glancing around as if he'd overlooked the village.

'Well you found it,' he chuckled and turned back indoors. His heavy tread was like a bear's lumber. He looked as if he'd be happier walking on all fours. As an afterthought he added, 'Come on in while I get my stick.'

Inside, the walls had been painted canary yellow. The worn checkerboard linoleum recorded the years of passage: table to sink, door to armchair. A porcupine-quill box was stuffed with screws, nails and curled photographs of a young woman. Above the television, with its aerial fashioned from a lobster pot, hung an engraving of fishing boats at Portree. A family Bible rested on the sideboard.

'I'm a Macleod of Skye,' said the old man as if he and his kind had been away from Scotland for only a few years. 'My people came out in 1791. It's them that knewed your granddad.'

'My great-grandfather,' corrected Beagan. The old man's distorted sense of time irritated him. 'I can't find much evidence of him.'

'Nothing left of him or nobody else.' Macleod poured coffee thick as molasses into chipped mugs. Beagan refused the offering. 'My people were the first on this stretch of coast so they settled the best land. The latecomers who came after us had to make do with the lots behind, in them highland places you know. Nothing grows up there so they were the first to move on. Then when the shipyard closed and the town's future hung on a fish-hook everybody started to go, eh? Young folks got lazy. They let the land get growed over and the nets rot.' A transport roared past the cracked window, 'Love that Crunch!' printed on its side. His voice rose in anger. 'When I was a boy I was brought up on porridge and the Bible. Now all I see is corn flakes and Nintendo games. Everyone's gone,' Macleod cried above the scream of an Irving Petroleum tanker. 'They even moved the old church to pave a road so folks could get out quicker. Ain't nothing left of Promise except me and the dead and we ain't going nowhere. No sir.'

Macleod found his stick and set off up a pine-needle path, stomped across the highway without a glance to left or right and sidled down the bank to the shore. Beagan scurried behind, darting between two logging trucks. The old man untied the painter and slipped a rowing boat out of its hiding place in a culvert. Beagan hesitated on the shore. He had forgotten his Kwells.

'Don't just stand there, help me push.' Macleod took the oars as Beagan launched the boat out into the bay. He turned the bow back towards the Clansman Motel and against a cacophony of thunderous lorries began to sing. 'Bet in the city you never heard the Gaelic. It was the language of Adam in the Garden. In your granddad's day it was Canada's third most common language. Now there's maybe eight hundred speakers left in the whole damn Maritimes, if you'll pardon my French.' The stroke of the oars left a trail of twisting whirlpools in the wake. 'Used to be that a man from this island was Scottish first and foremost. Second, he was Cape Bretoner. Third, he was a Nova Scotian. And fourth, if at all, he was Canuck.' A guillemot circled overhead and the cry of an air horn echoed across the bay. 'Don't know now what nobody is no more.'

I balanced on the bow behind the splendid fellow and looked back at the receding headland, the tartan cloak cast around my shoulders. Jamie wore a look of disappointment. 'I had hoped at least to see the old manse,' he sighed. 'I can't believe that there is nothing left.'

'Nothing physical,' I corrected sharply. The fate of Promise had distressed me too but doubt tended to strengthen my certainties. 'It is memory alone that endures. We saw that last night.'

'But I can't conjure it up like that,' Jamie complained. 'I haven't the knack.' He sighed too deeply for my liking. 'I would have just liked to touch the old walls.'

'Sentimentality does not become you, James,' I stated, then added with a hint of sarcasm, 'Is it yourself that hankers after your old body?'

'No. I was never particularly f-f-fond of it. There was that bandy limp and, of course, my stutter.'

'The finest thing in life, right enough, is growing older. The back goes, the hair falls out, the muscles sag and that's a disappointment but only a fleeting, physical concern. We die, yes, and that is sad for those left behind, yet the spirit lives on to glean the rich experience and wisdom of living.' I dismissed mortality with a wave. 'Promise is like a corpse, the discarded shell. But its spirit, its history, is alive.'

'Only as long as someone living bothers to remember it.'

'That is why he is here.' I gestured at my great-grandson. 'To grasp that which made him.' Beagan glanced uneasily towards the bow. I leaned close to Jamie and whispered as if Beagan and Macleod might overhear. 'But that apart I tell you this, he may be of our flesh and blood yet he is a person too fond of the fireside.' I sensed myself growing over-excited. 'In my time no man would be caught whistling on the Sabbath. Your mother used to peel Sunday's potatoes on a Saturday night. But in the name of Providence this Beagan contemplates fornication out of wedlock and reads newspapers on the Lord's Day.'

Jamie leaned back against the gunwale and put his hands behind his head. 'Tell me about Mother,' he coaxed. 'It was, what, the second summer when you met again?'

'That was a year of many blessings,' I relented. 'Within the space of twelve months I gained a wife, a home and a son.'

'Tell me,' encouraged Jamie.

'You will recollect my concern for personal hygiene.'

'Cleanliness is next to godliness,' he quoted. 'You were as careful as an Egyptian about your linen.'

'In those days I maintained the discipline of immersing myself every morning. I only succumbed to the bathtub when Bras d'Or froze over.' The recollection brought Jamie out in goose-bumps. He shivered and the boat rocked as if caught by a keen gust of crosswind. Beagan grabbed a lifejacket while Macleod cast a weather eye at the sky. 'It was my custom to swim far out into the bay before rising for air. But one day when I surfaced it wasn't the cold which took my breath away. A trading smack had gybed around the headland and heaved to in our cove. I heard familiar voices shout my name. They spoke the Gaelic and I fancied for a moment that I had traversed the whole Atlantic and swum back to the Hebrides.' I blinked the salt from my eyes. 'It was then that I recognised the *Good Intent*. Ewan Cameron had brought her to Promise for the timber. We had braw woods, right enough.'

'And Mother?'

'Kirstie was with him, yes. It was fine to see her gentle face.' Jamie waited for me to share my affections but none were forthcoming, it simply wasn't part of my vocabulary. Instead I said plainly, 'I can recollect her bridal dress, a grey material with deep blue stripes. The stricter members of the wedding party had thought it rather too gay. I myself found it to be very handsome.'

'There's a piece of it in the trunk,' said Jamie, nodding towards Beagan. 'At least I remember Mother putting one there.'

'Would you know that it rained that whole year from the day we were wed to the night Zachary was born?' I glanced up at a bank of snowclouds rolling in from the Atlantic. 'I caught the drips of rain leaking through the roof in pots splashed across the cabin floor as she wept in her labour. And mark you this, that sweet water doubled our blessings. No one had expected such a bountiful harvest, not from

95

the earth nor from a woman of your mother's age, and the congregation, enriched in soul and substance, bestirred themselves to erect us a manse.' My grip tightened on the Bible. 'To this day I have never yet seen a finer building and sure I am that I never will.'

Jamie remembered the plain, simple house; its kitchen with a black cast-iron stove, the bedroom where he and his brother had been born, the study with the few precious books shipped from Scotland. The globe had been set in pride of place on my writing table. The box trunk had been arranged underneath it as a footrest. Apart from a few letters from home the trunk was all but empty; I was a man who scattered words like seed, it was Jamie who would come to hoard them.

'Kirstie's father laboured too, organising the fishers then dressing, salting and shipping their catches in tierces to the West Indies,' I continued. 'The *Good Intent* traded our salmon and cod for cargoes of sugar, molasses and rum. Then when winter returned he stopped the men leaving for Sydney Mines by starting the shipbuilding. Aye, he constructed a workshop and moulding loft beside his salt store and fish shed. The cooper's yard was extended for a blacksmith. A forge with two fires was added. They felled timber to supply masts for Her Majesty's Navy – he had secured a profitable contract – and his first New World ship took shape on the shore.'

A delivery van down-geared to climb away from the coast highway and distracted me. 'They're g-r-r-r-eat!' was emblazoned along its length. I found it difficult to correlate the modern world's bold assertions with the sin of its lost belief.

'You can't get away from it, James; Ewan worked like the spring-tide. He had the three qualities necessary for success – judgement, industry and health – and it brought prosperity to Promise. Cabins began to be replaced by farmhouses. There was clapboard instead of squared logs. And

Red McNeil, well now, he built his wife a stone lodge with fretwork on the eaves. Not in Promise itself mind you but there across the bay.' I pointed forward beyond the Clansman Motel. 'Anne felt that stone lent a manorial air and told all comers that the pioneer days had passed. Here, she used to say, is genteel and civilised society. The best corner of the promised land, she called it.' I stroked my whiskers. 'Anne McNeil was a good soul, but as full of boasting as the egg is of meat.'

The rowing boat followed the direction of my finger. 'My responsibilities grew too. The kind and zealous ministry they dubbed it. It was as many as five sermons that I preached on the Sabbath, canoeing to the far reaches of the parish. And there were so few clergymen on the island that more and more people came from far afield to our church. They filled the pews, stood by the windows and crowded the gallery. At one point a hundred young adults and almost as many children, among them Zachary, waited to be baptised. I could not accommodate them all at the font and called for *am Baisteadh Mòr*, a great summer baptism.'

A storm-beaten dredger chugged past and in its swell, in the reflection of Beagan on the water, I saw fleets of small boats converge on the bay. The McLeods rowed their children across West Bay. Barra men coasted down from Iona. Lewis families sailed around Cape Dauphin. The McNabs tacked over from the Loch Lomond shore. 'We gathered together on the beach, plunged ourselves into the glimmering brine and praised God, calling for repentance, for a break with the sinful past. We washed ourselves clean in the name of the Father, the Son and the Holy Spirit.'

'And I was christened then with Zachary?' asked Jamie.

'You, *a bhalaich*, were baptised one bitterly cold February. I performed the sacrament with you in my arms. "I will give unto him who has thirst the fountain of the water of life." I reached into the font and touched cold ice. The holy water had frozen solid so I struck the surface.'

'As I recall your arm was always strong to smite.'

'Forget you not James, the devil does not beguile the disciplined,' I answered. 'The ice shattered into splinters but each shard was bone dry. There was not one drop of liquid between them. So I turned from the font and led the congregation out into the weather, down the winding path to the edge of the bay. There I knelt down, dipped my hand into the sea and anointed your brow.' I reached over the side of the boat. 'With this living water, my boy.'

As if by intuition Beagan's gaze dropped from the horizon and alighted at that moment on the ripple. It was for all appearances a splash from the boat's wake or the cold flop of a hungry fish, and not the touch of the hand of an angel that it seemed to be in his imagination.

THE TOWN WHICH had grown around the McNeil house clung to the end of a point like a clinch of limpets. Keith and Elie's Jingle Restaurant was up for sale. At the Caledonia Co-op a lone couple hovered by the meat counter comparing prices of individual chicken breasts. The United Church appeared to be as forgotten as its faded sign: 'Fight Truth decay, brush up on your Bible.' Broken beer bottles lay splintered on the overgrown playground and yellowed posters pleaded 'Save Our School' from grimy classroom windows. In the post office, where Macleod cashed his pension cheque, an unhappy freckle-faced boy swam in a vast hand-me-down baseball uniform. 'If it's too large you can change it with MacCodrum. Or is it MacCrimmon?' His mother hesitated. 'Who's the first baseman?'

The resident minister bought a lottery ticket and refused to be drawn into criticism of a lapsed parishioner. 'I don't speak disrespectfully of any people. She's a dear soul, drive anyone crazy.' He reminded Beagan more of a jovial game-show host than a God-fearing clergyman. When the postmistress added her voice to the litany he blathered more vapid pleasantries. 'I never heard a woman turn down the opportunity to speak. Especially you Aberdeen girls. You're good at it.'

'Where's that no good son of yours?' Macleod yelled at him. 'Gone to the city?'

'I am the son, Mr Macleod,' the minister replied. 'It's my father whom you knew.' He then noticed Beagan. 'And who is this young feller?'

'He turned up on my doorstep looking for Promise, if you can beat that,' answered Macleod. Beagan introduced himself. He hadn't felt seasick in the rowing boat, possibly because of the company, and wished he were back on the water.

'We don't know how the Lord works but His ways are wonderful.' The minister's laugh was like a fox's bark. 'That's why you're here today.'

'What did he say?' shouted the old man while stocking up on Crunchie bars and Maxwell House.

'That there's a parish concert this lunchtime,' Beagan bawled back.

'Cape Breton is an island of fiddlers,' the minister declared as he led them up the damp empty street. 'The music lifts people's spirits, stops them thinking about unemployment for a time. Did you know that the singing and step-dancing which live on here disappeared from Scotland with the Clearances?'

Beagan found it hard to believe that any performers lived on lonely Cape Breton but there were fiddlers aplenty in the steamy Parish Memorial Centre. The islanders had emerged from behind the closed doors of their scattered farms and gathered together for the Kinettes' concert. They swept in from the wet, stamped the cold out of their boots and shook themselves dry. Daughters swirled their tartan plaids and mothers wore high-necked blouses. The pizzeria owner practised a medley on the piano. At the bar the old men were speaking Gaelic. The minister gossiped with great good humour, paused to inspect the Bake Sale and bought a ticket for the quilt raffle. A handbell rang as he made for the stage. Fiddles and guitars were tuned. Grandparents took their seats between their great-nieces and -nephews. A slender boy with a ponytail darted into the dressing room to wish luck to his parents. The minister's welcome was short and familiar. Entertainers and spectators alike all lived within a dozen miles of each other. Beagan spotted no waterlogged day-trippers who had wandered in off the Ceilidh Trail.

'And to start us off here's young Carrie Macaulay, Libby's daughter, to sing "Sleep Sleep Bonnie Baby".' A voice whispered from the wings. The onlookers chuckled. The minister barked, 'Oh bless my soul, wrong again.' Life and his own jokes amused him equally. 'To sing *Mo rùn Geal, Dileas*.'

Thirteen-year-old Carrie stood off the stage's centre. The spotlight had fused but no one missed its illumination. Her gentle Gaelic air hushed the audience, its sad music washing away their chatter. Her mother's Polaroid flashed and cranked out a picture. There followed a dozen costumed performers with laments about emigration, ballads of mist-covered mountains and shanties for fishermen's fathers and fishermen's sons. All the songs were about Scotland and the pain of diaspora, providing solace in a place that had been economically depressed for generations. Everyone knew the words and joined in for each chorus.

These are my mountains and this is my glen,
The braes of my childhood will call me again.
No lands ever claimed me though far did I roam,
For these are my mountains and I'm going home.

As they shuffled on stage a troupe of seven MacAskills, shy and soft-spoken, seemed unlikely dancers until the music lightened their feet. The driving rhythm of the step-dance was in the fiddler's bow, in the piano player's right hand, in their lively footwork. A spinster schoolmistress sitting alone at the back of the hall, her torso rigid and face devoid of expression, tapped out the steps on the worn plywood floor beneath her chair. The quiet man beside Beagan introduced himself as a McKinlay. He had grown up away from the island and didn't know his great-grandfather's Christian name. 'But I always knew the day would come when I'd come back to Cape Breton,' he confessed. His tie was stuffed in his suit pocket. 'I love the hills and sea, to hear the Gaelic; it's like falling in love. How do you explain falling in love with a girl?' Beagan asked how long he had been back. 'Oh no, I still live in Ottawa,' he explained. 'I've got a good job with the government and I'm married, eh?'

The audience raised their styrofoam coffee cups and cheered as two sisters from Margaree Harbour sang 'Mairi's Wedding'. Beagan fancied, incorrectly, that the song might have been heard at Hector's wedding.

> Plenty herring plenty meal
> Plenty peat to fill her creel
> Plenty bonnie bairns as well
> That's the toast to Mairi.

'Watch your shins!' shouted the schoolmistress as she took to her feet, and Beagan realised that he had never before seen people so enjoy dancing.

Only Macleod remained silent. Once he cast a cynical look towards the stage then tried to polish away half a century's dirt from a yellowed fingernail. He seemed oblivious to the joy around the hall and grumbled to himself. At the end of the concert the minister took the stage, asked the flushed congregation to bow their heads and thanked God for making them stewards of this land.

Outside it had begun to snow. A spring flurry laid powdery flakes on the islanders' hair and coats. As they crossed the parking lot and climbed down to the water Macleod complained, 'What a waste of a morning.'

Beagan, cheered by the strathspeys and reels, pointed out that there had been a good crowd at the concert. 'And the minister said that most of them listen to the daily Ceilidh radio hour on CJFX.'

'Them that are left. All the others are in Ontario. Every summer they load up their big cars and drive up here for the Homecoming

Crab and Corn Boil on Belle Côte beach. They spend an evening at the Glenora distillery then drive away for another year.' He dropped on to the seat and his weight sent waves rolling down the beach.

'But they remember. They come home.'

'They do hell. The old folks die off and the young get educated until they know enough to leave.' Macleod swore as he took the oars. 'I should never have stayed home with my mother.' Beagan waited to step aboard. 'Come on,' shouted the old man. 'Come on and I'll show you something you won't forget.'

They rowed back across the bay towards the roar of traffic and beached the boat further up the coast. Macleod led the way through the bush, trudged along an overgrown path and emerged on to a small escarpment. 'They're mostly drownings,' he said. 'Drownings and women who died in labour.'

Two dozen gravestones, worn by weather and stained by the years, were hemmed in by the encroaching thicket. Beagan swept away the snow to reveal an elaborate carving of two entwined hands and a chiselled 'Memory'. Beneath the powder blanket the stone of Katie McNeil, 'the beloved wife of Donald Macdonald of Skye', told the living not to weep. 'She is not dead but sleepeth.' Meg Morrison was buried beside her only child. 'Born at Uist, North Britain,' the mason had recorded in stone. 'Life how short eternity how long.' Beagan brushed down the plain marker of a Hamish MacFie of Mull. 'Gone to a better place,' he uncovered. Annie Rankin of Loch Linnhe lay beneath the words, 'Three times a wife but never a mother.'

'Is your mother here?' asked Beagan.

Macleod shook his head. He had nursed her through thirty years of old age. 'My brother took her away to a hospital in Toronto. Said she would be more comfortable. She went and died anyway. So he buried her there.' Beneath his quicksilver eyes, in the folds of heavy skin, dwelt the sadness of the bereaved. 'This place were never no Canaan,' he sighed, 'but it was home. I'll wait for you by the boat.'

'I'll come with you.'

Macleod pointed to a corner of the cemetery. 'That's where they laid your granddad.'

Beagan stopped in his tracks. 'My great-grandfather?'

The old man groaned and heaved himself towards a single grave standing apart from the rest.

Beagan smoothed the snow off the inscription. 'Who's this?' he asked. The name carved on the stone was James MacGillvery.

'How many times do I have to tell you? It's your granddad.'

'My great-grandfather was Hector Gillean. He was the first minister here.'

'Gillean? I thought you said MacGillvery.' Macleod leaned forward and studied Beagan's face. 'You sure look like a MacGillvery.'

'My name is Gillean,' Beagan assured him.

The old man knotted his brow and reached back through the years. 'That was before my time.' He searched his memory and scratched his head. 'I never knew him,' he said then walked away.

Beagan slumped down on a tomb and wished for a drink. The island seemed to have been severed from its past, like the dead from the living, and the trauma of the split had left behind only bitterness, incuriosity and prettified theme parks. The Kinettes concert had been the single exception. In the box trunk there lay reams and reams of records, but as for finding any physical remains of his family's history in Nova Scotia, too many years had passed. He saw that only his memory, the fine, vital thread stretching back through time, could hold and embrace his heritage of the Word.

Beagan shoved his hands into his pockets and found the Improved Metallic Memorandum. He sighed, stood to leave, and then his eyes fell on the old stone. It read 'The Reverend Hector Gillean.' The marker hadn't aged well. A grey blemish ran down over the carved hand, with index finger pointing heavenward, and into the inscription 'Yonder is my home.' Beagan touched the stone, felt the chill of a sea breeze and shivered. He toyed with his great-grandfather's diary and for a moment it seemed that he might read a sermon aloud. Instead he closed the book and whispered, 'Are you there?'

'Is it himself that expects me to rise up out of the earth like a spectre in a Hollywood movie?' I asked Jamie, who had never been as slow-witted as his grandson. 'Who else was he thinking it would be? Aye, it is me that's beside you,' I replied and Beagan heard my voice in his head. He stepped away in shock, stumbled over his big feet and landed flat on his back.

SLIGH' AN UISGE

Waterways

CHAPTER IV

THICKER THAN INK

MOTHER'S TEARS SPILT down her powdered cheeks and dropped dusty clouds into the crystal waters of Bras d'Or. She sat rigid on the seat between Zachary and me, looking neither left nor right, not speaking, not even appearing to draw breath. All movement within her seemed to be suspended, as if her heartbeat had been clenched by the hand of grief. The skin on her face was taut and I felt the stiffness of her spine through the mourning crêpe. But when she released the gunwale to dab an eye, I saw her fingers tremble like winter herring trapped and dying in a fisherman's net.

The pall-bearers pulled on their oars and our cortège grieved across the empty bay, past the silent shipyard, to landfall beneath the headland. They hoisted the pale pine box on to their black flannel shoulders and staggered like a piebald spider through the twists of upturned roots which wreathed the shore. Mother did not take Grandfather Cameron's arm but stepped into the water and on to the beach. 'Has F-F-Father gone to heaven?' I whispered.

'He has gone home, Jamie,' she replied.

'He is dead,' stated Zachary.

She took us by the hand and followed the coffin up the steep, winding path to the graveyard in the wilderness. The bearers lowered it into the dark earth. A paper-white headstone lay on the tangled brushwood like a discarded book which had lost its cover.

Old McKinlay the Elder spoke without notes. He had

broken his reading spectacles. 'Though we are deprived now of his presence do not fail to remember the Word that our departed brother, husband and father has spoken but let it be a living influence in our hearts.'

My new shoes pinched my toes. I felt the bones in mother's hand as she squeezed my own. Fisher MacFie wiped his nose and picked up a spade. The first shovelful of soil landed with a hollow echo and I supposed that the casket was empty, that if I ran down to the village Father would be there making notes on the pier or standing at our doorway eating his bowl of porridge and gazing out over the water. I imagined that come evening the post would bring the month's copy of the *Island Reporter* or *Mac-Talla*. I saw the candles being lit, the neighbours gathered in and Father reading the newspaper aloud from the first to the last page. He would pause between each article to reach for his anti-quated globe and point out the location of the towns and cities of our new Dominion. 'This is Muddy York, the place that they now call Toronto,' he might say, or trail his finger across the continent explaining, 'It is here that they are building the railroad.' But when Macfie's second shovel-load struck the coffin with a deadening thud I knew that I would never see him again.

Zachary held back his tears. I knew that it was not done for a boy to cry but I could not control my heart and sobbed like a baby girl. The mourners either whispered tender Gaelic sympathies to Mother or boomed in English that the sorrows of the Lord Himself exceed those of His creatures. Red MacNeil's daughters patted my shoulder and walked away down the slope back to their home.

After the funeral our dark house was full of Mother's silence. She hung her veil over the mirror so its reflection would not trap his spirit. We ate a little cold cod with *col-cannon* for supper. As had been our custom we sat before the evening fire around Father's chair. I turned the globe around and around on its axis. The following morning we lay late in bed watching a beam of sunlight creep across the wall and over his bookshelf.

When my father had stood up in church and preached it was as if God Himself was speaking. To him the Scriptures were gospel, literal truths, not allegories. The Sabbath, the pulpit, the Bible, all were the pillars of civilisation, the pillars on which a better world would be built. He had brought this certainty to a doubting, disordered society. He, like many missionaries, had offered its dispossessed people continuity and reason by speaking plainly and clearly of good and evil, heaven and hell. Upon the settlers' changeable present he had fixed the regular pattern of religious ritual: early morning and evening prayers, grace before and after meals, a Sabbath devoted to church worship. His positive assertion of faith had restored their steady self-control. It had affirmed the belief that honest industry brought an abundant tomorrow. The Word focused the hearts and minds of the New World.

As a child I had thought my father to be like the Lord: tireless, all-seeing, immortal. But the relentless patriarch had not been infallible. New times had demanded new measures and new men. During the first half of the nineteenth century the population of North America had quadrupled. The industrial production of the old colonies had surpassed that of Great Britain. By 1867 the new continent had been spanned by thirty thousand miles of railroad, more track than had been laid in all the rest of the globe, and Canada had declared itself to be a nation. The confederation of the provinces had not been universally desired. In Halifax the occasion had been marked by the hanging of crêpe in store windows and the flying of black flags at half-staff. The New Brunswick government had fallen over the issue. Independent politicians in Newfoundland had warned voters that if the province joined the Dominion their homes would be sold off to pay taxes to Ottawa. But within twenty-five years the young nation had built the fourth-largest merchant marine to sail the seas. Man had triumphed over the obstacles of nature and by the end of the century millions of Europeans had turned their backs on the past and ventured west to embrace the present with a certain belief in the success of the future.

On the island windjammers were launched, coal was mined and timber cut. The steamer *Banshee* plied Bras d'Or, called at Boularderie and Wycocomagh, brought in imports and took away a more precious commodity. Cape Breton's greatest export came to be not her trees or minerals but her people. The exodus changed the community. Migrants pinned their hopes on tomorrow and neglected the duties of the present. The envy of those left behind festered into bitterness. My father had no sympathy with those who shirked responsibility. The selfishness of man could not be tolerated and he was not slow to reveal his feelings in unmistakable language. He continued to preach for evangelical obedience, chiding us for our sins, encouraging us to let the Word be a living influence in our hearts. But for many the ambition for earthly success came to exceed their faith in heavenly rewards. It would have been contrary to human nature to expect anything less in a promised land.

The changes brought him into conflict with members of his congregation. Some families withdrew from the church. Others fell into indifference. A few traders took to working on the Fast Day and after one wholesome reproof for sinful conduct Moody the publican began to cross to the other side of the street when meeting Father out walking. But those who strayed from the flock only increased his resolve. One disaffected parishioner came to church chewing Pictou twist tobacco. Another, who had been accused of taking money out of the collection plate, interrupted a sermon. Father banged the pulpit and raged, 'God hath put me here and the Devil will not put me out.'

He delivered over a hundred sermons between his last March and September. Each was charged with fire and wit.

He dismissed as poppycock Darwin's hypothesis that there was no Divine order, that God was irrelevant to Creation, that man was a talking ape. Man, he preached, was not at the service of his species, responsible only for its pro-creation, a novelty dangling on a limb of evolution. He was a noble work, created in God's own image, formed of the dust of the ground and given the breath of life by the Lord. He was a painter, a poet, a shipwright, a linguist, a maker of wonders for the greater glory of God Almighty. But many parishioners no longer listened. In the month before my father's death I asked him why he continued to lecture to the dwindling congregation. 'I used to think that I could change them, James,' he acknowledged. 'Now I keep preaching so that they won't change us.'

Father had been blessed with vigorous health. He took his physical well-being for granted. Then, almost overnight, it deserted him. He began to suffer from pain in his loins and a rise in body temperature. He passed blood and albumen in his urine. Doctor MacKay advised him to rest his kidneys but he paid little heed and went about his business. On a return trip from Sydney where he had bought a set of Communion Elements (for which he had given a dollar himself and paid for the rest with thirty-two donated quarters) the mailgig was caught in a storm. The wet cold sapped his remaining strength. He took ill and had to stay at home. Headaches plagued him and his nights passed with aching torpor. Old age came as a deep tiredness which blurred his sight, sapped his concentration and rendered him incapable of writing.

As the maples shed their crimson coats it pained him to see the people gather at the church and not to be able to preach to them. He hated idleness. There was so much work that remained undone. One September Sabbath he ignored Mother's protestations and went to the congregation to read the Scriptures. Though not strong his voice remained good and clear but it was his vision which began to fail him. He found it difficult to focus on the text. Before his eyes the printed letters seemed to shiver then come unstuck and slip one by one out of line. He placed his hand beneath the words as if to hold them in place but still they peeled away and fell off the page in a jumble which landed at his feet, a meaningless chaos of symbols. He bent down to grasp them but the letters slipped through his fingers like water through a sieve and vanished in the gaps between the floorboards. He stood up and saw that no word remained on the page. The Bible had been rendered blank. Betraying nothing he completed the reading from memory, closed the Book and returned to the manse. There he excused himself from lunch and lay down for a rest.

Later that afternoon Father began to complain about the untidiness of his room. He seemed to see a great deal of dust and, worse still, mites.

'There Kirstie,' he said, pointing at the floor before his chair, 'tiny, tiny mites. Dear God, there are dozens of them.' Mother explained that he was seeing only a flake or two of dry paint and suggested that his eyes might be tired. The week before she and Red MacNeil's daughters had distempered the walls to bring a little cheer to his room. He dismissed her sympathy. 'Those are mites and they are moving. Was there ever paint that moved? Kirstie, we must stop them from spreading.' I had a flake in my hand and took it to him. 'See that now, how quickly they run. James, put it down,' he ordered then insisted to Mother, 'I am not seeing things.' He became stern when roused. 'You'll not like it when they reach the foot of your bed.'

'Look F-F-Father.' I placed the speck in his palm. 'It is only paint.'

He tried to squash it once then twice then let out a gasp. In his mind the dust, his mites, had become letters. Words untangled at his feet scattering ciphers about the room. The alphabet crawled across the carpet. Sentences unravelled behind the chair. A web of characters, almost a whole psalm, spun apart in furious rupture then crept away into crevices. Columns of symbols slid out of the Hebrew Bible and swarmed over Young's *Concordance* then ran away down the legs of the bookcase. Phrases wormed into cracks in the wall and a dozen vowels took flight. He cried for me to hurry for the broom and I rushed to sweep away the shapes from the floor.

'There,' he shouted, 'and over there.' Father brushed the script off his hands, from his trousers, away from mother's skirts as she held him to her breast. Zachary stared in silence and I beheld the terror in Father's eyes as all that had been order descended into chaos.

By evening, after the doctor had given him a draught to encourage sleep, he was calmer. The letters had risen in a swarm and become motes of light which hovered before him like a cloud of silver dust. Father stared into space and the doctor waved his arm across his line of sight.

'You've put your hand right through them,' he complained then added sternly, 'Wait you now, MacKay, it is not my imagination. I am not going mad.' He then revealed himself as he seldom did even to his most intimate friends. The letters had converged into a single, resplendent beacon. He asked the doctor to look above the door where their light had become the eye of the All-Seeing One. Only a faded engraving of a Scottish loch hung there but MacKay believed that the radiance was upon the minister. There was no longer fear in his eyes. My father spoke of the presence of God. He had no doubt that this was the fulfilment of the promise of His presence through the Dark Valley.

In all my life my father had touched me no more than a dozen times, half of which were hidings, yet in that last night lying on the horsehair mattress he took my hand and held it as if the force of his grip might anchor an ascendant spirit. 'God gave a promise to Noah so that the world might be started anew,' he told my brother and me. 'He gave His promise to Abraham, "Get thee out of thy country, and from thy kindred and from thy father's house unto a land that I will show thee."' His ink-stained finger left a smudge on my palm.

When we awoke the next morning his room was empty. In the night he had tossed aside the blankets and left the house. The bed was still warm and damp from his fever. Every corner of Promise was searched before Fisher MacFie noticed that his canoe was not on the shore. They found Father on the water later that day. His complaint had assumed the character of dropsy and sometime before dawn the hour of his departure had come. He had heard the voice that called him home.

In the old box trunk there is a photograph, a family portrait taken not long after Father's death. Mother sits before the camera wearing a solemn face and a worsted wool dress, its skirts ballooning beneath the Bible on her lap. Zachary stands at her side in the centre of the group, his hand posed on her shoulder and collar button snapped tight around his neck. His long thin features give him a puritanical look. He appears more concerned with the need to uphold rigid morals than to enjoy a little carefree fun. 'There's not a devil in Hell that'll pluck a pin-feather from you,' Grandfather Cameron had often told him.

I had been set on a stool to his left and told not to fidget. The face which looks out from the portrait is round, even chubby, and wears like book-ends the enormous ears which I had inherited from Mother. My cock-eyed collar, well, it had popped undone just before the flash of the photographer's powder, but I had managed to hide from the lens the gravy stain on my cuff.

Father had enriched our souls but not our purse. The few

dollars that he had saved had been loaned to the needy without record or receipt. In the days following the funeral many repaid his generosity with their honesty. Strangers knocked at our door and returned the loans to Mother. To help I busied myself with beanpoles and pea vines, tending to our rows of onions and cabbages. Still there was barely enough to see us rehoused, so at the age of four-teen years Zachary left Promise. His great wish had been to join the army and pursue a military career, but with-out the money to buy a commission he chose instead to be-come a teacher. He gave Mother a single goodbye kiss then shook her hand. He was frugal too with time; not an idle minute slipped through his net, and he quickly earned his matriculation certificate, the first vital step on the road to financial success. His first post was at the little red school-house over Cape Breton's Skye mountains. Every Friday evening he walked home with a single silver dollar in his pocket.

'Facts,' he would instruct me while reading a borrowed copy of *Mac-Talla* by the coal-lamp, 'are what one needs to get by in this life. Facts dispel ignorance and dark-ness.' Zachary studied the reports on commodity prices while I whispered to myself the newspaper's Gaelic stories.

It was some fact which he read that convinced him that my future lay in mechanical engineering. He secured for me an apprenticeship two dozen miles away in Sydney, and at the ripe old age of thirteen I was sent to work for Hiram Whistle, Manufacturer of Steam Engines, Gas Machines and Compression Boilers. The devices that Whistle produced were noisy, noxious and temperamental. His 'Lark' Vertical Steam Engine puffed and wheezed and once spat a comet of flaming coals clear across the yard into the privy. It burst into flames and caused Mrs Whistle to have an attack of neuralgia. His 'Nightingale' Silent Gas Motor tended to overheat and shriek more like a tortured tern than a song-

bird. It later blew a six-foot hole through the iron hull of
the only steamship ever built in the region. There was pleasure in crafting sheets of tin and casting iron pistons but
within a year I was sick tired of the trade. The dirty dark
workshop with singeing forge gave me a headache every
day. The cheap metal tinged my hands with a gleaming
silver sheen that could not be washed away.

I tried to explain my unhappiness to Mother but could
never find the right words. It was my failing, not hers. I
was unable to unlock my heart and let words speak the
truth like Father. In the months after his death we had
been forbidden to enter his study. Mother slipped in alone
at night when she thought we were asleep. We heard the
lock click open and the door sigh closed. The key was hidden
in a brick behind the stove. One day when the house was
empty I took the key, opened the door and stole inside. I
stood in the half-light ringed round and round by the shelves
of books. I took down a volume of sermons, ran my finger
over the spines of pamphlets, breathed in dust and memory
and felt a deep sense of contentment well up within me. The
library surrounded me with his words.

· But Mother came home early from a Presbyterian Society
meeting and found me. I expected my disobedience to earn
me a beating but instead she knelt down beside me, her
black silk of mourning rustling with the movement, touched
my hair and whispered, 'When I come here I feel that he is
still with us. I feel him near.'

I searched for the right words, grappled to communicate
the secrets of my heart, tried to speak with his clarity
and eloquence, but my lips were drawn shut like window
blinds on the Sabbath and I could only utter a crabbed
babble of ugly sound and untruth. 'No. He's not here,' I
lied. 'I don't f-f-feel him.' I too was frightened. I too missed
him. And I never deranged the papers as Zachary later
accused.

My dissatisfaction was not eased when the Dominion

government withdrew shipbuilding bounties to promote the westward expansion of the nation. Canada wanted silver rails not wooden boats. Whistle closed his workshop, mounted a 'Lark' Vertical on a barge and steamed south to Boston. The change of policy meant that even Grandfather Cameron could offer me no employment. His yard too was threatened with closure. I was of little use at home, helping Mother to put up twenty quarts of beans only to be rewarded with a length of Zachary's tongue for growing a single, unprofitable sunflower. I felt myself to be an ideal candidate for the cutty, the kirk stool reserved below the pulpit for delinquents. My brother instructed me to join the newly-formed Dominion Coal Company but I remembered Father's guidance. 'Much has been given to you and much will be expected of you,' he had said and every night I prayed for his blessing.

In spring after planting the early potatoes I boarded the Quebec Steamship Company's SS *Campana* at Pictou Harbour for passage up the Saint Lawrence River. I had never before sailed in a real steamboat and she seemed to be a very fine one. The snow had melted and the blossoms swirled around the wharf in great pink clouds of petals. Beyond Montreal the new province of Ontario stretched a thousand miles from east to west with all the Great Lakes in between. There were polar bears and tundra in its north, peaches and industry in the south. I felt the draw of its rich, thriving capital, Toronto.

I could not afford a berth but found a protected corner on deck out of the wind. My father's globe was tucked under my arm. Mother had reached into his study and out of her grief to give it to me, though I cannot think why as Zachary had the greater ambition and industry. Maybe she knew that it made me feel close to him. As dusk fell the sky wore a string of red rubies. Among my fellow passengers there was a party of Scots who sang through the night. Their enthusiasm did little to help my sleep but it didn't matter for my hopes glowed like the luminous trail of embers flung into the clear air from the steamer's funnel.

> We're sailing west, we're sailing west
> To prairie lands sunkissed and blest –
> The crofter's trail of happiness.

EVERYTHING IN CANADA moves from east to west: the sun, waterways and postal codes, explorers, history and hopes. Beagan would be no exception, provided he could get out of Pictou. He sat on his trunk at the waterfront looking west, past the unemployed youths playing volleyball, out towards the Gulf of Saint Lawrence and sensed something of the vastness of the country. It brought to his mind the story of an expanding English firm which established its first overseas bureau in Vancouver. One day the head office cabled the west coast with news of a prospective client in Nova Scotia. 'Can you go and meet him?' asked London.

'You go,' replied Vancouver, 'you're nearer.'

There seemed to be no reason for Beagan to dawdle in Pictou. He had been in town only a morning and its main attraction was a svelte, underclad volleyball player. The shops along Water Street seemed tired, their windows were empty. A Native woman slumped in an alcoholic haze on the steps of the Highland Beverage Room. The harbourside park petered out into a vacant lot of rough stone and quarrelsome gulls. Apart from the Heritage Quay, a fine museum which commemorated the province's first Highland settlers, the only vibrant part of the sleepy port seemed to be Smiley's Video Shop. It was doing a lively trade in Nintendo games as Macleod had forewarned.

The meeting at the grave had unsettled Beagan. It was difficult enough to communicate with the living; one did not expect the dead to strike up conversations too. The flood of readings, discoveries and fancies sloshed about his head like spring run-off in a brimming lake. He wanted out of Nova Scotia and scanned the harbour looking for a boat, any boat. His 'Doers and Dreamers' Official Guidebook could suggest no ferries, no freighters and certainly no passenger ships which might follow in the wake of the SS *Campana*. It seemed that none existed. Only a small catch of lobster skiffs and an erstwhile summer holiday cruiser moved on the water.

He stopped by the office of Scotty's Taxis to ask for advice. The sign above the door read 'We're not here to make a mint, we're here for the business.' The young, tam-o'-shantered owner had a Walkman wired to his ears. 'What do you know for sure?' he said in greeting.

'I beg your pardon?' replied Beagan, looking blank.

Expressions had changed in the last two decades. Scotty translated, 'I mean, like, what's happening, eh?' Beagan's answer caused him to snap off his earphones and fill the little room with the high-pitched hiss of Led Zeppelin. 'Say, you crazy or what?'

'I'm following the route that my grandfather took late last century,' Beagan explained, having decided that blunt confession was the only way to confront his distress. 'His name was Jamie Gillean and he travelled by water so that's the way I'm going too.'

'All the way to Vancouver?'

'Eventually, yes. But Toronto will do for now.'

The tam-o'-shanter shook in disbelief. 'Get out of town.'

'I'm trying to but there don't seem to be any boats.'

'The only way is by road, eh? You want a cab?' When Beagan's spirits slumped Scotty added, 'Looks like you need a drink.' It struck him as a fine idea. 'Come have a swish and we'll talk her over.' Beagan hadn't noticed the matching pairs of half-barrel flowertubs in every front garden. 'Hey, you never heard tell of swish before?' Scotty exclaimed and invited him into the backroom.

Alcohol in Canada is heavily taxed; a bottle of spirits can cost more than twice its American price, so enterprising Maritimers took to buying the empty fifty-gallon oak casks which had been used to import liquor.

'We put into 'em ten gallons of water, five of sugar, then seal 'em up and swish 'em − turn 'em − every day for a month,' explained Scotty while drawing two paper cups of amber liquid from an unsevered barrel. 'Like, spirits are shipped at 100 proof so the wood is real saturated with Bacardi, Johnny Walker, Hennessy, whatever. What we get out after four weeks' swishing is a mean 40 proof. Go figure!' He laughed and raised his cup. 'And not only can you do each barrel twice, but then you cut her in half and give it to a girlfriend to plant flowers. Makes a nice birthday present.' Beagan tasted the smoky peat of a fine malt. 'Trouble came when everybody started doing it and stopped buying their drink at the liquor store. The government don't like losing the revenue so they went and put a tax on empty barrels, if you can believe it. Stopped the whole thing dead.' Scotty removed the tattered cap as a mark of respect and patted his cask, 'This here's the last swish barrel in Pictou County.'

Egg-white meringues of cloud, their bases flat as if dropped on to a great glass baking sheet in the sky, stretched away to the west. A seagull scuttled up Water Street in a sideways crab-like run. Beagan might not have found a route out of town but as he wove back to the pier it seemed to be a less urgent concern. He slumped down on his trunk and into the whisky's numbing warmth. He smiled in the general direction of the svelte volleyball player before noticing the frothing white bow wave of an approaching boat. He rubbed his eyes. 'The third glass is always the killer,' he thought, looked again then tumbled off the edge of the pier.

'F-F-Father, what on earth are you doing?' cried Jamie.

The Reverend Hector set down the end of the trunk. 'That boy is intoxicated. Again,' Beagan heard as he fell, fancying that Hector had tipped him off his seat and into the harbour. 'This behaviour will make the very stones shed tears,' the Reverend added as his great-grandson flailed his arms and spouted water like a manic fountain.

'It looks to me more like he's drowning. And anyway, Beagan only really took to drink again after your melo-dramatic visitation at the burial ground,' accused Jamie. 'Your conduct there was, if you'll f-f-forgive me, quite unnecessary.'

'The boy called for me. It would have been faint-hearted not to reply.' A lick of water splashed Hector's shoes. A gurgling cry reached their ears.

'He hasn't had a wink of sleep since leaving Promise. All night he sits up in bed expecting to see your face appear before him.' In response to the shouts Jamie kicked a life ring off the pier. 'To my mind it would have been more prudent to wait.'

'There's many a slip between ship and quay, James. Mark my words.'

Scotty and the volleyball players bolted down the pier, 'Stairway to Heaven' hissing in their wake. Scotty dropped a line to haul Beagan and the ring on to dry land. The others, seeing him soaked but safe, watched his mirage transform into an approaching thirty-five-foot Bayliner motor yacht. The streamlined bow and moulded decks gave the ship the look of a silver submarine. Her bridge bristled with antennae and aerials, the horn sounded and somewhere a small dog barked.

The splendid craft throttled back and swung broadside to the Pictou gas bar. On her stern beneath a fluttering maple leaf was her name: *Szerencsès*. Two stocky boys wearing baggy shorts and 'Save the Whales' T-shirts appeared on deck holding the rope like a coiled snake. They cast it out suddenly as if the serpent had hissed and licked their fingertips with a cool forked tongue. The volleyball players ran to catch the painter but it fell short into the water. 'Jeez, how stupid,' said the elder boy. 'Mum, it was Randy's fault.'

'Try again and this time concentrate,' advised a gentle voice from the bridge. The twin Volvo Penta diesels reversed to avoid hitting the breakwater.

As the two boys began to retrieve the rope a terrified, auburn-haired hamster darted between their legs. It was followed by a yapping, shaggy mongrel. 'Oh man, Tufty's going to eat him alive,' wailed Randy. The boys dropped the line to chase their pets. As the Bayliner drifted astern they yelped and shouted over the foredeck and around a hatchway. 'If your dog eats Sniffy you're dead meat.' But the hamster had no intention of being anyone's supper. He vanished down a small porthole. Tufty tried to follow but became stuck halfway. His muffled bark echoed out of the air vents. During the commotion a young woman descended from the bridge and coiled the rope. Her throw was so accurate that Beagan had only to bend to pick it up from the damp pool at his feet.

'Fill her up, please.'

As the boys set upon a plate of baloney sandwiches a small crowd gathered to admire *Szerencsès*. 'It means "lucky" in Hungarian,' explained the woman. Her accent was as mellow as eight-year-old Tokaj.

'You can say that again,' observed Scotty.

'She's not that big,' she said with genuine modesty, then added, 'But she is ours.' The young family seemed to be unlikely owners of an expensive yacht. They gave themselves no airs. The boys were even prevented from buying doughnuts from the nearby Tim Horton's as they hadn't earned the treat.

As Beagan looked around the pier for a place to change into dry clothes they offered him the spare cabin. It wasn't hard to engage them in conversation. 'We're going to see the belugas,' enthused Joel, the elder brother.

'The boys are crazy about whales,' confirmed Piri, their mother, while doling out another round of sandwiches. She wore a maple leaf badge on her cardigan. 'I wanted them to see the Saguenay breeding ground before it was too late.' Her movements were fluid and considered. When Beagan explained a little of his plans her invitation was spontaneous and sincere. 'I don't know much about the Pacific but you can come along as far as Lake Ontario.' Her features seemed to be softened by kindness. 'I could do with another pair of eyes on the bridge.'

'I'd be pleased to help,' he replied.

His smile faltered when she added, 'My husband had to fly back to Toronto this morning. Hey, you don't speak French, do you?'

'Some.'

'In Hungary when I grew up French was considered to be a capitalist language. It wasn't taught at school. As a result on the way downriver I nearly ran into a Haitian freighter.' She looked up the pier towards Beagan's bulging trunk. 'You can have the third bedroom, but I don't know where we'll put your luggage.'

'She is a beautiful boat,' confessed Beagan.

'We won it,' said Joel.

No Canadian could ever resist a lottery. The federal, provincial and local governments all operated dozens of games – Wintario, Lotto 6/49, *Le Millionaire*, Scratch 'n Win – and most people almost always had a ticket for an impending draw. It had been suggested that the dream of winning had come to compensate for disappointment in the promised land. That didn't seem to be the case for Piri.

Szerencsès cleared Pictou Harbour and sprinted across the Northumberland Strait. In the picture-window bridge Sniffy the hamster dozed beside the throttle while Piri steered north-west across the waves. 'Before I came to Canada I never thought I'd even learn to drive a car.' Her lips curved into a gentle smile. 'So this is a real thrill.'

'I can imagine,' replied Beagan. He had taken a hot shower, changed and stuffed his wet clothes into the onboard washer-dryer. 'It would have been for my grandfather too. He followed this same heading aboard a steamboat called the *Campana*, though not at quite this speed.' A spume of spray slapped over the deck. Piri switched on the three all-weather windscreen wipers. 'I think he'd only ever been out in a canoe before.'

'When was this?'

'In the late 1870s.'

'Gosh, a long time ago.'

'He was a tireless correspondent. After he left home he wrote a letter to his mother every week for over thirty years. That's what's in the trunk,' Beagan said, gesturing below-decks.

'Wow,' enthused Piri. 'And you've still got them.'

Beagan had begun to feel at ease, though not because of the swish. In Piri he sensed a need to share both family and the experience of emigration. 'It's almost like having him – and his father – travelling with me.'

'That's neat.'

'In one of the letters Jamie – that's my grandfather – mentions a pod of small white whales that encircled his ship and entertained the ladies until someone onboard opened fire with a shotgun. The sportsman, as Jamie called him, killed two before the others vanished beneath the surface. It upset him.'

'It would me too,' she shivered. 'The Gulf must have changed a lot since then.'

'Yes. For a start there weren't ten thousand ships passing through it every season. The great auks would have been gone by then. The last colony had been bludgeoned into extinction about the time Jamie's father arrived from Scotland. But he would have seen the last big herds of walrus. And some Eskimo curlews.'

'Like the boys and me seeing the last of the belugas?'

'Maybe the end of another species,' replied Beagan and caught his reflection in the windscreen.

The Nova Scotian shore was ironbound with moist green sweeps of fertile farmland descending to a silver estuary and tidal mudbanks. *Szerencsès* sliced through the top of the waves and cast great swirling billows in her wake. Piri's confident control and the electronic stabilisers ensured a smooth, comfortable ride. 'She's quite something to have won,' admired Beagan.

'And it's not the best thing that's happened to me.' Piri's eyes seemed to glow with excitement. 'My luckiest day was Monday 18 August 1975.' The exactness touched Beagan and he laughed. 'That was the day when I met a wonderful man, a photography student from Toronto.'

'When you were in Hungary?'

Piri nodded. 'It was the last morning of his holiday and he stopped at the restaurant where I worked as a waitress. He ordered seven cups of coffee just so he could speak to me. Later I learnt that he hates coffee. We wrote each other too, every day for twelve months, then he came back and asked me to marry him.'

As the Maritimes dropped away below the horizon a little of

Beagan's despair went with it. Piri's trusting nature and confidence strengthened his sense of well-being. 'You know I admire your grandfather, leaving home like that,' she said. 'Of all my siblings I was the homebody. We lived in a tiny village. The only time that I travelled to Budapest I got train-sick.'

'Jamie wrote that he felt queasy aboard the *Campana*.'

'Our family was very close, very loving. It had never occurred to me to live anywhere else. But there I was one week after the wedding hugging and crying and asking my parents to forgive me for leaving them. It was the hardest thing I ever had to do.'

'Did you know much about Canada?' Beagan asked.

'I knew that it was far away and very cold, that there were big houses for everyone and big cars. I knew that the people spoke English and French and wondered how the heck I was going to communicate with them. I didn't speak English either back then.' The radio crackled and Piri reported their position to the Coast Guard. 'I'd never been in an airplane before, a bit like your grandfather in the steamboat, so Peter held my hand through the whole flight. He didn't let go once. You see I was only eighteen years old at the time and filled with a lot of insecurity. I worried that his parents wouldn't like me, that I'd never see my family again. But then I remembered the belugas. We'd done a school project on whales and I thought that they were so beautiful. I realised that belugas bred in the Saint Lawrence and asked Peter if one day we might be able to see them. He promised me that we would.

'Although the flight hadn't upset my stomach the drive to his parent's apartment made me really nauseous. I wasn't used to such big cars, or any car for that matter, and going up in the elevator I started to feel sicker and sicker. Peter's parents welcomed us with a wonderful dinner of chicken soup, cabbage rolls, the works. They'd even baked a "Welcome Home" cake. I tried to eat, I didn't want to insult my mother-in-law, only after two spoonfuls I had to run to the bathroom to throw up. "Holy cow," I thought, "I really blew it this time." I hadn't of course. They saw how much Peter and I loved each other and made me feel at home.

'We rented an apartment in the building opposite. We didn't even need a moving truck, just walked across the street with all our stuff. I couldn't believe it; I'd been in Canada only three weeks and already had a place of my own. I thought, "What a great country." But you know it was kind of scary too. In our building lived more people than in the whole village back home and Peter had to leave me with them to go to work.' Piri eased back on the throttle as a surge of cross-waves reared their angry heads. 'He gave up his photography and got a job in Mississauga at the Bay, you know, the department store?'

'It used to be called the Hudson's Bay Company,' explained Beagan. 'It's the oldest company in Canada.'

'Older than Woolco?' asked Piri. Beagan nodded. 'I ask because my mother-in-law helped me apply for work there. They invited me in for an interview and I wasn't sure if I could handle it. What should I say? How should I respond if they asked when I wanted to start? Peter taught me to say, "As soon as possible." I rehearsed the line in the bath, on the bus, over and over again. In her office the manager, Mrs Singh, asked me a few questions, seemed satisfied then really said, "When can you start?"

'"As soon as possible." I said it without a mistake.

'"Be here tomorrow morning at eight o'clock," she replied. I nearly fell off my chair.

'I started as a sales clerk at the fast food counter; you know, candies, burgers, milkshakes, that sort of thing. At the store opening I was so scared that I thought my legs were going to give out on me. My workmates encouraged me to serve the first customer. "Go ahead. You'll be fine," they said.

'"I'm sorry, this is my first day," I told the man, "and I don't speak English very well." I didn't know the name of anything but he kept on pointing and pointing until I got it right. He was very patient. Other customers weren't so nice. They made fun of my accent and I had to sneak away a few times to cry in the toilet but I got by. Six months later I was chatting with a customer who wanted some chocolates.

'"Your English is very good now," he said. I hadn't recognised him. "Don't you remember me? I was your first customer." I was so happy. It made me realise that I was starting to have a history in Canada.'

The lines of cliff and pine wrapped themselves in the ultramarine veil of dusk. Sea and sky entwined into a weave of single hue and the stars came out like diamonds across a black velvet heaven. *Szerencsès* dropped anchor below Rocher Percé, the pierced rock behind which explorers' caravels and emigrant tubs had once weathered the Gulf's storms.

'Do you like whales too?' asked Randy while leading Beagan on a tour below-decks. There was a beechwood cocktail bar and ice machine, three cabins and a hot tub. The yacht's custom-built interior had been fitted out by Finnish chandlers. The cutlery was David Mellor, the china came from Delft and the video had a Dolby Pro-Logic Surround Sound System manufactured by Sony.

Beagan noticed the photographs of fin-backs and great blues hanging around the galley. 'Did your mother take these?'

'Joel did.' He showed off the underwater camera outfit. 'We think whales are the greatest.'

Piri cooked a spicy Hungarian *gulyás* for supper. The side dish was a cool cucumber salad. For dessert she served a honeyed *strudel* of cherries and raisins wrapped in translucent pastry. 'I'm sorry that I bored you with my story,' she apologised as they loaded the dishwasher. 'It was real dumb.'

'You didn't bore me,' insisted Beagan. The boys had settled down to watch a Jacques Cousteau video. 'I'm interested why people leave home and what they find in their new country. You know, the search for a promised land? I feel very bitter towards Canada; it's wasted too many opportunities and broken too many hearts.'

'It didn't break my heart. No way.'

'I see that,' he acknowledged.

Piri stacked away the last of the plates then pulled a small bottle from the cupboard. 'I've a soft spot for apricot brandy,' she confessed. 'Would you like a glass?'

They folded themselves around the galley table. 'A few months later I was transferred to the stationery department. It was a big challenge and the supervisor gave me a huge order book.' Piri hesitated, 'Are you sure you're interested in this?'

Beagan nodded. 'My grandfather once published a journal for the stationery trade.'

'Really? Well, maybe my supervisor should have read it. She talked fast and I was too embarrassed to tell her that I didn't understand. So of course after a few weeks of people buying pens and paper clips and whatever I ran out of stock. The supervisor was really upset and told the store manager that I didn't want to learn. I was totally humiliated. I thought that he would fire me there and then. "There is no stock," he said, turning on the supervisor, "because you didn't teach Piri properly." He made her explain it all over again and from then on I worked really hard. I couldn't let the manager down and everything was soon under control. In fact at the end of my first year some visiting big shots told me that I had the best-organised department of all the Woolco stores in Canada.' Piri blushed. 'Not to brag or anything, but I felt such a sense of accomplishment. I can't really put it into words. I was no longer some Hungarian girl who hardly spoke English but the Canadian who put together a great stationery department.' She beamed with pride. 'I even started to beat Peter at Scrabble.'

'How long did you stay at the store?' asked Beagan, reaching for the brandy. The sudden, loud slap of a wave against the hull made him jump.

Piri put a hand over her glass. 'Not for me, thanks. Five years, hardships and all, and Peter kept his promise, driving us up to the Saguenay every summer to see the whales. At first it made me a little sad, the belugas reminded me of leaving my family, but with the birth of the boys my life really did come to be here. That's why it's important for them to see them. It's funny, when I visit Hungary now I feel that I'm going home, but when I fly back to Canada I am home again.'

'I lived in Scotland all last year on an island that I'd never seen before, eating oatmeal for breakfast, walking in the rain along the seashore, and I felt like I was a part of it. And it was part of me. But here, in the country where I was born, well I can't say that this is home,' Beagan sighed, 'but it is.' He pushed the glass away from him and added, 'Tell me about your other good fortune?'

'Do you mean the lottery?' she asked. 'People say that winning a lottery changes your life, and I guess it does but I was kind of used to change. I was so lucky to meet Peter, to move to this beautiful country, to be blessed with the boys. The money was like icing on the cake. Peter could give up his job at the Bay and take up photography again. We could treat the boys to real special holidays. I could help my parents. People think that there's a science to it. When we won one reporter asked me what system I used. I told him that all I had done was choose the right ticket. It's only a question of luck.'

The next morning *Szerencsès* cut across to the north shore and made for the mouth of the Saguenay, last breeding ground of the beluga whale. A kittiwake veered across the bow then swooped up a cliff chasing its shadow. The valleys and peaks of the Charlevoix, moulded by millennia of rain and wind, had the look of sleeping giants. Their hips and shoulders wore crests of caribou moss. Over their waists and between their toes rushed clear blue streams. For thousands of years they had watched the beluga migrate down the icy Labrador Current to feed, mate and calve between their outstretched arms. Then in the last century the giants had felt their rivers being dammed, smelled the dumped mercury and heard the cries of fisherman as the whales were butchered. At Rivière Ouelle during the 1870s as many as five hundred belugas were slain in a single tide, more than the total number that remained alive in the Saint Lawrence today.

Piri heaved to and let the Bayliner wallow on the deep black waters of the Saguenay fjord alongside tourist steamers and hotel boats. Majestic capes jutted out into the river, their cliffs towering high above the hopeful flotilla. Camera lenses flashed in the sun. Joel and Randy helped their mother lower the photographic apparatus into position. The whale-watchers waited patiently, expectantly, fruitlessly. No pure white tail broke the surface. No dolphin-like face crossed Piri's viewfinder. At the end of a long, empty afternoon the sleeping giants watched *Szerencsès* pull up its sea anchor and slip away from the fjord.

After Piri had put the boys to bed she joined Beagan on the bridge. 'It's a shame,' she kept repeating. 'I've watched their numbers shrink over the years but there's never been a summer when we haven't seen any at all.' Disappointment weighed on her like a heavy cloak. 'Would you mind if we cruised through the night?' she asked Beagan. 'If we take it in shifts we might make Montreal by morning.'

Szerencsès chased the sunset west up the Saint Lawrence. Navigation lights glittered on blunt-nosed Lakers. Buoys blinked and clanged on either side of the channel. Piri turned up the stereo and filled the bridge with Bartók's Magyar folk songs. The river rolled in inky blackness beneath the towering crags. The Bayliner passed Québec City long after the *calèches* had been locked away and the last horse clip-clopped into its stall. Delphis Duhamel was still awake and noted their passing with a vocal rendition of 'O Canada', but it was a *fleur-de-lys* that fluttered on his flagpole. Above them starlight flashed and strobed through the struts of the Pont de Québec.

Szerencsès's custom-built bridge also twinkled and glittered, though it was lit by diodes rather than heavenly bodies. On board were radar, weatherfax and a depth sounder. The Raystar Chart-plotter glowed with the vaporous outline of channel and shore. Beagan brought up from his cabin Hector's old terrestrial globe. Piri gazed at its faded panels and pointed at the Austrian Empire.

'There's Hungary, and look, Sopron is marked too.'

'I like Budapest,' he said, recalling an earlier trip to gather material for a guide book. 'All those curves and colonnades and crescents. And the smell of violets.'

'Peter says this machine can track eight satellites simultaneously.' Her Furuno plotter pinned their position on the real globe. 'I guess it's good to know that we can never get lost.'

A tremble in her voice reminded Beagan of the first maps of Nouvelle France which had marked the great wilds of trackless unknown with the inscription, '*On ne connaît point le Cours de toutes ces Rivières.*' The course of these rivers is completely unknown. 'You know, sometimes in Canada,' he whispered, 'gazing out over the bow or looking through the darkened windows of a night train, I'm overawed by a feeling of unimaginable vastness, a sense that out there is wilderness without end.'

The morning was warm and everyone in Montréal looked as if they were off to a beach party. They wore shorts, floppy tops and muscle shirts covered with slogans: 'Peace through Unity', 'White North Hockey Club', 'Je me Souviens'. The only exception appeared to be an anglophone businessman who, admiring his reflection in spit-polish patent leather shoes, stormed up and down the river walk shouting into his mobile telephone, 'Are you still there? Can you hear me?'

In New World cities one needs only to scratch the surface to find the original reason for settlement. As Piri veered *Szerencsès* past the container terminal Beagan gestured above the island city's glass and steel towers to whale-backed Mont Royal. 'That's the hill which Jacques Cartier climbed. You know, the French explorer who named Canada.'

'I'm sorry, but our version of history never included him,' confessed Piri. She eased back on the throttle to give way to a nippy harbour tug. 'But I can tell you the name of the first Russian dog to be launched into space.'

'Cartier was the first European to sail upstream,' persisted Beagan, anxious to tell her their shared history. 'We're a thousand kilometres from the sea and the Saint Lawrence is still, what, a mile wide here. He reasoned that such a broad expanse of water could hardly be a river. To him it had to be the promised passage to the Orient.'

'What made him stop?'

Beagan pointed forward towards the first Seaway lock. 'That rough water there. It blocked the river and his ship could go no further. His search for China ended and he wistfully named the rapids Lachine.'

Piri swung the boat towards a vacant slip. 'Could you look after the bowline, please?' She wrapped an arm around Joel and Randy as they climbed on to the bridge.

'He was looking for a western waterway,' explained Beagan, raising his voice while walking forward, 'a dream inherited by Samuel de Champlain, the father of New France and history's most travelled explorer.' Beagan coiled three loops of rope in his right hand. 'Champlain established Canada's first permanent white settlement and set out by canoe over Lachine. In 1614 his voyageurs paddled west as far as Lake Huron looking for the legendary *"Mer de l'Ouest"*.'

Piri spun the wheel and went hard astern. 'Did he find it?'

'It wasn't there to be found, even though it's marked on many of the early maps,' he replied. 'But the energy and faith of those first *habitants* was remarkable, surviving terrible conditions, the bitter cold, complete isolation. It nurtured in them a savage love for the land.' Piri slipped the engine into neutral and *Szerencsès* drifted alongside the petrol dock. 'Champlain traced the lineaments of half the continent. His discoveries opened the interior, laid the basis of the fur trade and gave Britain and France a reason to go to war.'

As Beagan tied up, a middle-aged attendant idled towards the pumps. Montréal was the second-largest French-speaking city in the world and Piri was anxious not to cause offence. She asked Beagan to order the fuel.

'Don't speak to me in French,' snapped the attendant as he tugged at the hose and clanked the nozzle into the tank. 'I'm Greek. Speak to me in English.' He wore a nylon short-sleeved shirt and a scowl. His silver-olive eyes seemed to shimmer and dance in the rising diesel vapours.

Beagan watched the irrepressible Canadian urge to diffuse aggression swell up in Piri. 'You sure are lucky living in this beautiful province,' she said, trying to make conversation. 'We've been right up to the Gulf and back again.'

'Québec has been ruined by the politicians,' retorted the Greek.

'Hey, *calmes-toi*, Andreas.' A second attendant had overheard the conversation. It seemed not to be the first time that he had tried to pacify the Greek. 'They just getting us a better deal, eh? The idea of Canada still moves most of us, except for the hardliners.'

'What? A tolerant land of opportunity away from old world prejudice?' snarled the Greek. 'Tell me about it.'

'Isn't that the ideal which brought the French and English – and Greek – settlers?' suggested Beagan.

'Yeah, sure,' nodded the Québécois attendant.

Unable to restrain herself, Piri chatted about Beagan's interest in emigration. The Greek scoffed and glared at him. 'You want to hear a good story, do you? I came here twenty-five years ago and stayed too long. Now it's too late to move. I'm stuck here. My life is wasted. End of story.'

His anger disturbed Piri. It subdued the boys who slunk back below-deck to watch television. When the tanks were filled Beagan cast off and they drifted past Île Notre Dame. 'We were just trying to be friendly,' Piri said.

'He's frightened of being stranded,' replied Beagan, catching sight of a referendum billboard which translated as 'We have the right to be different.' In a handful of months the province was to vote whether it wished to remain part of Canada. 'You know it's not Québec that is distinct but its French-speakers. The separatists prefer to overlook the fact that one in five Québécois isn't *pure laine*, or pure wool as those of old French stock call themselves.'

'It sounds arrogant. I thought this was the country where different people were meant to get on?'

'That's what the majority want. But then the new populist version of history already omits those who transformed Montréal from a small mission and military post into the commercial capital of Canada,' remembered Beagan. 'After the defeat of Nouvelle France it was British entrepreneurs who came here looking for riches not in the Orient but along the road towards it. Their fervent search for pelts, and later for timber, gold and hydroelectric power, enabled the wilderness to be developed.'

By the 1890s about a hundred Montrealers, most of them Scots, had come to own the wealth of more than half the nation. On the hill from which Cartier had gazed west they had built High Victorian homes with Romanesque arcades and fairytale towers. They had constructed so many banks, universities, hospitals and places of worship that Mark Twain had observed that Montréal was a city where a boy could not throw a stone without breaking a church window. Throughout those years the French, grand-children of the first pioneers who had rooted themselves in the soil, were excluded from the boardrooms and clubs of the élite.

'Now only a century later the old Scottish families are gone, driven out by improvidence and French nationalism,' continued Beagan. 'Since the election in 1976 of the Parti Québécois, 150,000 English-speakers have moved away from the province. Even many new emigrants have voted with their feet.'

'Shifting the country's economic centre three hundred miles west to Toronto.'

'And providing the separatists with a scapegoat,' added Beagan. 'The years of British domination are portrayed as an era of exploi-tation rather than enrichment. Partisan politics promoted this false perception, telling the francophones what they wanted to hear to win their votes, setting them at odds with other Canadians.'

'Nationalists distorting the past?' said Piri. 'That's something I'm familiar with. It reminds me of Yugoslavia without guns.'

'This does not please me well,' sighed Hector. It was not in his nature to succumb to despondency, but the incident with the attendant had affected him too. 'Noah, Abraham and Jacob all died in faith, not having received the promises, the place which they should receive as an inherit-ance. But here I see no faith, no charity, neither on the left hand nor on the right.' He and Jamie sat astern as *Szerencsès* slid into the concrete canyon of a Seaway lock. The heavy steel doors closed behind them and cut out the morning sun.

'It's all down to geography,' suggested Jamie, anxious to lift his father's spirits. He had removed his shoes and his feet dangled above the boat's wake. 'It was Lachine which hindered the inward development of Canada for more than three hundred years. Without it France alone might have dominated the great white north. "*La belle province*" could have been "*le beau pays*".'

'That may yet be the way of it,' replied Hector, remaining grave, 'and it is not to my liking.' The surface frothed beneath Jamie's toes as the boat was lifted to the upper river level. 'If I recollect aright, the two defining elements of nationality are a wish to be governed together and a common sympathy; that is, shared language and beliefs. You'd see that here as soon as a mote in an oystercatcher's eye.'

'F-F-Forgive me, Father, but you're missing something. When you settled in Promise the land was very young. There was no past, only a present. Now there is a shared history.'

'I see nothing shared here but distrust and delusion. Your grandson has reason on his side.'

Szerencsès plied the channel which skirted the turbulent rapids. A jetboat kicked up plumes of spray as it ran joy-riders over the swift, choppy waters.

'Take Lachine,' suggested Jamie. 'It prevented the French from colonising the interior and made Canada a f-f-fractured nation. That history unites us. The rapids can even be blamed for inciting the American War of Independence.' Hector frowned in disbelief. 'Really,' continued his son. 'In the last half of the eighteenth century the American colonies were reaching west over the Appalachians. The expansion was driven for the most part by land speculators, among them George Washington.'

'James, you are as great a liar as a cat is a thief.'

'It's true,' insisted Jamie. 'In the trunk is a copy of his advertisement from the *Maryland Journal* of 20 August 1773.'

'In our trunk? How on God's good earth did that come to be in there?'

'How did any of it come to be there?' Jamie answered

with a shrug. 'Please, hear me out. Washington's sales pitch enthused, as I recall, that no lands exceeded his on the Ohio "in luxuriance of soil, or convenience of situation. They abound," he boasted, "with fine f-f-fish and wild fowl of various kinds, as also in most excellent meadows, many of which are, in their present state, almost fit for the scythe." I read it again over Beagan's shoulder only yesterday,' he explained. 'Well, the advertisement went on to assure prospective settlers that they "may cultivate and enjoy the lands in peace and safety". But that was the problem, the land was still Indian territory, so Washington and his fellow speculators could guarantee their customers safety only by demanding British military protection.'

'He asked England to protect his speculation?'

'And London tried to oblige. The Saint Lawrence was the best route for shipping troops into the expanding colonies, but with the need to cross the Lachine rapids, the operation was very expensive. The British public had become less and less willing to shoulder both war costs and the colonial burden, so Parliament chose for the first time to tax Americans for the protection which they demanded. The introduction of this levy inf-f-furiated them and when it was extended to a tax on tea they – led by Washington himself – rose up in revolt.' Jamie leaned back against the stern staff. 'It's this sort of story, these events and choices, which made the country. The one element which unites Canada is its history.'

'That's fine in theory, James,' replied the Reverend, his heart still chafed, 'providing someone remembers it.' On Szerencsès's stern the maple leaf flag flapped in the wind, was caught by an updraught and wrapped itself twice around Jamie. Beagan watched its motion out of the corner of his eye.

*　　　*　　　*

BEYOND MONTREAL THE alluvial plain was dotted with the isolated mountains of the Monteregian Hills. The shore rose in sweeping slopes to ridges crowned by lush woods. The boys had exhausted their library of videos and were restless during supper. Beagan tried to entertain them with stories about the explorers who had once canoed along the same gentle banks. As they paddled, he told them, Champlain's voyageurs had sung, '*Youpe! Youpe! Sur la Rivière*'. He recalled the open immigrant bateaux and broad, pony-drawn Durham boats that had followed them. Their settlers had camped at night on the shore dreaming of a glad arrival in Belleville or Port Hope, fearing an impoverished landing in Port Credit.

'Is that where they invented credit cards?' asked Randy, holding Sniffy the hamster in his lap.

'No, stupid,' said Joel, excited by the sense of adventure. 'Just shut up and listen to the story.'

At the Long Sault rapids, where *Szerencsès* climbed through another lock, Beagan told them of later migrants who had paused to eat at a weatherboarded wayside tavern. They had stolen apples from orchards skirting the towpath while awaiting the double-hulled steamer *Iroquois*. Later still travellers had boarded the *Rapids Queen*, whose shallow draught enabled her to navigate the wild chutes, and the grand paddle-wheeled *Kingston*, with her potted palms and carpets in three shades of crimson, to ride up the waterway which funnelled settlers from the Atlantic to the Great Lakes.

'In the old days there was so much competition along this route that the navigation companies needed to fight for trade,' Beagan recounted as Piri whisked a chocolate mousse. 'In 1857 two steam-boats, the *Montréal* and the *Napoleon*, challenged each other to a race. Each claimed to be the fastest boat and each stoked its boiler with boosters of colophonium and barrels of grease.'

'Wicked,' said Joel.

'They set off to the cheers of passengers and the wail of bag-pipes,' Beagan continued. 'There were lots of Scots aboard among the migrants. But twelve miles into the contest the *Montréal* burst into flames. The crew tried to contain the fire with a single hose. The travellers helped out with water jugs. Only the flames spread too quickly and the captain turned the ship to shore. Eight hundred feet from the bank she ran aground with the tide running downstream. The blaze drove all the passengers towards the bow. One of the two lifeboats capsized while the other became overcrowded and sank. People jumped overboard, fell on top of one another, drowned holding their infants in their arms. In fifteen minutes the 253 immigrants who had come in search of a promised land on earth found instead their paradise in heaven.'

'Man, I guess they just weren't lucky,' said Randy, tucking into his dessert.

As *Szerencsès* lay at anchor beyond the last Saint Lawrence lock on the north shore of Lake Ontario, Beagan sat cross-legged in his cabin, the contents of the trunk spread around him on the floor. By his side there was a child's pouch of cat's-eyes marbles, love notes wrapped in hair ribbon and a well-thumbed book of elegies. He lay down the fragile copy of the *Maryland Journal* and picked up a bundle of his grandfather's letters. Piri had put the boys to bed and appeared at the door with two tumblers of apricot brandy. A breath of jasmine followed her as she settled beside him on the thick pile carpet. 'What sort of man was Jamie?' she asked, nodding at the papers.

'Well, good,' Beagan replied. 'Relentless in promoting the good.' He handed her the family portrait taken after Hector's death. 'Much like his own father, though Jamie's definition of it was more liberal. That's him on the right.'

Piri saw two lonely boys and their widowed mother frozen in Victorian formality. She sensed too the loneliness in Beagan. 'It's difficult to know what he thought, or felt, but I like him; look, he's trying to hide a stain on his cuff.'

'This is the first letter he wrote home. It's dated 16 May 1879.' Beagan unfolded a sheet of creased paper and read, 'I arrived early

Saturday morning and our steamer appeared to float through the thick fog into Toronto harbour.'

Piri stretched to look over his shoulder. The page was covered with a neat hand but without paragraphs. 'The writing is so dense.'

'Paper would have been expensive for him.' Beagan read on, pleased to have a sympathetic listener. 'The shoreline was obscured by mist and the buildings seemed to soar above the earth like enchanted castles. Churches shot their spires towards heaven, the Saint Lawrence Hall lifted its copper dome like a hot-air balloon, even the roughcast Parliament appeared to break free of both gravity and civic burden to levitate into the firmament.'

'It can still look like that today, if the pollution's bad. Sometimes you just can't breathe downtown.'

'I don't know if I'll recognise it. I've been away so long and cities change so quickly. I saw that when I lived in Australia. I worked there as a travel agent for a time.' He winced, recalling his attempts to make a home in Brisbane. No sooner had he settled into an apartment and hung his pictures on the wall than the building was demolished and a modern development constructed in its place. It happened three times in as many years. 'So you'll know Toronto better than me now. The new office blocks and roads and all that.'

'Maybe, but you know who made it.'

'The noise of sawmills and smell of distilleries' corn mash assaulted my senses,' Beagan continued to read. 'A cloud of white dust drifted over Gooderham and Worts' flour mill then swirled skywards with the steam from a puffing Grand Trunk locomotive. The steamer whistled its arrival. Baggage porters cried, armfuls of babies wailed and mothers wept on seeing their husbands ashore. An Irishman slipped and fell into the water between the wharf and ship's hull. His friends hooted until they saw him go under a second time. They then lowered ropes that were tied to barrels and other impossible life-preservers before a strong fellow jumped into the water and pulled the drowning man to safety. The rescuer swung lightly on to the wharf, shook himself as if he had been a

Newfoundland dog and walked off into the crowd. Toronto has over a hundred miles of streets, most of cedar-block planking with long-board sidewalks, so every corner of the town resounds with the sound of hooves and boots on wood. Everywhere there is, as Father would have said, so much of a bustle and a stir.'

'It must have felt so busy to him. I'd never seen a shopping mall before I came to Toronto. They were so big that they made me feel a little sick at first. There were so many things to look at, so much choice.'

Beagan shuffled through odd-sized printed sheets and tightly-written cards. 'He had thought that his first week would be spent tramping every board-foot of the town looking for work, but by lunchtime on the first day he had a job.'

'Even faster than me.'

'Here we are.' He showed Piri a Niagara Navigation Company timetable. Across the top Jamie had inscribed in red pencil, 'My First Assignment.' On the back of the leaflet he had noted, 'I am employed as a printer's devil, making rollers and setting type in a small newspaper office on Bay Street. I enjoy the work but my weekly pay is only $3.00. Accommodation costs $2.50.'

'His room backed on to a slaughterhouse,' Beagan explained, looking up from the page. 'He says somewhere that the lows of the cattle ensured he was never late for work. But he had to pawn his overcoat and live off biscuits for a week. In the end he wrote to home for help. His mother sent him money on the condition that he spend it "in a right way". She worried that life in the city would lead him to sin.'

Beagan handed Piri his great-grandmother's letter. Six single dollar bills had once been pinned to its corner. 'Be sure you go regular to church and attend Bible classes. The Lord will be with you; lay hold of Him for He will guide you.' She read out the careful hand then took another sip of brandy.

'Kirstie had grown up as a herring girl in Scotland. I like to remember her as a child gathering tangle for the kelp-making, following the fisherwives home, their scaly creels shining like silver in the moonlight. Later she and her sister followed the herring, seizing and sorting their father's freight of fish. The music of their cries, as they chaffered their wares, would have rung through streets of towns down the length of the west coast. But the years of living with a stern moralist like Hector took away a part of herself.'

'Not her love for her sons,' observed Piri. 'Did Jamie have any friends in Toronto?' Beagan shook his head as he refilled her glass. 'When I first arrived I spent a lot of time alone too,' she said. 'I remember our first Christmas. We had a small artificial tree but I wanted a huge pine with tons of chocolate ornaments on it like back home. Peter really tried to make me happy and bought some *szaloncukor*, the traditional Hungarian candy, to hang in the tree, but then he had to work right up to Christmas Eve. I stayed in the apartment missing my family, crying my eyes out.'

'I think Jamie was lonely,' acknowledged Beagan. 'He worked five and a half days a week in the print shop. Sunday was set aside for worship. Only Saturday afternoons were free, and he took to paddling a borrowed canoe around the island.' Beagan passed her a flyer announcing a public demonstration of Edison's incandescent electric light. On the back Jamie had written, 'The harbour is protected by an arc of flat islands which lie so level with the water that they appear to be half-submerged. It is a place apart from the city with deserted bays, scattered raggle-taggle homes and lakeside cottages. At dusk I like to come ashore on an empty beach, make a driftwood fire and cook a sausage for supper. Sometimes if I'm feeling bold I sing "One More River to Cross" or "The Canadian Boat Song". Last weekend the sound of a piano and a woman's voice reached me from across the water and not long afterwards, although it filled me with guilt, I treated myself to a straw hat as my Scotch cap looks shabby. Cost $1.00.'

'Here his mother writes back asking him not to be too bold on the water,' laughed Piri. She read aloud, 'I enclose a camping quilt of cloth similar to a Paisley shawl so you can spend the occasional night sleeping under the stars away from the clatter of town and the bellow of condemned cows.' She turned the letter on to its side. 'What's this in the margin?'

Beagan leaned close to her. 'That's his brother. Zachary liked to give orders to everyone, especially Jamie.'

'You must decide on the course of your career. Be precise in your objective. I have been informed by an associate that, if you are not too lazy to study, you should attend the School of Practical Science. On taking a course there you can obtain an excellent situation as a Mechanical Engineer.' Piri looked up from the page. 'He sounds a bit like a sergeant major.'

'Zachary had a gift for organisation.'

'Did Jamie listen to his advice?'

Beagan shook his head. 'He had already chosen his career. Both the brothers had.'

Hector glanced over Beagan's shoulder as he reached for a photograph album. On its cover was a snapshot of Jamie standing by a canoe with paddle in hand, his britches held up by a braid belt and sporting the straw hat. 'As I recall a dollar was not an insignificant sum,' chided Hector. 'I hope that garment was not bought with the money your mother sent.'

Jamie removed the hat from his head and suspended it in space between them. 'Even if I had had the inclination to be thriftless there was never the time to spend my wages on anything other than essentials. I watched my money carefully, F-F-Father. In two years I did not once allow myself to take the street cars home, even though I was tired and the road was muddy.'

Hector examined the boater then spun it away towards the *en suite* bathroom. It hit the mirror and knocked Beagan's toothbrush into the sink. He and Piri looked up from the album. 'Your headgear smacks of ostentation,' Hector told Jamie.

'I was no city swell, nor had I ever any intention of becoming one.'

'Nor did you intend joining the ministry. It disappointed me that you did not hear the call.'

'I heard a different voice. In the newspaper office I found

a deep satisfaction in f-f-forming the words letter by letter in the compositor's hand-type. It excited me hearing the lick of ink on the plate and transforming a blank white sheet into thoughts, information, communication. I could find the right words, set them in type, press, preserve and prevent them from ever slipping away. My stutter didn't matter, F-F-Father. I could hold an idea in my hand and share it with another, send it to Mother at home, broadcast it like seed to ten thousand readers.'

Jamie sat up and drifted Buddha-like across the cabin. 'Canada was then a young land of scattered communities. The new railway, reaching west mile by mile towards the Pacific, would soon carry newspapers to every farm, mine and lumber camp in the Dominion. Print was the means of communication. Words could fuse the disparate people into a united nation. It made me determined that I would become a publisher.'

'I am glad, James, that you saw fit to work with your brother.'

'And I too, despite all that happened. You can read of my pleasure at Zachary's decision to move to Toronto.' Jamie gestured at the trunkful of letters. 'There was little love in him but he was a man of great devotion. I looked forward to sharing his company. Yet even in our most optimistic moments neither of us foresaw the fullness of expansion that would grow from our f-f-fine f-f-folly of enthusiasm and ideals.' He pointed down at the album. 'Look there, Father.' Beneath them in the darkened cabin Beagan and Piri were leafing through the black and white photographs. A youthful Jamie and Zachary stood together on Bay Street pier. Their cheeks were clean-shaven and their eyes bright. 'It was you who made it possible.'

'Providence was good to you, right enough,' admitted Hector, who would have flushed had blood still pumped in his veins.

Piri flicked through a dozen pages and two lifetimes. In an early colour print Jamie paused to catch his breath aboard the RMS *Kipper* as she steamed up the Muskoka lakes. By the album's last leaves his hair had thinned and he had taken to wearing a trilby. Slip-knot ties had replaced black satin stocks. He acquired a ruddy complexion, maybe from the trials of the first years, and grew portly. Zachary, on the other hand, maintained his agile wiriness on page after page. His moustache, which in the span of the album had been transformed from copper brown to snow white, always remained neatly trimmed. Jamie's whiskers tended towards the unruly.

'Look here, they are getting too far ahead of themselves,' said Jamie as Piri turned over another decade of pages. 'Don't you find, Father, that clock-locked linear time, with its ticking off of days, is a pattern only the living follow with ease? For me it is like a swallow trying to keep track of a turtle's progress. I want to let go of the eph-ph-phemeral moment, to soar away and to ride the winds and currents of time.' But Hector was not listening to his son. Instead his zealous eye glared at Beagan.

The rocking of the boat and the brandy had conspired to relax the couple. Beagan and Piri imagined voices in the drone of the engine. Its rhythm conjured up the unheard music of the belugas' serenade and Jamie's song to the stars on Toronto Island. In the warm cabin Beagan reached forward to take a bundle of letters from Piri's lap, then laid his hand on her knee. But as his body shifted towards her there was a sudden cry. Randy had woken from the depths of a nightmare. Piri pulled back, stood up and left the cabin.

Jamie put his hands on his hips and turned towards the Reverend. 'Father, what are you doing?'

'If a man looks at a woman with lust then he commits adultery in his heart,' hissed Hector. 'O Lord, lead us not into temptation but deliver us from evil,' he prayed, wrestling in travail with the Holy Spirit, then added, 'This boy seems determined to be a wisp in every bed.'

For a moment Beagan did not move. He took a long, deep breath, looked right and left, then gazed into the empty air around him.

CHAPTER V

WRITING ON WATER

'OW DOES A poor man enrich the w-w-world?' By hard work, by improving himself, by self-trust. 'Concentration,' I quoted from Emerson, 'is the secret of strength in politics, in war, in trade, in short, in all the management of human affairs.' It matters not if a man is rich or poor, only that he has discipline. Capital and good connections may help to begin a career but they alone will not secure the future. Zachary and I were fortunate to have inherited a zeal for productive labour and a belief in honest industry. We aspired to make our own success by helping other people to prosper.

If I stood on a chair balanced on my bed I could glimpse the glint of blue water across the rooftops. I found comfort in its sight, remembering that it was little more than a century since white men had first sailed around the island and into the sheltered harbour. The early settlers had cleared the oak from the mainland and planted red Fife wheat, as in Promise. In late summer the ripe russet heads of grain had bowed and swayed in the balmy breeze. They had eaten the dense flocks of wild pigeons which roosted so low on the trees that they could be knocked off the branch with a stick.

'F-F-Fisher MacFie and I caught sea-salmon at home,' I enthused to my landlady, her cheeks slashed with rouge bought from my rent money, 'just as the pioneers used to do here on the Humber River.'

'Pigeon pie tastes dandiest with crab-apple jelly,' she replied.

John Graves Simcoe, the first lieutenant governor of the new province of Upper Canada, had led the colonists to the site in 1793. In a canvas house which had originally belonged to Captain Cook, he had laid out his grandiose plan for a great capital city. His surveyor, Captain Gotherman, had then attempted to transform the limitless wilds into an orderly town of geometric splendour. The central business section was to be a precise grid of 121 regular blocks surrounded by a noble common. But the magnificent plan had utterly ignored the terrain and with the first spring run-off the new capital turned into a swamp. The resulting swarms of mosquitoes had brought with them the danger of malaria.

As I trudged around the puddles between my boarding house and the print shop I understood how Simcoe's Muddy York had come to be dubbed Hogtown. His tight-buttoned, tight-lipped gentlemen in uniform, among them the young aide Arthur Wellesley who was destined to become the Duke of Wellington and defeat Napoleon at Waterloo, had sung 'God Save the King' then lain down on their blankets in the mire to sleep. One day, they had foretold, Hogtown would be a cosmopolitan metropolis. But this was still some time off when the province's attorney-general, John White, was mortally wounded in a duel with John Small, clerk of the Executive Council.

The first families, anxious to rise above the common pioneer life, assumed airs and graces and renamed the quaggy city. Toronto, they claimed, was the Huron word for 'meeting place'. Others maintained that the Indian name meant 'trees in the bog'. The discrepancy between how things really were and how Old Toronto wished them to appear to be ruffled me no end.

This disparity spawned newspapers that were a strange

hotch-potch of politics, religion and abuse. Few column inches were ever set aside for accurate and detailed information. The titles of the first broadsheets proclaimed both their allegiance and their attitude: the *Royal Standard*, the *Church*, the *Porcupine*. The publisher of the radical *Colonial Advocate* was William Lyon Mackenzie, a wild wiry Scot who covered his baldness with a flame-red wig and led an unsuccessful armed rebellion against British colonial rule. Tory bully-boys once threw his printing press into Toronto Bay. The second editor of the *Toronto Telegram* was a staunch Royalist. 'Black Jack' Robinson won cheers and circulation when he announced the eleventh Commandment: 'Thou shalt not bear false witness against the British Empire.' Even the political parties themselves launched newspapers. 'We must start the *Empire*,' wrote Conservatives to their prime minister John A. Macdonald, 'or prepare for defeat at the next general election.' In Upper Canada the press was committed not to freedom of expression but to the manipulation of public perception.

In a small society that is stable and not in flux, the line between truth and falsehood is sharp. Words are rooted in a known and knowable context. On Cape Breton, Father as parish minister was heard and trusted. We all knew that old McKinlay would sooner play fiddle for the devil than tell a lie. But as society grows its citizens are obliged to accept information without evidence. Each fact cannot be verified by first-hand experience and language is subjected to the pressure of a changing environment. Words taken on trust may be corrupted by those bent on self-interest. Politicians collect information by secret means and withhold details that do not serve them. Businesses can distort statistics to influence their investors and customers. As words are devalued people begin to lose faith in what they hear, as Promise's parishioners had ceased to listen to Father's sermons. Individuals become confused and start to mistrust their institutions. Society begins to unravel, scattering its parts like the letters of a nightmare alphabet. It was to my mind only an independent press that could counter this descent into confusion by obtaining accurate intelligence and disclosing it to the public. The responsibility of newspapers is to make truth the common property of the nation.

When I met Zachary at the pier he wore a new, natty bow tie. He shook my hand and said, 'You should trim your moustache. Speed on the road to success depends on appearance as well as substance.' His arrival was a day later than expected because Mother had asked him not to travel on a Sunday. As I collected his valise he trotted out her fond saying, 'There is no blessing in the gain made on the Sabbath.' My brother turned his back on the lake, looked up towards the heights of Deer Park and marched inland. He had inherited some of Father's missionary spirit. He too was a man of vision, exiled for the sake of the Word, but instead of the Lord's Commandments the tenet which he strove to impart was the gospel of fact. 'Facts,' he would say, 'are all that a man can depend upon. Words are everybody's business.' In the uncertain world after Darwin, when the Bible had come to be seen less as a literal truth and more as an allegory, irrefutable facts were my brother's certainty.

We walked the city streets all afternoon so Zachary could orient himself. He inspected the business district as a soldier might survey the field of battle, looking for the high ground and taking particular interest in the location of newspaper offices. I made a point of taking him to the intersection of King and Simcoe Streets. On its four corners stood a handsome set of buildings: Upper Canada College, Government House, a tavern and Saint Andrew's church. Education, legislation, damnation and salvation were gathered together at one crossroads. Zachary was unimpressed until I mentioned that the editor of the *Telegram* was an old boy of the college. At suppertime I suggested that we might like to indulge in a celebratory Tom-and-Jerry at Clancey's but he declined. Instead we had a quiet meal at home. Zachary professed little need of physical comforts. Nevertheless he readily accepted my offer of the bed, which left me sleeping on the floor. The next morning he set off early to begin his career.

In Cape Breton he had admired the *Mail* and so he now secured himself employment on the commercial page. Almost at once he deemed its market reports to be unsatisfactory. Inadequate space, he judged, was provided for trade information. The sporting section was his page's main competitor, and in the battle for column inches the Amateur Golf Championships took precedence over the collapse of the Panama Canal Company. Pork belly prices, claimed the editor, never did a damn to increase circulation.

Zachary's frustration only stiffened our resolve to establish an independent trade newspaper. 'Shared knowledge is the foundation of modern civilisation,' he told me over a dinner of fried potatoes. There were two slices of bacon. He ate the larger piece. 'The propagation of accurate information dispels ignorance and darkness.'

The commercial press of the time offered little that was worthy of emulation. Publications lacked independence; their reports read like advertisements and their statistics like fairytales. All the facts were out of date. Paper stock too was of a low standard. Print density was inconsistent and in winter ink froze on the plate in unheated printshops. We calculated that a reliable journal devoted to the interests of the grocery and kindred trades could provide a useful public service. Storekeepers could improve their sales with knowledge of public tastes and manufacturers' wares. Farmers could plan, plant and trade with greater efficiency. It became our ambition to produce a paper of an editorial quality and typographic art then unknown in Canada.

Zachary gave up his post at the *Mail* and we became the brother publishers; proprietor, editor, advertisement solicitor, book-keeper and office-boy of the Gillean Publishing Company Limited. Our days began on foot. One of us walked to the east, the other to the west, first to the abattoir and then to the King Street Produce Market, to reconnoitre for prices, facts and trends. We quizzed traders at the Saint Lawrence Market and questioned dealers at the Exchange. At lunch we hurried back to the office to write up the copy, neither of us dawdling long behind the desk in our nine- by twelve-foot office as we had been able to afford only a single chair. We devoted the afternoon to canvassing for advertisers. Within two months the first number of the *Canadian Vegetable* made its appearance as a monthly periodical. Ten thousand copies were sent out to general storekeepers across the Dominion. It was the intention to show that our new concern would provide them with a proper vehicle for the conveyance of reliable market reports. Our first editorial declared, 'The *Vegetable* is entirely independent and will state facts and express opinions regarding topics of importance to the trade in a fearless and independent manner. We will also pay our bills promptly.'

But the appeal for support which accompanied the initial copy met with little success. One solitary subscriber was the result of the mountains of labour. We were disappointed but not disheartened and tried again, collecting and distilling facts, then distributing another ten thousand free copies to merchants. This time our reward was a mere five further subscribers. Our enterprise was flawed. The *Canadian Vegetable* was not a going concern.

'Old facts don't pass muster,' proclaimed Zachary. It occurred to us that in the ever-fluctuating grocery market a monthly paper was a poor guide to prices. One day's bargain broccoli could be sold at a premium after a spell of drought. Information had to reach the trade promptly.

'Pigeons,' I said in a flash of inspiration. 'It's a pigeon that we need.'

'Don't be sassy with me, chap,' Zachary replied.

We invested in a single homing pigeon with fine white wing patches and a rusty breast. I named her Harriet. Zachary called her Bird No. 1. Every morning I carried her away to the markets, scribbled the latest prices on a tiny roll of paper and released her to carry it back to the office. Zachary, who did not like to be seen with the bird, then updated the produce report. With the last of our borrowed capital we printed a third number and this time issued it as a weekly. The trade appreciated the change and their response was immediate. The requests for subscriptions arrived by the postbag and circulation grew at a remarkable rate.

The alteration also appealed to advertisers. It was the practice of the day for advertisements to appear only in the large daily and commercial newspapers, where not one quarter of the circulation reached the people who were interested in the goods on offer. This approach scattered much seed upon stony ground. Our innovation was to guarantee advertisers direct access to interested readers. In addition it had been the established custom to revise notices only once every six months. We encouraged our clients to update their insertions every week. 'Let your advertisements speak to your customers as your travellers would talk to them,' prompted our handbills. The Gillean Publishing Company applied itself to making advertisers' space, no matter how large or small, profitable.

Our ideal was to conduct business on honest principles, to be independent of any clique, house association or other guild. We strove to resort to no schemes nor use undue influences to secure advertising patronage. As a result a vista stretched before us, an ever-widening avenue of ambitious service.

The formula enabled us to extend ourselves and to

purchase *Paper Fancies*. The official organ of the book, stationery and fancy goods trades had been reduced to a sad, tatty pamphlet. We infused the periodical with energy and, dare I say it, merit, determined to make it an ornament to journalism, and produced it too as a weekly. Modern photo-engraving replaced woodcut illustrations. *Paper Fancies* became a satisfactory index for its patrons and in the first year made a profit of $1,100 after the payment of all expenses. Zachary calculated that we could double the figure in twelve more months. We did.

The key to the success of any venture, with or without pigeons, is good timing. As I reached the age of majority Canada stood at the threshold of a period of remarkable growth. Capital poured into the young Dominion from the London money markets. Investments were repaid with wheat from Manitoba and the riches of the Canadian Shield. Eastern factories manufactured goods as fast as foundries cast the rails to carry them west. Settlers from every corner of Europe swarmed off fast Atlantic steamships and crammed aboard trains bound for new homesteads across North America. Our population began to increase by 10 per cent every decade. Alexander Graham Bell invented his telephone. The Statue of Liberty rose at the entrance to New York harbour and we bought six more birds. The New World spirit was transforming the wilderness into an industrial nation.

We worked hard to expand our papers and did well under the increased responsibility. Each week we met our local customers and tried to understand their requirements better. Our canvassers travelled with a pigeon under their arms to see the more distant merchants. Many of our patrons were general dealers, handlers of hardware and dry goods who made frequent representations to us to serve their branch of commerce. In response to their demands we launched our third venture. The *Hardwareman's Nuts & Notions* met with appreciation and its success required us to move to larger offices. Our advertising patronage increased and brought large additions to the subscription list. Within three years the Gillean Publishing Company was free of debt. We hired two full-time journalists and a girl as a shorthand writer. She set her desk alongside the cages and relieved us of a great deal of letter writing. She also fed the birds. Her pay was four dollars each week, a salary at which I felt her well able to afford a new hat.

The novelty of profit enabled us each to draw ten dollars every week from the company. All our income had before been spent on improving the papers. Zachary deposited his salary in the bank. 'Come what may it goes there,' he declared. 'With this money I will form the nucleus of a fortune.' My deposits in the Home Savings and Loan Company were less frequent, but I did manage to economise enough to buy a fine Peterborough lapstrake canoe. When weather and work permitted I paddled it around the island or sailed under a spread of standing canvas as far as the Etobicoke River. Some evenings I didn't return home until ten or eleven o'clock.

One summer when all the giddy people had gone down to the beach and the cloying heat prevented even Zachary from working I proposed that we take a week's canoe trip together. At first he was suspicious of the luxury – we had never before indulged ourselves in a holiday – but I convinced him that the rest would improve our concentration.

Muskoka is a lake district of lonely pines and pastel pink granite that lies a hundred miles to the north of Toronto. The train dropped us at the Gravenhurst railhead and we paddled the Peterborough towards Shadow River. We dived off blueberry islands, swam through the embrace of cool black currents and dried ourselves within the canoe's cocoon. In late afternoon we slipped through sun-warmed shallows and pulled our boat over sandy beds ridged like a mackerel sky. At dusk we pan-fried fresh trout for supper. The lonely call of the loon echoed across the waters and we fell asleep listening to the flip flop of waves on the shore. Although Zachary spoke of nothing but work we shared the week there, watching deer step out from behind bleached white birches and cross black rocks to drink, drifting shirtless across the lazy afternoons and sheltered bays. It was all too soon that we had to return to the city's noise, hustle and bustle. Zachary was anxious to get back. He missed the work. His skin had also taken on a brilliant red tinge from the scalding sun and I needed to apply an oatmeal powder poultice to his face every morning.

As our train rattled south the thickly-wooded hills became seamed with roads and clearings. Here and there fields appeared dotted with huge pine stumps. We passed a threshing machine and a horseless carriage. Zachary's excitement rose as I sank into disappointment. The fair pastureland around Lake Ontario was fertile but too flat to please me. I knew then that I lived too much right inside myself but, even if I had managed to cobble together the words to explain my feelings, Zachary would not have listened. He was looking forward, trying to catch sight of the city over the cornfields. He got a cinder in his eye. I sat with my back towards the locomotive, gaze fixed on the northern woods, and soothed my sadness by daydreaming of canoe trips around Toronto harbour, unaware that its island was about to change my life.

The island had long been a sanctuary from the rigid conformity of mainland society. Once it had been connected to the mainland by an isthmus and revellers had cavorted in the merry-go-rounds, bowling alleys and abundant taverns of the Peninsula Pleasure Grounds. The amusements and arcades catered for the worst sort of new immigrant, the more prudish Old Torontonians had claimed, and there were calls from the pulpit for authorities to curb the intemperance. In 1858 the prayers of the pious were answered when divine judgement came in the form of a great storm which washed away the landbridge and destroyed the most notorious of the island saloons, Quinn's Hotel.

Thirty years later it was the absence of a regimented grid pattern which drew the less conventional citizens to build simple summer cottages along the winding, leafy lanes. Every June families left their solid Victorian townhouses and moved across the bay to casual wooden homes with open front doors and broad verandahs cluttered by wobbly armchairs. They feasted on watermelon in picket-fenced gardens of lavender and fragrant grey-green mignonette. The girls bathed in the lake, dried their hair in the sun and walked to the Baths to have a little lunch at the pavilion. Afterwards they dawdled at the table to read each other's fortunes in the tea leaves. Their brothers paddled to Hanlan's Point to see a strong man perform, then met their sisters on the beach for a taffy pull. Their mothers called on friends or shopped at Walker's for new blouses while their fathers finished work early and caught the puffing ferry back to the serpentine streets of the summer place apart.

It was the head of such a family, Eden Prosper Goode, who as the Invention & Progress Correspondent of the *Toronto Globe* had provided the capital to launch the *Canadian Vegetable*. He was a man of great enthusiasms, although his technical knowledge was at best hazy. He had been born in the Bishop of Kerry's palace in Ireland where his mother had taken shelter after her Catholic neighbours had burnt down her house. They hadn't been keen on having an Irish Protestant living in the vicinity. Later he and his young parents had been shipwrecked in the West Indies and reached Toronto by way of New Orleans and Boston where his father, who could not spell, had held an editorial position on the *Farmer's Advocate*.

Goode first invited us to the island one humid Saturday

afternoon soon after our return from Muskoka. His summer house nestled in a grove beneath a clump of stately pines. Hammocks and geraniums hung between the trees. A caged canary sang along with a piano playing inside the cottage. Zachary and I mounted the wooden front steps and, the door being ajar, knocked on its frame. A terrier lying in the shade barked once, rolled over and went back to sleep. A child, her hair waved in curls, peeked out from behind a lace curtain and ran away. The piano stopped playing.

'Lizzie,' a woman called from within the house. 'Lizzie?' A breath of cool air wafted out from the shadowy front room. We were dressed in our three-piece suits and it was hot on the verandah. The child reappeared at the window and stared. Zachary knocked again which evoked a third call, this time more insistent. 'Lizzie!'

The child turned and addressed the voice. 'Lizzie is making cocoa-nut cake.' She returned her gaze to us and added, 'I am having mine with raspberry syrup.'

'It is Mr Zachary Gillean to see Mr Goode,' announced my brother, ignoring the child and clearing his throat in an impatient gesture. 'Is Mr Eden Goode at home?'

Footsteps padded across the hardwood floor and a gentle sweet face appeared at the door. Its owner had fair ruffled hair, blue eyes and a graceful figure clad in a spotted cotton blouse and serge dress. 'I'm sorry,' apologised Bessie, Goode's eldest daughter, 'but I thought Lizzie would come.' She stepped into the sunlight and we saw that she wore neither shoes or stockings. Zachary bowed and introduced himself. I had never before seen a young woman's feet and blushed.

'Well, the pigeon publishing brothers,' said Bessie, making us sound like a circus trapeze act. 'But aren't you awfully hot in your suits?' She was as startled by the state of our dress as we were by her undress. 'It is real warm today.'

'Our appointment with your father is to discuss business, Miss Goode,' explained Zachary with due formality. Her lack of respect had irked him.

She raised a hand to cover a smile. 'I am sorry. I try to be quite good-natured but ... but it just comes out all wrong.' She shrugged her shoulders and laughed brightly. The planks of the verandah were painted grey and the shadows of the lattice created by the sun criss-crossed the floor. Bessie skipped from cool shadow to shadow, past the potted palms and on to the grass to avoid burning her soles. 'Father has been experimenting with his photo-camera all day,' she explained, then, catching me looking at her feet, blushed too. 'He is out back, gentlemen, if you would care to follow me.'

We followed her skipping run behind the house to where her sister Daisy was suspended by her feet from a tree. An intricate web of fine supporting wires upheld both her skirts and her modesty. Their brother Arthur was attempting to fasten a hat to her head but it kept falling off. 'We could use a dab of molasses, Pa,' he suggested, at which point Daisy shrieked.

'Just retie the ribbon, Art,' instructed Goode. 'And remember the parasol.' A new Kodak was mounted upside-down on a tripod beside him. He tried to keep apace of innovation, indeed he had encouraged his publishing friend George Brown not to turn down the offer of exclusive British Empire rights to the telephone. Brown, unlike Goode, did not think that they were worth the $150 price asked by Bell.

Goode caught sight of us. 'Excellent; the Messrs Gillean. You're just in time to witness an experiment to prove that the truth is not the facts. Come quickly.' We stepped forward and shook hands. In the sunlight Goode's balding head gleamed like newly polished rosewood. A forgetful house-maid appeared to have left a small chamois of blond hair on his crown. Zachary pointed out his mispositioning of the camera. 'Ah, there you are wrong,' Goode informed him. 'It is just where I want it to be.'

'But the subject recorded will be upside-down.'

'Not so,' said Goode, turning away from his family. 'You will agree that the camera cannot lie.' We nodded our assent. 'Then you must also accept that it preserves an individual perspective.'

'Not individual, no,' disagreed Zachary. 'It records a scene objectively, without interpretation.'

'But I as the camera-man choose where to point the apparatus. I decide what facts are to be included in and excluded from the field of vision. My selection is my interpretation. Yet you maintain that the resulting photograph will be objective. What then if you take a photograph, composing it with whatever facts and elements you choose. Will it be any less true?'

Rather than agree that both perspectives would be valid Zachary said, 'No, but there is always the accepted view. The facts should be allowed to speak for themselves.'

'Facts don't speak, Zachary, they are spoken. An accepted view only comes about because it is preached to or held by the majority, not because it is objective. And in any case it does not negate the individual perspective. Look at Daisy. There can be no such thing as an objective view, not in photographs or paintings, books or journalism.'

Bessie climbed up the ladder as Daisy's skirt slipped loose from an ankle wire. Her flushed and inverted face brought to mind the new red tulips that Dutch florists on Yonge Street had begun to sell. Zachary gestured to the family set-piece. 'But this is a manipulated truth.' I thought it looked like fun.

'It is my truth,' replied Goode. His domed pate coloured as he grew excited. 'The photograph will portray my daughter as the only right-minded lady in a topsy-turvy world. And who is to say that isn't the case? It is the way that I see it.'

'But is that useful?' asked my brother.

'I have an abhorrence of pursuits which are useful and profitable alone. Our family excelled because we liked doing something and not because of any ulterior motive such as making money.'

Arthur passed Daisy the handle of an open parasol. She held it beneath her head and leaves shaken from the tree sailed down into its canopy. 'Father?' she breathed.

'I hope your support of our enterprise,' said Zachary, 'came about because as well as liking it you believed in its usefulness.'

'Every time I see a spark of vision I water it. I nurture the flames of dreams. The Goodes have always done that. Fernando Espero Goode supported Dias de Novais, the Portuguese explorer, and was honoured in the naming of the Cape of Good Hope.'

'Father, we are ready.'

'The English poet Barnabe Googe, who spelt the name in his individual way, inspired Good Queen Bess with his "Cupid Conquered" and became one of her gentlemen-pensioners.'

'Daisy is turning quite red, Father,' said Arthur.

'Think too of Goode's *School Atlas* and *Good Housekeeping*. And consider George Brown Goode, the zoologist, who encouraged the National Museum of Natural History to open its doors to the general public. He also recorded 156 new species of fish.'

Daisy rested her hand on her sister's head and whispered, 'I think that I shall be sick.'

'I don't see what this has to do with facts,' interrupted Zachary.

'The fact is that it's my true story. You will find a Goode in every port of the world and for all of them the means are always the end.' He waved an arm as if encompassing them and the world in his grasp. 'I like pigeons too.'

'Father, Daisy is feeling unwell,' said Bessie. She had taken charge of her younger siblings all her life.

'I am with you, my child.' Arthur removed the ladder. Goode studied his tableau. Daisy's feet appeared to perch on the underside of a branch. Her skirts, held up by the wires, seemed to billow in an imaginary breeze. The book open in her hand completed the impression. Goode clicked the shutter to preserve his vision. A woman of calm countenance stood reading beneath a parasol in an upside-down world.

With a flick of his hand the subject was released and fell groaning to the ground. Bessie took her sister into her arms and comforted her, a spontaneous physical compassion the like of which I had never seen. At Goode's invitation we retired to the parlour to discuss business. Later Bessie stole in to our meeting and left us each a peeled snow apple, its flesh white and cool, and a smile.

The following weeks found me often at the cottage on the pretence of discussing business. I tended to arrive in a rush, declaring that I could only stop by for a minute, then stay all afternoon. Bessie's bright sunny ways drew many young people to her and together we sailed to Victoria Park and played pig on the verandah. I knew no card games and so found myself at somewhat of a disadvantage, especially as Bessie cheated outrageously. She threw back her head and laughed at my endeavours, her face overflowing with such pleasure that it seemed her whole being existed only to share joy. I took pleasure in teaching her how to ride a bicycle but she needed no lessons in canoeing. At the Grand Aquatic Regatta she won the silver medal in the skiff race. She insisted that the prize had really been awarded for her irrepressible chatter. 'I am such a desperate talker,' she told me, and when we stayed up late gathered under the porch's red light playing charades and shouting proverbs, I believed her. Bessie had a kind word for everyone and there was always a story poised to trip off her tongue.

We began to correspond with each other on the days when business kept me in the office. At that time a letter written in the city at breakfast would reach the island by lunchtime and a response could be on my desk before the end of the working day. If we used a pigeon our messages could be exchanged in an even shorter time.

'Go thou in well-doing,' she preached in the morning after a meeting had forced me to cancel our canoe paddle around the island. 'I am quoting scripture today as I suppose you notice.' But it was her Irish heart which spoke in that afternoon's letter. 'Oh do run over here and quarrel with me or find fault with me. I do get so tired of people who always say the right things. You let me scold and grumble at the world and in return explain things as to make me good-natured. I don't have to talk to you unless I have something to say and then you talk to me as if I was a sensible girl instead of flattering me up as if I were a spoiled lady. You are so good to me and I would be awfully glad to see you.'

One Sunday the island church was too crowded and we sang our hymns under the trees on the lakefront. The coots and green-headed mallards paddling around us added their peeps and quacks to our prayers. On the long walk home Zachary talked about social conditions. Although not fond of the extravagance myself I brought her a box of chocolates and took the liberty of addressing her as Miss Bessie. 'It is not good for man to be alone,' I managed to tell her without a stutter.

'Or woman either I think,' she replied.

The days grew shorter and the nights cooled. Even Arthur stopped bathing every morning. The cottages were closed at the end of September. Weatherboards were fastened over the windows and dust-sheets laid over furniture for off-season ghosts. Field mice made their nests in the upholstery. Water pipes were drained before the freeze-up. As families sailed back across the harbour to the confines of city life the launch of a new paper, the *Lumberjack*, stole all my free hours. Zachary and I set up camping beds in the office to enable us to work through the night. The soft cooing drove him back to the boarding house before the end of the week, but it was not the birds that disturbed my sleep.

Bessie spent the autumn calling on friends with her mother, doing her needlework and dancing at society balls in a mauve silk party dress with pearl bead trimming. She went home to a hot footbath and a glass of punch. Yet the social season disappointed her. The rich coat of gold and red which adorned the trees meant the coming of winter. Her spirit seemed to shrink. It curled up in a dark corner to hibernate until spring.

It was in early November that I found both the time and the courage to invite Bessie to the Grocers' Ball, a gala dinner-dance which was renowned for the finest fare and entertainment, but when the evening arrived a spanner in the press prevented my attendance. The junior printer had knocked over his bag of jelly babies and it took me all night to ungum the works. My letter of apology arrived too late and Bessie's feelings were wounded.

'When a girl crimps up for about two hours, arrays herself in silken sheen, soaks herself in *Highland Heather* perfume, it gives one the idea that she rather intends going somewhere,' she wrote. 'But when she sits all muffled up for three hours or so, keeps assuring her family that she knows he will come for her and all the time knows he won't, it rather means that, that, well, that matters are a little mixed.'

The hurt which I had caused distressed me. It seemed selfish folly to toy with Bessie's feelings and I resolved that my time would be better employed in productive labour. But despite great application I could not concentrate on my work. Indeed I could hardly eat, playing with my breakfast at the lunch counter, and an absence of appetite had never been one of my failings. Zachary's just criticism of the lapse of discipline increased both my sense of guilt and my misery.

The first snow fell, settled in the carriage ruts and turned the roads into a quagmire. On Front Street my boot stuck in the mud and was trampled beneath the hooves of a Baker Carpet Cleaning cart. That evening I rode home aboard a flying demon of the Toronto Street Railway. The high-voltage flashes crackled from the overhead wire and trans-formed the bare wayside trees into beheaded corpses. Their broken and twisted limbs swayed to the discordant music of steel wheels on frozen rails. I closed my eyes, pulled my coat around me and forced my thoughts back to summer. The tram jerked and bucked and shook me out of my reverie but not away from the realisation that my life had become joyless without Bessie. It was my timidity which had pre-vented me from embracing her affection and, aware that I would never be able to say the words to express my feelings, I resolved to write to her that night.

I sat up until dawn spoiling half a ream of good paper and breaking the nib of my pen. My landlady knocked at the door twice. She worried that I suffered from delirium or had a fever in the head. In an attempt to make myself understood I wrote about the three books on my shelf: *The Reveries of a Bachelor*, *Les Misérables* and *Grandfather Grey*. 'What I am trying to get at,' I scrawled, 'is more than I can explain.' It was as if I had taken a crazy fit but some-where in the scribbles I asked Bessie to marry me. The writing was so bad that she would hardly be able to make it out. I drank six cups of tea and did not sleep. The envelope was too heavy to be carried by a single bird so I made a cat's-cradle of fine string and suspended it between the feet of my two favourite pigeons.

Her response was with me by dinnertime. 'Your letter tells me that you love me but please Jamie tell me with your lips. Make me understand.'

Bessie drew me out of myself and unlocked my heart. At

our wedding she wore myrtle and carried a shower bouquet
of white bridal roses. Her dress was simply made, heavy
corded silk trimmed with Brussels lace and the orthodox
veil of tulle. An orchestra of mandolins and guitars played
at the reception. A buffet of dainties was served. I wore a
red geranium and small green leaf in my buttonhole. My
bride held on to my arm through the whole afternoon.

The success of the firm enabled us to buy our own cottage
on the island. Every evening I returned home from work to
find a peeled snow apple set beside Father's old globe. We
traced the journeys which had made our families, by way
of Promise and a West Indies shipwreck, and brought us
together. After supper Bessie played Irish airs on the piano
and I sang Scottish songs. If we felt daring we risked a duet
of 'Seeing Nelly Home'.

She had our bedroom painted blue. 'Now James,' she said
as I reached to turn down the lights, 'you are getting bold
again.' I picked at the lace trim of her night gown. 'Shall I
take it off?' she offered.

'Oh yes; well, if you don't mind.'

'I don't mind.' She pulled the shift up over her head and
I held her sweet beauty.

We were never far from each other's touch. On Saturday
afternoons the breeze carried our canoe along the lakeshore.
Bessie lay on a bed of cushions, a slender arm curled around
the bow, her fingers dabbling in the water. The material of
her skirt clung to her thigh. In the autumn we went to
Joseph at the Strand and saw the Robin Hood Opera Company. Some days she did feel poorly and stayed in bed.
When I had to travel away from home we wrote to each
other every day. On my return she once welcomed me in a
feather boa which had been discovered at Walker's. 'Don't
you think it makes me covetous?' she asked. Nine months
later Claire was born.

The child lay in cotton tucks and pleats on the butternut
chaise longue chattering at her mother. Bessie stretched out

above her as if she were an angel about to take flight. My girls were both desperate talkers. When they grew over-excited I cooled them with a fan and whispered them gentle lullabies. Bessie threw her hands behind her head and laughed and laughed.

Aged eight months Claire died of cholera infantum, a constant diarrhoea which prevented her from keeping food in her stomach. I could never again bear to hear a child cry. Bessie gripped me in her arms and made love like an animal, wailing and sobbing out the terrible sadness. She took to visiting a neighbour's house and begging to hold their baby. She felt her arms so empty.

Sandy was born the next November. In time he would father Beagan. But the Boy was not six months old when Bessie lay down for an afternoon nap in the blue bedroom and did not wake up. On our bed I embraced her with all my strength, gripped her skin, tried to break through to the unbeating heart but the flesh which had brought us close lay cold between us. Bessie was twenty-five years old. Her eyes were closed, her tongue was silent, the silver cord had been loosened and the golden bowl was broken. I wrapped her letters in waxed paper and tied up the package with string. The sealing wax dripped and burnt my hand. I locked it away in the old box trunk with her wedding veil, white satin slippers and the spotted cotton blouse which she had worn. Half an hour after the funeral the Boy was baptised. The funeral boat was crowded and Toronto harbour covered by fog. As the cortège made for the mainland all the steamers in the bay whistled for guidance.

My losses heightened the importance of letters. I began to save all my records. I sorted Mother's correspondence. I filed away my journals. I cherished Father's sermons. The books and papers became my greatest possession. Without the continuity of a family village or old comfortable home all that linked me back to a shared life were words.

I threw myself into work, trying to find distraction in activity and routine. The devil chased me for his copy, the foreman insisted on new type, a subscriber wanted to stop his paper because we had omitted his name from a list of businessmen. Pigeons were replaced by telephones, Bell's not Brown's, and our publications continued to expand. New editors, circulation managers and a corps of correspondents helped strengthen the papers' columns. I oversaw the building of a new plant on the broad boulevard which approached Ontario's Parliament Building.

Zachary came more and more to be influenced by – and influence – the opinions and tastes of society. He enjoyed the power that money brought. He also found reward in the discipline of the militia. All his spare hours were spent with the regiment. He rose to the rank of honorary colonel and in the process learnt to manage people, to delegate responsibility and to direct the corporate attack. His life too came to be run more like a military operation, a well-organised affair of business trips and social engagements, hard work and daily horseriding. There was little room for spontaneity and none for emotion. He never commented on my bereavements. It was not in his nature.

At the opening of the new City Hall with its three-hundred-foot clock tower Zachary stood beneath the Union of Commerce and Industry stained-glass window. His thick, confident moustache and splendid dress, worn with a precision that touched on the pompous, set him apart from the other dignitaries. The evening before, he had been elected by acclamation to the Presidency of the Canadian Newspaper Association. In his acceptance speech he had spoken of the fourth estate usurping the position once occupied by the Church.

'It is powerful and reverenced as a force to help every-thing good and do justice to everything evil.' He no longer tried to reflect thought but instead aspired to mould opinion. 'It is my aim and hope,' he had told the Old Toronto audience, 'that our publications will provide leadership for the promotion of common interests and help to build up a great nation within the British Empire and in alliance with the United States.'

But Zachary's ambition and our success were no longer enough to inspire me. I needed to mourn. I took to walking through the city at night. The anonymous movement comforted me and I found vicarious pleasure in glimpsing intimate moments through half-opened windows: a couple dining by candlelight, the silhouette of a woman washing her hair, a husband drawing the bedroom curtains. The city had begun to introduce electric street lighting at main intersections and the great arc lamps hissed and spat much like the local politicians who declared that night had been banished. 'There is no more darkness in Toronto,' they lied. The electric glare obscured more and more of the sky. I missed seeing the stars. I seemed to have lost the firmament.

I sold the island cottage, let go of the townhouse and asked Zachary to buy my share of Gillean Publishing. I took to travel and moved west to start trade papers in Guelph and Windsor. The boy Sandy was left behind, placed temporarily in the care of the Goode maiden aunts. I had no other choice. It pained me to look upon the face which remembered his mother's. When he saw me put on my hat and pick up a bag he spoke his first sentence. 'Papa no go,' said my son.

I was once again a wanderer but in time there came to be one place where I could immerse my loneliness. With the settlement from the firm I bought a rag-taggle fleet of coal-burning tugs and supply boats, pinewood scows and puffing steamships which carried freight, mail, passengers and newspapers through a land of thirteen hundred lakes. The Muskoka & Magnetawan Steamship Company was the largest freshwater flotilla in North America. Every summer I travelled north to the pink granite waterland and relaxed into a sort of family life. The Boy was sent up to join me. We paddled my canoe and let the Irish terriers run free. I bought him toy bagpipes and he filled the lakes with his raucous music. At night we cut the motor of my Ditchburn launch and drifted over the black waters counting stars. I never stayed with him for long or explained why I had to go away but I did tell him a story, a story that one day he would tell to his own son, Beagan.

CHAPTER VI

MOSQUITO FLEET

'I HATED GOING to bed on nights like that,' recalled Jamie, gazing up into the heavens. Twilit waves lapped against the side of his canoe. 'I liked to stay up listening to the crickets and waiting for the morning star.' A breath of wind ruffled his thin strands of red hair. 'Look, F-F-Father; there's the Big Dipper. And aren't those the Pleiades?'

'It was the ancient Greeks who considered navigation safe at the rising of that constellation, *a bhalaich*,' said Hector, his celestial reflection shimmering in the moonlight. He trailed his fingers in the cool water. 'They've helped a good many navigators, including the *Good Intent*, right enough.'

'The Boy, Sandy, loved looking at the stars. He always sat with me there, where you're sitting, until he grew bored of his moody old man and got a boat of his own.'

'A stiff measure of discipline would have served him well. As would an absence of that Muscat woman.'

'Rosa was a fine photographer, F-F-Father. No one else managed to capture Pike and the steamships in their prime. That passion for preservation made up for any other failing.'

'There would have been little succour for her in my congregation,' dismissed Hector. 'Look you how her story affected your Beagan. He has all but dismantled the box trunk looking for her photographs.' He was wary of unbridled affection. 'All this feeling can only lead to mishap.'

'It is rather a mystery that, the disappearance I mean,' said Jamie, glancing again at the Pleiades.

'It would have been best had she herself never appeared.'

'No, F-F-Father, you're wrong, because of the love in it, even you cannot deny that. She and Pike are part of the story and Beagan needs to hear it, only, well, I can't do it myself. So would you, please?'

With a theatrical flourish Hector raised his wings above him. Before their eyes night became day, the setting moon transformed into a rising sun and the cluster of stars were bound into red ruby sparks puffing out of a sooty funnel. Captain Pike sounded his two-tone whistle as the RMS *Kipper* rounded Wigwassan Point. In the crickets' chirp Jamie heard the wheeze of the Doty engine and to his delight a little gasoline-powered motorboat sliced through the tossing, rocking swells to catch the old ship's wake.

'I REMEMBER IT,' said Beagan aloud, leafing through the albums again, the contents of the trunk spread around him, every envelope and file emptied out on to Gravenhurst's deserted town pier. 'In the photograph my father is laughing.' He had left Piri and the *Szerencsès* in Toronto harbour, skirted the city and driven north to Muskoka. 'I can see his skiff skimming over the water. I can picture his hair glistening, his eyes sparkling, I can even hear his laugh.' Beagan looked out on blueberry islands and lonely pines. He tasted spindrift on his tongue. 'We cherished that photograph but it has disappeared.'

The photograph was signed Rosa, Rosa Muscat. With her Kodak and a small canvas bag she roamed the Muskoka lakes during the last summer of her short life. Before the First World War her camera drew her into the green dark forests, the wheelhouses of ships, the northern hotels where guests sipped iced tea and lounged in wicker chairs. She travelled alone because her parents were dead. They had been performers who had emigrated from the Azores to Canada. Their speciality had been synchronised swimming. At the Toronto Summer Show Colonel MacKenzie's diving horse – the star attraction – had missed its cue and dived on top of Mr and Mrs Muscat during their popular 'Fallen Angel' routine. The tragedy had closed the show for the day but Rosa had been orphaned for life. She was alone. 'My life is like a piece of old bread, dry and hard, and the sun shines meanly on me,' she had said. So when she fell in love with the captain of the *Kipper* she knew that it was a gift from God. But the Daughters of the Empire (Gravenhurst Chapter) didn't see it that way. God's gifts were reserved for the afterlife, not for common harlots who laughed in church and enticed respected citizens into sin. Society cut her dead. There were no invitations to the Port Carling Water Carnival or Victoria Day picnics on Browning Island. Yet Rosa was used to it. She believed in miracles and had always been either loved or feared for it.

Theodore Pike, the captain, had puffed, whistled and wheezed ships up the lakes since the first logging days. He knew every shoal, every hidden rock, the call of each loon in every bay. He'd seen the old *Nipissing* burn at its moorings. He'd walked on the water of Gravenhurst Bay – from shore to shore, from sawmill to sawmill – across a boom of logs. Like many immigrants he had come to the middle of the vast continent – far from the Atlantic, far from the Pacific – to escape. But Pike wasn't running from persecution or poverty or even failure. He was running from the terror in his heart. On the day he had sailed from Glasgow forty years before he locked it away behind a wall of stone.

It was the lakes which drew Pike to Muskoka. The clear blue-black waters and untamed maple hills helped him forget the inner wilderness. Other settlers were enticed from Muddy York up the Muskoka Colonization Road by free land grants, but the topsoil was too thin to farm so they cut down trees instead. The great oaks and pines were felled on the upper lakes and rivers, lashed together and punted downstream. At the wild rapids the vast rafts were often sucked underwater by the cross-current, their rough cabins swept away in the backwash, and the raftsmen either held on tight to their red pine oars or stayed beneath the waves. They drove the logs down the waterways to the mills and tanneries of

Gravenhurst, then dubbed 'Sawdust City'. The pioneer woodsmen named their townships Watt, Stephenson and Brunel in honour of engineers who had harnessed nature but they called the waters Fairy, Otter and Moon.

The steamboats came so migrants could reach the great stretches of fertile land that lay beyond the lakes. A. P. Cockburn's first boat, the paddle-wheeled *Wenonah*, was made of planks cut from the finest timber on Sparrow Lake. Her massive keel was hewn with broadaxes from a single white oak. Her name was the Ojibway word for 'first-born daughter' and Pike worked aboard her as a stoker, wooding up the roaring sweating boiler and polishing her gleaming brass valves. His formal manner and taciturnity won the respect of the locals and he grew with the Navigation Company. He became a deckhand on the iron-hulled *Nipissing*, with her ornate paddle-boxes and pagoda pilothouse, helped crew the elfin *Oriole* and was promoted to mate on the *Medora*. On hot summer nights when the crew took turns cooling themselves in the Cockburn's Phillips Perfect Refrigerator, Pike sat on the hurricane deck teaching himself to navigate by the stars. He earned his Master's Certificate and by his sixtieth year was the senior officer of the freshwater flotilla. The company's fine new palace steamer, which Jamie named the *Kipper* in salty memory of Kirstie's herring days, was placed under his command. Her high razor-shell bow cleaved the waves. Two full-length decks curved around her fantail stern. An erect red and black single stack mounted her amidships. She had a Doty triple expansion engine, two Scotch marine boilers and a handsome circular dining lounge finished in weathered oak and burlap. Pike steered her around drifting logs and surly lumbermen, carried the mail and, as her luxurious interior appointments had not been built for the penniless immigrant, prepared for the arrival of a new type of traveller.

At dinner parties in Toronto, Pittsburgh and Cleveland the talk was of the lake district. Its soft healing waters were said to lower blood pressure and alleviate heart disease. When the rails of the Grand Trunk reached Muskoka the optimism of the age transformed the backwoods into a fashionable waterland.

The Muskoka Midnight Special, its brass bell clanging sleeping passengers awake, arrived at Gravenhurst from Buffalo and Toronto every summer morning. Young men in white ducks and striped blazers crossed the wharf to the waiting steamers. A moustached banker took his wife's gloved hand as a gust of wind dislodged her broad-brimmed hat. Jamie often sat alone at the end of the pier, watching not speaking, as the crew rolled up their shirtsleeves to load the wicker baskets and leather trunks, buckets of fishing worms and bundles of Gillean newspapers. A blond boy in a sailor suit chased his sister. Her ponytail swung like a pendulum. Their footfalls beat a tattoo on the wooden dock. The purser checked his manifests. A yachting cap blew into the water. 'This steamer,' announced the blackboard, 'is for Windermere.' The chalked destinations read Beaumaris, Rostrevor and the Royal Muskoka Hotel.

The rich holiday-makers cruised up the lakes to the new luxury wilderness resorts. Their gables, turrets and wide sweeping veran-dahs towered above sandy bathing beaches. The rocky terrain and mossy spruce bogs hindered the construction of roads so the only way to explore the miles of broken shoreline was by water. The hotels organised steamboat outings for the mornings, shuffleboard and croquet matches in the afternoons. Dinner was served by uniformed waitresses in picture-window dining rooms. In the evening guests danced on waxed hardwood floors and drank chilled claret from punch bowls.

The very wealthy moved on from the resorts to build private summer cottages in intimate hidden bays. Their cook, maid, family silver and linen were all transported north on the annual trek from city to country. Their fortunes financed a forty-year flourish of skilled boat-building. Long, sleek motor launches were fashioned from teak and Honduras mahogany. Sweeping windscreens edged in chrome, silver running lights and morocco upholstery set off the varnished decks. The more ostentatious cottagers rode astern and employed a uniformed pilot to attend to the wheel. The handsome pleasure cruisers shuttled between cottages and hotels, meeting trains at Lake Joseph Station and Bala, exchanging passen-gers in mid-lake transfers. They snubbed together with Jamie's steamers then, while music wafted on the breeze, secured lines and gangways for a moment's coupling. On the *Kipper*'s aft deck two members of the company orchestra played a medley of popular airs on the xylophone.

It was in the spring when young deer lick maple sugar from the lower branches that Pike met Rosa. He thrust a boathook down her dress, snared her corset and saved her from drowning. It was long after midnight and Rosa could not swim. As soon as he had lifted her aboard she dived back into the lake to rescue her camera. The snow had only just melted and the waves snapped the thin ice around the hull. Pike took her back to his cabin to warm by the stove. In the lamplight he saw the honey-pale hair of her forearms then noticed that her fingers had turned blue. She shivered and cast a gentle shower of rain over the deck. A tin tub sat full and steaming by the stove. Pike divided the room with a screen, found a clean towel and offered her his bath. As she wrung out her skirt the water ran across the floor to gather in a pool around his feet. Rosa lowered herself into the warm water and startled the minnows in the tub. They had been sucked up by the pump when Pike had drawn his water from the lake.

The cabin was his home. He hadn't slept on dry land since the nineteenth century, and around her she saw his collection of memorabilia: a carved whalebone, the golden toe of a Burmese Buddha, a Pomo coiled boat basket decorated with clam-shell beads and tufts of red woodpecker feathers. A shard of marble from the Great Pyramid served as the soap dish. His towel rail was the bronze censer from a German monastery. Through the course of his seafaring youth Pike had gathered curios and relics from around the world. There were dinosaur bones and petrified eggs, two Roman amphorae filled with American copper pennies and a fleet of schooners in a dozen bottles. Beneath a Saracen scimitar between two sheets of glass was a minute fragment of manuscript, its Greek letters faded and edges singed, the only page to survive when the books of the library at Alexandria were burnt to heat the city. Beside his bed was a tennis racquet used for expelling bats.

'This is my ark,' Pike explained as he passed a dram of whisky around the side of the screen. Rosa was encircled by flashes of silver. The bodies of the minnows were so translucent that they seemed to be more a suggestion of life than its substance.

'It was one of those moments,' she said later, 'when you can no longer put on the shoes that you thought you would wear all your life.'

The drying clothes filled the cabin with her scent. Pike sat in his cane armchair and tried not to watch the young woman's shadow dance over his nautical prints and Chilean engravings. Rosa did not stay. She was anxious to develop the photograph which had almost cost her life. The Kodak sat in a puddle on the deck. After she departed all that remained of her was a damp handprint on his sleeve.

It was her photographs which next touched him. They seemed to see below the surface and capture the essence behind the image. The sensation was so powerful that Pike had to turn over the pictures and look behind them for the perceived depth. His long fine fingers stroked his white walrus moustache but the mosquitoes buzzed around his ears. Women were portrayed without hats. Labouring men were photographed in their shirtsleeves. The Daughters of the Empire didn't approve. Public morals were at risk.

As spring blossomed into summer Rosa discovered the lakes from the bridge of the *Kipper*. She photographed the puffing ships, the belching mills, the prosperous cottagers. Her camera followed their caretakers as they took down the snow shutters and let the cool May sunlight flood into the chalets. Her broom helped sweep away the clam shells discarded by scavenging racoons and the carcasses of dead mice frozen during the winter. She photographed pearl-white boathouses on emerald curved bays and watched the sleek Ditchburn launches being lowered from the rafters into their slips. Through her lens the supply steamers *Mink* and *Newminko* plied the lakes to stock the cottages. Their crew of four – captain, engineer, butcher and grocer – brought staples and gossip to kitchen maids. Fillet steaks and roasts were supplied by McCulley's

Meat Market. Hardware, clothing and shoes were carried on special order. Every week the *Smelt* brought Pike his newspapers and a dollar pot of Quick Cure, a patented remedy used with success in curing colds. He had never shaken off the cough contracted on rounding the Horn and a teaspoon heated on a piece of old tin filled his cabin with fumes which eased sleep. Every Sunday the long-bowed, canvas-canopied church boat nosed from dock to dock gathering the faithful. The *Spray* from Orgill's Point collected and delivered laundry. Bill Campbell peddled fresh farm produce from his tug *Ida*. Private yellow pine launches, their fly-wheels spinning amidships, spat smoke and sparks into the sweet air. The diminutive *Gypsy* from Clark's Mill took more than a day to tow its log boom the few miles from Skelton Bay to Snug Harbour. She often blocked the waterway leaving no passage clear and the other boats whistled their irritation at the sawmill's pointers.

'In my heart there are clouds and thunderstorms,' Rosa told Pike when the days warmed and the air filled with the drone of insects. On a stormy night in June she returned to his cabin and took him as her lover without fuss or formality. As the sway of the ship rocked them to sleep he called her his angel.

'You know how angels behave, don't you?' Rosa replied. 'They always go back to where they came from.' Then she anchored herself to the bed, one foot locked over the edge, the other thrust between their two mattresses and wrapped the sheet around them like the spirals of a conch shell. The great stone wall around Pike's heart cracked and miracles became possible. The prophets had walked on water. Jonah did live in the stomach of a whale. Saul was blind and then could see. Pike was forty years her senior and Rosa had faith.

AS THE *KIPPER* whistled for the *Gypsy* to clear a passage Hector strode from shore to shore, though not across the boom, beside himself with indignation. 'No angel that I've ever met wears lipstick, especially cherry red. And that Pike runs too much from his own doubts and demons, just as does Beagan.'

Jamie followed behind, leaping cat-like over the loose logs. 'Maybe if you stopped attacking her vice you might begin to appreciate her virtue.'

'It was not myself that laboured all those years to tolerate such undirected, unbridled passion.'

'Isn't it better than just being dull and decent?'

Hector stopped in mid-stride, starboard of the *Kipper*'s bow, and the swells lapped over his shoes. 'My role is saving souls, not condoning sin. This sort of behaviour unstitches the fabric of society, right enough. Your brother understood that.' A light laugh sparked across the water and Hector stared up at the ship. 'Bless my soul, is it herself onboard?'

'It is, F-F-Father,' said Jamie. 'And we do need to continue the story for Beagan.'

'That we will. There is responsibility in this memory and that, at long last, he begins to appreciate, though devil enough remains in him to damn a dozen sinners. Now stand aside James, it is time to call your brother.' Hector looked over his shoulder, spread his cape then shouted at the trees, 'Zachary!' A clutch of startled chickadees took flight. 'Zachary!' The *Kipper*'s Union Jack rustled in the breeze. 'Where on God's good earth is he?'

AT FIRST THE Daughters of the Empire (Gravenhurst Chapter) tried to ignore the liaison, but as it was the juiciest gossip since Amanda Dung had eloped with the snakebite-elixir salesman they couldn't restrain themselves for long. Word of the scandal spread through the community, up the lakes and portages, from Bent

River to Swampy Bay. The more prudish citizens who lacked anything better to do refused to travel on the *Kipper* so the town council became concerned, especially as the mayor was married to the chairwoman of the Daughters of the Empire.

One afternoon in late July on her way south through Lake Rosseau the *Kipper* called for passengers at Windermere House. The Daughters of the Empire stepped aboard to find Rosa with her captain on the bridge. Winifred Stubbs suggested that they refuse to travel but, as the chairwoman's bunions were aching, they agreed to compromise their principles. The mosquitoes joined Rosa, the Reverend MacGill and Blossom, Ed Kingshott's prize heifer, on the *Kipper*.

On the approach to Port Carling the *Kipper* hit a deadhead, a submerged log, and the force of the blow snapped the drive shaft clean in two. The current was very strong where the waters of Rosseau rushed towards the Indian River rapids and the steamer was dragged towards ruin.

The women screamed. The Reverend prayed. Blossom mooed. The captain leaned on the wheel but without her engine the elegant ship became sluggish and refused to respond. He pulled the lanyard and a plaintive steam whistle wailed for help. The first mate, an old lumberman with arms tattooed, distributed lifejackets and whispered of demons. It seemed that all hope was lost until Rosa removed her corset. The Daughters of the Empire recognised her as the Jezebel whom they had always feared but Pike saw her corset, the one from which he had released her on a dozen summer nights, as their only chance of salvation.

Together the lovers descended to the bilges. Soaked in grease and oil they crawled forward of the thrust bearing, beyond the pistons and cranks, to locate the break. They fashioned a splint and wrapped the corset around the join. Back on deck the Reverend had lost faith. He prayed aloud while Pike engaged the engine with infinite gentleness. The whalebone stays gripped. The propeller turned. The *Kipper* held its ground against the current and edged back upstream to the pier. Blossom, the prize heifer, never realised her luck. In her excitement and in full view of the passengers Rosa embraced Pike. 'You are the best of men in the world,' she laughed. 'Now kiss me without breathing for one minute.'

In Ontario no one says thank you to a whore. Evil disguised as the common good can spread like a forest fire in August. Mosquitoes bite and the incident fabricated substance to claims of negligence. The council revoked Pike's licence. They would allow no fornicators at the wheel. They barred him from the ship, evicted him from his cabin, banished him from the ark. Pike and Rosa didn't give a porcupine's fart for the Daughters of the Empire (Gravenhurst Chapter) and settled into a hotel. 'Life is a cake full of stones but hope is my motto,' she insisted as September's gusts blew through the open window. But their money was limited and at night Pike hung his cap over the lightbulb to save electricity. The dark room stood still and the air was heavy with the smell of stale beer from the tavern below. After so many years afloat Pike awoke sweating and crying that the wind had changed direction and the bow line snapped. In the grounded sawdust hotel he grappled with imaginary ropes before falling exhausted back to bed.

The townspeople who owed their lives to the unlacing of a corset shunned the lovers. Shopkeepers, farmers, even Blossom's owner refused to serve them. A rumour was spread about that Rosa was pregnant. Winifred Stubbs claimed to have overheard the couple talking. 'We will name him after a river or a lake,' Rosa had whispered. Winifred had to sneak up close to hear their conversation. 'A name not bound to anything just as water isn't bound to anything.' Then the days grew colder, the leaves turned crimson and Pike bought a canoe. He boxed up the Buddha's toe and dinosaur bones, the pyramid soap dish and the Alexandria library parchment. One autumn morning while the mist clung to the surface of the lake they slipped out of town never to be seen again.

'It was shortly before they disappeared that Rosa took the photograph of my father,' remembered Beagan, alone on the pier. 'Years later, after he died, the print was mislaid. I'd always hoped that the negative would be in the trunk, but I've looked right through it and it's not here.' On the strip of negative where the image had once been there was only blank emulsion. The photographs taken before and after it were perfectly preserved but the laughing boy had vanished.

CHAPTER VII

TREES IN THE BOG

'PIKE?' FUSSED ZACHARY. 'I don't remember anyone called Pike.' He straddled the roof of the wheelhouse like a cocksure phoenix, adjusted his splendid evening dress and brushed a fleck of dust off his lapel. The plume of his silk scarf snapped in the breeze. 'Bally fool of a name anyway.'

The ship's bell rang and the whistle sprouted a moustache of steam which curled and wrapped itself around the stack. A trail of smoke spiralled away over the stern of the **RMS** *Segwun*, the sole survivor of the Mosquito Fleet. Jamie sailed along beside the bridge, paddling the air in an ersatz sidestroke and kicking his feet as if under water.

'I'm not surprised that you have f-f-forgotten him. You hardly ever left the office, except for society soirées.' He tightened the shoulder strap of his bathing costume. 'You never had time to visit me.'

'In all labour there is profit,' spouted Zachary. He was in a particularly pedantic mood. 'And the Lord rewards him according to his works.'

'I will not have the Apostles quoted in vain,' snapped Hector as a guffaw of irreverent laughter chased him up on to the bridge. His inspection of the relaxed holiday-makers on the lower decks had put him in a severe humour. 'Were there ever two boys who forgot so fearfully much learning?'

'James always lacked concentration, Father. He confused the business of work with the matter of life.'

'Be that as it may, you are not the highest tree in the

181

orchard, Zachary,' reproached Hector. He cast his critical gaze about the modern lakeland. A water-skier slalomed past the steamer, kicked an arc of spray over the dockside satellite dishes and took a spill below a garish billboard which advertised Great North Log Homes. 'That trollop should be in church, like all the other lie-abeds down below.' The ski-boat cut across the *Segwun*'s bow, its passengers raising their beer bottles in salute, but before Hector could pass judgement his attention was distracted by Jamie's aerial ballet. 'And what would it be that you are now doing, James?'

'Swimming, F-F-Father.' Jamie rolled over and flailed his limbs about in an erratic backstroke. 'Or at least trying to remember how to. It's been a long time.'

'It would seem that both memory and elegance have deserted you.'

'Not memory, no.' A startled seagull squawked and swooped away from the foremast. 'I remember that this is the very bay where Zachary and I began our f-f-first holiday together.'

'Our only holiday together,' corrected his elder brother, his back as rigid as the red and black funnel. 'Vacations never agreed with me; all that excessive sun and wasted time.'

'It is not laziness that ever built anything worthwhile, especially a good ship.' Hector paused to consider the *Segwun*'s lines, handsome enough to please the most fastidious sailor, then nodded in approval at the trail of steam. 'Right enough, she has a lively sheer, James. You should feel justifiably proud.'

Zachary stamped his foot on the roof and startled the captain, who looked up from the nickel-plated hand controls. 'I never understood what James saw in old boats. I would have sold out and been shot of Muskoka years earlier.'

'I grew fond of them,' confessed Jamie, breaking into a

back-crawl. 'They were like a f-f-family: little *Mildred*, the busy *Newminko*, grouchy old *Cherokee*.'

'A decidedly unreliable family in my opinion,' tut-tutted his brother. 'The *Mildred* blew a gasket and ran aground. The *Newminko* sank in the Port Carling locks and the *Cherokee* impaled itself on a shoal.' He did not share a love of boats. 'She sheared her propeller blades and was left to rot. The wreckers smashed her wooden superstructure to remove the engines. I warned you that the new highways would stop people travelling by water but you didn't listen. So you lost a fortune.'

'I sold my share in the Navigation Company for a modest sum.'

'Maybe a quarter of its real value. And you gave away the *Sagamo*.'

'Her name meant "Big Chief", and she once carried eight hundred passengers,' Jamie explained to their father. Hector had sat himself in the restored cedar-strip lifeboat and begun pulling on imaginary oars.

'The new owners removed her boilers to convert her into a floating restaurant but a heater exploded and set her ablaze. I heard a rumour that the Fire Department couldn't be bothered to save her and let her burn.'

Hector stopped rowing, scandalised. 'It is only a fool who squanders his inheritance.'

'The whole business was a bad investment,' pronounced Zachary.

Jamie sighed, drank in the clear clean air as deep as his breath would permit then held it as if diving under water. He counted to ten. His brother's zealotry tested his patience but he was determined not to show irritation. 'The *Kipper* didn't sink or run aground. It was bureaucracy which wrecked her,' he recalled. 'Do you remember that fire aboard the SS *Noronic*, the pleasure cruiser on Lake Ontario?'

'Of course. We were the first to have a reporter on the

scene. The tragedy had a considerable impact on marine insurance premiums.'

'One hundred and eighteen excursionists were killed in one tragic night.'

'A sad event but it brought about changes that were good for both the public and business. The Ministry of Transport reacted by imposing exacting regulations on all passenger vessels. Safer ships were built. Insurance companies prospered. Two of my papers, *Great Lakes Shipping* and *Insurance Digest*, had very profitable years.'

'But under the new rules wooden ships never sailed again,' stressed Jamie. He had stopped his thrashing and glided alongside the wheelhouse. 'The *Kipper* was condemned as unfit, stripped down to her main deck and converted into a barge. Muskoka Wharf station was also dismantled, the rails torn up and the trim building replaced by aluminium-clad boathouses. The f-f-fleet simply wasted away.'

'The price of progress, James. I told you to sell your interest.'

'Progress?' said Hector, stroking the lifeboat's caned black-cherry seats. 'Did you say progress?' The further he travelled from his islands the more the lyricism left him. 'It is the old days that I understood better, you can't get away from it.'

'No one can hold back the tide, Father. The successful man goes with it, directs it.' Zachary peered over the heads to spot Beagan's balding pate among the tourists on the foredeck. 'And talking about inefficiency, what is your grandson doing here on this relic, James, other than wasting my time?'

'I suppose he's looking for me,' blushed Jamie.

'He could have saved us all a great deal of bother and stayed in Scotland with the trunk.' Zachary pulled a fob-watch from his waistcoat and gave it a testy shake. Timepieces do not run in the hereafter, yet he could not break the habit of a lifetime. 'There's nothing for him to find here.

Your halcyon retreat now looks like suburbia and you are forgotten.'

'That's a bit unf-f-fair.'

'You left no monuments. Why didn't you donate a ward to the local hospital or establish a Chair of Journalism at some small university as I advised? At the time it was not beyond your means.' Zachary tapped the crystal of his stopped watch. 'But now it's too late to do anything at all,' he added with a flash of bitterness. 'Is that sluggard going to get a move on or what?'

IN GRAVENHURST NO one could remember Beagan's grand-father. Jamie's cottage had been sold and the new owners couldn't be bothered to sail over to the public wharf to pick him up. The *Kipper* was gone and nobody had heard of Rosa or Pike. At the town pier Beagan had opened the trunk and searched for the missing photograph, stretching his memory back to embrace his father's stories. He had then joined the queue of holiday-makers and boarded the oldest operating steamboat on the continent for a two-hour 'fun, romance and history' cruise up the lake. There had been no concessionary fare for the grandson of a past owner.

The RMS *Segwun* slipped through the Narrows and summer-brown children waved from the sweeping sundecks of plush pine residences. Replica Coca-Cola signs hung behind their broad windows. A trained dog scampered out of a cottage, rang a bell with its muzzle and the captain replied with another whistle.

On deck families unpacked their picnics and laughed in the sunshine. Older passengers ordered Ship's Champagne and sat down to lunch in the Royal Muskoka Salon. A lean, bow-legged man sporting a kerchief and worn leather boots swaggered fists first into the lounge. He dropped into a chair, suspended his Ray-Bans from his collar and asked for coffee, black.

'Yes sir, this is a great place in the summer,' he said to a friend up from the city for the weekend, 'but you can't beat the winter.'

He leaned forward to make his point. 'Four busloads of divorcees at Hidden Valley every week. You don't even have time to go skiing.' He thought the waves lapping against the hull sounded like applause. 'Like last year there was this girl who was rectifying her life with her husband, eh? She came up at Christmas, my own little elf.' The coffee arrived. 'But every time I did it to her she said, "You only want me for my body." You know, I like to think I'm more into spiritual growth.' Behind them a tanned, bored day-tripper read his ketchup bottle. His date straightened her shorts. 'So one time she comes up and finds me poking this other chicken and she goes crazy and starts breaking up the place and grabs my snowshoes and takes off.' He swallowed his coffee. 'One week later I'm here in town at the post office getting my mail, you know, and she comes in and she's got the snowshoes and she starts hitting me with them.'

'She still around?' asked the friend.

'Yup.'

'She still got the snowshoes?'

'Nope, I got them back.'

At the next table Beagan ordered a slice of blueberry pie and waited for the president of the company. He had agreed to give him an hour of his time but had been delayed inspecting the new electronic fire-detection system. Beyond the window a towboat pulled forward and another skier rose up out of the water. The outboard's whine drowned out the shrill call of a tree frog. It was somewhere beyond the rotating Kentucky Fried Chicken bucket that, according to the story, Rosa had saved the *Kipper*.

The waitress noticed him staring out at Indian River. 'The best place in the world,' she said and meant it. Her T-shirt read 'Muskoka: The Greatest Lakes'. She tucked a tip into her cut-off jeans and balanced half a dozen plates on her arm. 'I've been coming up every summer for longer than I can remember.' Her family had owned a cottage on Echo Point for over a century. 'It's sort of our touchstone.' She placed a frosty glass in front of Beagan. 'Hey, don't worry, you can drink the water. It comes out of a bottle, not the lake.'

The president could rave all afternoon about hull plates and retubed boilers. His kind, pudgy face was dominated by the wide, rabbit-like eyes of an enthusiast. He talked to Beagan about the history of the line and the coming of the automobile. 'If your grand-dad were alive today,' he said, 'I'd sure like to enquire why he didn't cut the larger ships, forget about serving the distant cottages and run pleasure cruises only?'

'I guess he didn't want to let anyone down,' replied Beagan. He asked about the company records, which had been lost, then added, 'Is there anyone around who knew my grandfather?'

The president leaned back and thought. 'Didn't old Doris Pilch work for him?'

'Sure, for most of her life. But, well, I'm really quite angry at her. My father left her this trunk to give to me on my twenty-first birthday, but she got the timing wrong and waited twenty-one years instead.' His eyes flashed with a moment's bitterness and he gripped the edge of the table.

'So she's gone a bit soft in the head,' shrugged the president. 'Big deal. We had her hundredth birthday party on board last year and she spent the afternoon wandering all over the ship looking for your grand-dad. That's how I remembered that she worked for him.' His eyes widened as if caught in a car's headlights. 'The only thing that keeps her going is the determination to outlive her daughter. Cheryl's spent the last twenty-five years trying to kill her off, waiting for the inheritance.' The president chuckled. 'You should go see them. They live like cat and dog up at old Tobermory House.' Beagan tried to picture the summer resort. 'You know, up on Lake Rosseau, across the bay from your grand-dad's old place.'

North of Port Carling knots of cow parsley, excited by the breeze, nodded their heads in a frenzy like dizzy blonde teenagers, or even après-ski divorcees. The earth's crust erupted through the topsoil. The thin ribbon of highway was hemmed in by great pink outcrops of the Precambrian Canadian Shield. The blueberry pie too was like granite, although Beagan's indigestion was more due to nerves. Doris Pilch had known his grandfather and raised his father, sailed aboard the *Kipper* and watched the Mosquito Fleet rot away. His stomach grumbled and he fished in a pocket for a Kwell when something in the rear-view mirror caught his eye.

His forefathers crammed behind him in a row along the car's back seat and argued. 'Twenty-one years wasted,' repeated Zachary, who had measured out his life in annual reports and inter-office memos. He commandeered the centre of the back seat like a pompous pasha. 'A man makes his own opportunities, James. Fate does not hand them out in turn to all and sundry.'

Hector paid his sons little attention, preferring to sit in silence. A truck accelerated by his window, 'Simply the Best for Less' emblazoned along its trailer. 'Progress,' he reflected then watched Beagan glance again into the empty mirror.

'Who is this Pilch woman then?' demanded Zachary from his throne. 'Another irresponsible friend of that Pike, I dare say.'

'Doris Pilch was my housekeeper; a gentle, mild, diminutive Scot,' explained Jamie.

'Not the one who wore those ridiculous flapper hats?'

'She wore sensible shoes, spoke French and F-F-Flemish, travelled across Europe as a governess and came to Canada to marry the Gravenhurst postmaster. They lived together under the town hall clock but it rang all night and drove him to an early death.'

'May he have found his peace in heaven,' said Hector as Beagan again pulled on to the hard shoulder.

'Why does your Beagan need to check that confounded map so often?' flared Zachary.

'Other side,' whispered Hector into their descendant's ear.

'I wish you wouldn't do that, F-F-Father,' sighed Jamie.

'Look now the two of you, it's well enough that he's coping with it,' insisted Hector.

Beagan turned over the road map and located the route. He took another long sideways look in his mirror then pulled back on to the highway. The acceleration was slow, as if the car was somehow overloaded.

'And yes, Zachary, it was Pike who suggested that Doris might like to be my housekeeper,' continued Jamie. 'She arrived at the cottage by steamer and after a short interview said, "Mr Gillean, it is most extravagant of you to keep the boat waiting. Am I to dismiss the *Kipper* or do you no want me to stay?" I hired her on the spot.'

'It was she who attended to your Sandy?'

'She cared for the Boy as if he were her own, then looked after me until my death.' The car lurched on to a side road kicking up a swirling trail of chalky pink dust. 'I never f-f-forgot her.'

IT WASN'T INCOMPETENT map-reading alone which hindered Beagan's search for the resort. The once grand Tobermory House Hotel had been closed for a decade. The forest had advanced on to the earthen drive, throwing out creepers and reducing it to the width of a footpath. Brambles screeched against the side of the rental car like fingernails drawn across slate. The parking lot was so overgrown that he mistook it for pasture. Bulrushes and marsh flowers had taken root on the beach. Weeds had split the patios and shuffleboard court. The tally of the last match was rusted on to the players' scoreboard.

A weather-worn 'For Sale' sign swung against the central rotunda. In the office lay a dozen table tennis nets, spools of unravelled adding-machine paper and a single flip-flop. The chapel was empty save for a discarded auctioneer's catalogue: '25 oak high chairs, 170 beds, 6 stags heads, 1 row boat (no oars)'. The corral of wood-beamed cottages which surrounded the central building had been ravaged by time and drunken boaters. Rags of curtains blew through jagged window frames. Rat-chewed guidebooks rotted on moulding carpets. Swallows nested under the eaves. The stone chimneys which had been cracked by the frost reminded Beagan of the cleared crofts of Scotland. He remembered the rusting iron bedheads lost in a tangle of gorse, a widow's smashed quern, a child's shattered cup, and shivered at the thought of another generation being cast out from their bay.

Beagan waded through the waist-high grass to the buckled steamer dock. Its spine had been broken by ice floes and the cribs spilt stones on to the lake floor. He knocked at the boathouse door. Seagulls rose in excited white flocks. A woodpecker tap-tapped on a maple, tree frogs sang in the pines and an indignant toad, its sleep disturbed, hopped under a birch branch. Dragonflies mated on the lakeside lamp-posts, their bases eroded and collapsed on the fine white sand. He knocked again and as an afterthought shouted. His voice sounded out of place, as if mankind no longer belonged. Above him a window creaked open and a television jingle drowned out the sound of the waves. 'How do you handle a hungry man? The Man-handlers; bah bah boom boom bah bah.'

'Who's there?' cried a shrill tongue. A head appeared against the sky and though he couldn't make out the face Beagan recognised the voice. He almost heard the electrostatic swish of the acrylic pant-suit. 'Oh, it's you. I guess you'd better come up.'

He climbed the dark stairs towards the announcer urging him to succumb to the temptation of tinned sauces – 'Mix the sauce with your cooked chicken, some mushrooms, peas, parsley, top it with puff pastry and in half an hour, real home-baked chicken pot pie' – and into the apartment over the boat slips.

'You've come to see Mom,' moaned Cheryl. She seemed to distend the compact sitting room. Like many country people she ate a traditional diet, one heavy on bread, fried potatoes and pies, and her metabolism hadn't adapted to a modern, sedentary life. Instead of labouring in winter fields she eased power-steered cars to heated shopping malls and grew obese. Her body had the exaggerated proportions of a plasticine figure lumped together by a schoolboy in art class. The neon pink outfit didn't help disguise her excesses. 'Mom's been poorly and a bit forgetful.' The towered boathouse seemed to sway with Cheryl's movement. 'I doubt she'll remember you.'

While he waited Beagan watched an episode of *The Waltons* sandwiched between ads for antacid tablets and chocolate bars. 'I still remember getting my first candy from my grandfather,' prattled an actor. 'I'll never forget that first taste; sweet and creamy and just plain good. I felt I was really somebody special.' He wondered if the chime of the town hall clock had been more restful than the racket of the television and stood up to turn down the volume. A corn dolly on a paper doily adorned the set. The lampshade was wrapped in store cellophane. Prints of kittens torn from an old calendar and hundreds of losing lottery tickets were tacked all over the chipboard walls. Unlike Piri, Cheryl had never chosen the right ticket. In contrast Doris's few possessions were crammed into one corner of the room. The sheets of used wrapping paper, carefully ironed and refolded, matchbooks and bars of soap from hotels long ago demolished reflected her Scottish frugality.

Beagan peered around the drawn curtains and out across the waters which Jamie and Sandy had shared until he heard the soft shuffle of slippers behind him. 'Oh, you look wonderful,' Doris rolled in her Highland burr. Her slender frame had shrunk in the years since their last meeting. She had the bones of a bird and it seemed that a breath of wind might blow her out of the window and away towards Wigwassan Point. Her frailty so moved Beagan that he forgave her the lost years as she fluttered in his embrace. 'You look just like your grandfather.'

'You're not the first person to tell me that.'

She took his hand and they sat on the sofa. A ghost would have made more of an impression on the cushions than did her featherweight. 'I had pneumonia,' she told him.

'That was two years ago, Ma,' said Cheryl, who had parked herself behind a plastic asparagus fern.

'Was it?' asked Doris and twittered like a sparrow. 'I lose track of the time.'

'She was sick and wouldn't go to hospital.'

'I'll not leave this old bay until the death watch is in my ear.'

'Then why won't you take your cyanide?' jested Cheryl. 'Ma, don't look at me with those beady little eyes.'

'I wish you wouldn't say that.'

'Me too,' said Beagan.

'Great price, friendly advice,' chimed the television.

Cheryl rose to her feet and Beagan imagined her care combined with sudden bursts of impotent rage: incurious, unmotivated and imprisoned by avarice. 'At least you didn't bring her candies.' She stabbed a thumb towards the spare room. 'There are boxes and boxes back there.'

'I never much cared for sweets.' A wrap of medical tape still repaired the bridge of her spectacles broken before the last war. 'Too improvident.'

'Birthday after birthday they've been stacked up in there, unopened, wasted. She won't let me touch them . . . luxuries.' Cheryl picked up a dog-eared scrapbook, dropped it on to her mother's lap and kissed her head. 'She hits me sometimes,' she told Beagan.

'I'm not surprised.'

'Oh, don't hit me again, Ma,' she added, playing the child. 'Bet you didn't hit his dad.'

'You do look so much like your grandfather now,' Doris repeated to Beagan as she examined the tatty leaves one by one. The glue had dried out and all the photographs slipped on to her lap. She remounted each before turning the page. There were pictures of her family home on Loch Fyne and her grandfather's ship, the *Ossian*. Her husband stood beneath the Gravenhurst clock and a brother posed in merchant marine uniform. There were postcards of all the Mosquito steamships. 'What a strong family resemblance.' She lay a finger on Jamie's portrait. 'You know he was a gentleman of the old times.'

'Why not give it to him now, Ma?' proposed Cheryl. 'You'll never look at them again.'

'I might.'

'Then put it in an envelope with his name and address on. It'll be easier to mail after you've gone.' Beagan felt her resist the temptation to ask for a dollar to cover the postage.

'Didn't I already send you something?' asked Doris, her brow knotted with the strain of recall. 'A letter? No, your father's box trunk.'

'You did,' sighed Beagan. 'Eventually.'

'I was glad to get shot of the dusty old thing,' said Cheryl.

'It seemed a long time to hold on to it but your father always had his own way of doing things. Is everything there?'

'Almost. I'm going through it now, trying to follow the family through the papers, and for my trouble getting soaked in Scotland, seasick on the Atlantic, even spooked in Cape Breton.' In the familiar company of the forgetful Beagan laughed suddenly, unexpectedly, as he hadn't done for years. 'It's funny, but it has sort of anchored me, at the same time as guiding me right across the country. By following them I'm finding something that was missing in me.'

'Here he is.' Doris's hand hovered over a snapshot of Sandy as a boy then turned the page. 'And here you are. Or is that his father?'

'It's my brother Alex.'

Doris became confused by the overlapping generations and started to address Beagan with his grandfather's name. 'Did you bring some pictures with you then, Mr Gillean?'

'I've brought back the trunk.'

Beagan ran out to the car and drove it through the tall grass to the boathouse. He eased the trunk upstairs, its memories scraping on every step. They spread the contents over the floor while Cheryl went off to get a Coke and some pie. 'Call this number now for your free personal involvement kit,' instructed another earnest advertiser. 'An operator is standing by to take your order.'

The photographs of bentwood chairs, potted palms and corn-flower-blue china eggcups transported Doris back to Tobermory House's golden days. There were Navigation Company timetables and a blank envelope containing a single lock of red hair. She picked up Hector's globe and wrapped a slender arm around it as a mother would cradle a lost child. Together they turned over a decade's worth of letters from the Boy to Jamie. Beagan read his father's words aloud. 'My dear Dad: I had a fine birthday. I got from Nan a toll set.'

'I was Nan,' interrupted Doris. 'Master Sandy's nanny.'

'The tolls are dandy like this: a fine screwdriver, a fine saw (big one), a dandy plane, a great big stell hamer.' He had added, 'I spalt this myself,' and concluded, as all his letters had concluded, 'Please Dad come home soon.'

'He was very good with his hands. He used the tools to build his first boat,' remembered Doris. 'What was it called . . . ?' She strained to name the shapes in her cloudy memory. '*Maud*, that was it; a log raft with a hole cut in the middle. He covered the hole with a tea-chest cabin and a stovepipe funnel and hid inside burning damp leaves in a McVitie and Price biscuit tin while walking along the lake bottom.' She perched on the edge of the sofa. 'Smoke belched out both the funnel and cabin's eyeholes and he came in covered in soot. He was filthy.'

In a sepia print the Boy beamed at Rosa's Kodak, a spanner clutched in his hand, standing chest-high to the engineer aboard the *Kipper*. Doris's voice took on a disciplinary tone. 'No, not clean enough, Master Sandy. Wash those hands again and this time use the nail brush.' She then asked Beagan how his father was getting on at school.

'Please do not expect another long letter this term,' he recited from Sandy's postcard. 'The exams really start on Friday and I shall be fearfully busy, that is if I want to pass them all.'

'Of course he must pass,' insisted Doris. 'And he can't go on getting minuses.'

Beagan studied the headmaster's comment on the term's report card. 'Sandy has taken a keen interest in machinery and has a practical knowledge of internal combustion engines probably unsurpassed by anyone of his age.'

The Boy wore a folded paper hat and rowed two woolly dogs across the bay which lay beyond Doris's window. 'Yesterday,' Sandy had written and Beagan read, 'I was looking over the

Scripps gasoline engine catalogue. A price list is enclosed giving full particulars. These Scripps seem to be a very straight bunch and their Reliability Engine is the plain, sensible motor with no freaks that powered the little launch *Detroit* across the Atlantic.'

'He promised to meet Mr Gillean off the *Kipper* at Port Carling on Saturday night,' Doris scolded. 'But his wee *Primary* had been in three speedboat races and was much too dirty.' Sandy's first motorboat had been named *Primary*. She had been powered by a Kermath four-cylinder four-cycle engine with reverse gear which produced twelve horsepower. He had fastened a shelf from the cottage refrigerator to the boat's transom at an angle that gave extra lift and she made a good ten miles per hour.

Cheryl had no interest in reminiscences and sat back down in front of the television. 'Years ago it was just vast, open space but then Canadian National opened the way,' blethered a railway commercial. 'Towns sprang up, business boomed across this country.' Doris was distracted by the sound and pointed at the flickering screen. 'Look at that child's posture. It's disgraceful.'

Beagan's hand fell on to an envelope addressed in Jamie's neat script. It was postmarked four months before his wedding. 'If you think you could get those feet of yours to work properly,' he had proposed to Bessie, 'I should be delighted to accompany you to the Grocers' Ball. It promises to be a splendid evening. Will you honour me?' A dusting of a scented powder settled on to Beagan's palm.

Doris fell silent for a moment. She ran a length of silk ribbon through her fingers then reached into the trunk and drew out a small leather album of honeymoon photographs: Montreal in a thunderstorm from the Windsor Hotel, the good ship *Sardinian*, a glimpse of York from a flying train, the ruins of Duart Castle. In a snapshot captioned 'Mother's happy island home' Bessie threw her hands behind her head and laughed. Doris looked up, took Beagan's hand in two of her own and spoke with sudden clarity to his grandfather. 'I think that I know something of the great love you keep for some locked up in your heart.'

Beagan remained silent. Cheryl switched to another channel and turned up the volume. 'Once upon a time in the land of Great Canadian Cheeses was a mighty cheddar bursting with flavour, a mild melting mozzarella and, imagine, delightful parmesan.'

'You live so much alone in so many ways and in her you found one who had the key to your heart,' affirmed Doris. 'Well she is gone and your life is empty.'

'Ma, don't tire yourself out,' said Cheryl without taking her eyes off the screen, then added, '*Lassie*'s on next.'

'Not tired,' snapped Doris, who had used up all her mothering with Sandy only then to give birth to complaint through genetics. 'I sleep all day in this cage and I'm so bored.' The programme's opening credits began and a collie performed a trick. 'Look at that dog, he's put all the rubbish in the bin. What a clever dog.' Beagan started to move away but Doris gripped his hand with sudden force. 'Your life but not your heart for she is with you still,' she continued. Her cheeks were flushed. 'Dear Mr Gillean, she is still alive in your memory, helping you be good and true, still standing by your side. But the Boy,' she pleaded. 'You must not forget your boy.'

Cheryl sniffed the air, sighed and put down her plate. 'Ma, do you want to go to the little girls' room?' Doris looked away as her daughter took her arm. Her lower lip was quivering. 'She wears a diaper now,' confided Cheryl.

During the thirty minutes that it took Doris to clean herself Cheryl harangued Beagan about the Queen. Was she the wealthiest woman in the world? Wasn't it unfair? Beagan said little as he repacked the trunk. 'There's a million dollars in total cash prizes available to be won,' chirped the TV. 'Don't let somebody beat you to the really big money.' When Doris shuffled back into the room her flannel housecoat was buttoned up to the chin. The excitement had exhausted her and she began to repeat herself. 'The first time I came to the cottage the *Kipper* waited for me. There wasn't a soul about so I opened the door and shouted "Hello!" Your grandfather came out of his study and said, "Oh that Fred Flintstone is a cheeky devil."' She had been distracted again by the television and laughed with Cheryl at the cartoon's antics. Beagan closed the trunk. 'Are you leaving so soon?' she asked him.

'I thought I might go for a swim.'

'Will you come back to see me?'

'Not this summer. No.' He explained about his journey west and the inheritance of the Pacific island.

'You mean there was more than just old papers in the trunk?' asked Cheryl from her chair. 'Like valuable stuff?'

'Oh yes.'

'I knew you'd get something. You always got something.'

'But next year? Will you come back next summer?' appealed Doris. 'With the trunk?' Beagan smiled and promised to do his best. She watched him nurse the family papers down the dark stairs. A jingle chased him out to the car. 'You need Fluff Fluff Fluff to make a Fluffernutter, Fluff Fluff Fluff and lots of peanut butter.' Cheryl pulled her mother away from the window and closed the curtains.

Beagan hung his jacket and towel on a tree, lay his clothes on a rock and pushed through the bulrushes on to the beach. He waded into the flip-flop waves then launched himself into the fresh water's embrace. As the gentle currents caressed and tugged him the memory of an entry in his father's notebooks sprang to mind. 'We had for many summers come to these parts and it was here that the love of water and of ships enmeshed us willingly.' Across the lake he heard the laughter of children diving from a dock and floating in rubber inner tubes. Somewhere far away a screen door squeaked and slammed. 'The family's love of words and water was by no means developed in a single generation,' continued the thought. 'It was hereditary.' Beagan felt that he recognised the curve of the bay, the lie of the land and the smell of jack pine which wafted through the dark woods down to the shore. The sun came out from behind a cloud and its glare dazzled him. Two figures were reflected on the rippled surface. He looked up but the shore was deserted. The line of the beach was broken only by the tree on which he had hung his jacket and towel. Yet in the mirror image of the sparkling water Beagan glimpsed a father and a son. Jamie's hand was on Sandy's small shoulder as they heard the two-tone whistle and waited for the Mosquito Fleet to round Wigwassan Point.

On Highway 400 Southbound the cars slowed to a crawl. A truck had overturned and shed its load of flags. The wind lifted them and they soared like rays along the asphalt. Tricolours flew between the lines of traffic. The Mexican eagle swooped above a Lebanese cedar. The colours of Poland, Trinidad and Tanzania flipped and flashed through the warm currents. A motorist tried to grab a Turkish crescent but it slipped through his fingers and skimmed away over the hard-tops. The ensigns became a school of extra-ordinary flying fish swimming free from a net, excited by their new freedom. For a moment the multicoloured beasts cast a spell over the roadway but then, as they crumpled to the ground, the horns started blaring and frustrated drivers became anxious to move on. Like the flags, they and Beagan were destined for the most ethnically diverse city in the world.

Canada is the country of the American counter-revolution. In the late eighteenth century the losers of the War of Independence moved north across the border. Many of the so-called Empire Loyalists were government officers, surveyors and tax collectors who owed their livelihood, and hence allegiance, to the Crown. Between 1783 and 1788 their numbers trebled the existing population of Novia Scotia and New Brunswick, and formed the nucleus of the future province of Ontario. Britain rewarded their patriotism with grants of free land and positions in the colonial administration. In turn their conservative influence and abiding distaste for republican democracy ensured that the orderly hand of government disciplined the rugged pioneer individualism for generations.

As late as 1910, 90 per cent of Toronto's citizens were still of British origin. Their city was renowned for being good and dull;

an ambitious town of strict churches and virtuous labour. On the waterfront, down the Spadina sewer and up in sewing lofts its citizens aspired to prosper. In mills and factories they produced the goods which built the nation. Their Model-T Fords spluttered along the streets which only a decade before had echoed with the clip-clop of milkmen's carts. On the Sabbath Eaton's, their dry goods and department store, drew reverent black blinds over its display windows. Their magistrates fined sportsmen five dollars for playing golf. The streetcars did not run for fear that their operation might lead to Sunday papers, saloons and theatres. Their city was law-abiding, God-fearing and conformist.

But the Toronto that Beagan found one Sunday in June was neither good nor dull; it was disparate. The city had grown into a conurbation of ethnic enclaves. Little India bristled against the Pakistani community. Chinatown expanded west into Polish Roncesvalles. Along the Bridle Path successful Slavs built ostentatious mansions and pushed out rich Greeks. The old Commonwealth Club had been renamed the Multi-Culti Drop-In Centre. Eden Goode's imposing townhouse in Rosedale had been bought by a Jewish property developer, razed to the ground and replaced by terraced condominiums. Its resident film-makers and lawyers, the great-grandchildren of Empire Loyalists, got together for barbeques and self-congratulation or to visit their parents in Forest Hill, the Anglo-Saxon neighbourhood which smelt of freshly cut grass and two-stroke exhaust. The hum of lawnmowers lulled the warm afternoon air as Russian gardeners manicured the wide verdant lawns bordering streets named Dunvegan, Kilbarry and Strathearn.

'The typical Torontonian has always been the new Torontonian,' pronounced Zachary from his back seat dais in Beagan's car. It pleased him to be in the city again, for he cared little for the world beyond its limits. Clean, modern streets flashed past the car's open windows. Electrum skyscrapers glittered beneath the CN Tower, the world's tallest free-standing structure. The United Brotherhood of Black Educators shared offices with Elusions Cypriot Dinner Dance Club. Next door the Saigon Village restaurant offered a special smorgasbord buffet lunch ('Today only: Surf 'n Turf *à la carte*').

'It was the Europeans who came here after the British,' he explained to his father. 'The Irish arrived looking for work. The Germans came after the shame of defeat. When the Saint Lawrence Seaway opened the port to ocean commerce every other nationality on earth followed them. The Jews migrated to escape pogroms and genocide. West Indians and Asians came in search of economic prosperity. Newcomer followed newcomer year after year.'

Hector stared wide-eyed at the passing scene. He had only once met a black man, a freed slave who had migrated with the Loyalists to Nova Scotia, but never before had he set eyes on an Oriental. Yet outside the Big Land Chinese Supermarket there wasn't a single white face to be seen. 'See that now, Celestials,' he said, pointing at the throng of shoppers buying fresh fungi and crisp *bok choi*. 'I would not be so sure that it wasn't Cathay that Cabot discovered after all.'

'The city is home to almost half a million Chinese, Father,' stated Zachary. 'Also to fifty thousand Somali refugees and thousands of Greeks.' The facts reassured his own sense of authority. 'More Italians live in Toronto than in Venice. Why, in the last thirty years the city's population has doubled, and one resident in three speaks a mother tongue other than English.'

'What then of the first residents? I see no Native faces like the Micmac Gogo who saved my life.'

'The Indians,' dismissed Zachary, 'are mostly dead, drunk or driven west. They won't bother you here.'

In a single block of Bayview Avenue Hector counted two synagogues, a mosque and a Buddhist temple. It was not until they passed south of Steeles Avenue that he saw the first church. 'What would it be that bonds these people together?' Moishe's Kosher Meats nestled beside the Curl Up & Dye Afro Hair Salon. 'What do they all share?'

'Common values,' volunteered his elder son. 'Tolerance, not judging their neighbours, the acceptance that one man's meat is another's poison.'

'There is honey on your lips though there should be a blister on your tongue,' said Hector. He did not understand such an attitude. 'What would it be that you are saying, my boy? That the drunkard is tolerated? Or a father who deserts his family?'

'Today the individual's rights are valued above all else. It is the state which offers help to those in need.'

'But the state would be certain to tell the drunkard to be ashamed of himself, would it not?' asked Hector. 'You would not be saying that it sanctions these values?'

'No man can judge another. It is a matter of freedom of choice.'

Hector was confounded by Zachary's response and began to pray. 'Be Thou a smooth way before me, be Thou a guiding star above me, be Thou a keen eye behind me, this day, this night, forever.'

The car cruised past a vast shopping centre. Listless gangs of youths idled outside the store windows while their parents wound through the acres of parked cars clutching bag-loads of shiny plastic purchases. At the edge of the mall an old woman danced alone around a park bench talking to herself and holding an imaginary partner. 'This is a terrible becoming,' whispered Hector. He stared at his descendants with incomprehension. 'The wind shall subside before I embrace these easy values. Where are the absolute virtues – thrift, self-reliance, respect for the law – the rocks that are not to be compromised? Where is the self-discipline and hard work that launched Jamie's *Segwun* and began your newspapers?' he asked. 'A man cannot improve himself without a moral authority.'

'Torontonians do respect the law, Father; indeed for most the government has replaced the Church,' said Zachary. Hector was too shocked to reply. 'And they share the belief that labour today is rewarded by their children's success tomorrow.'

'They also hold in common a disregard of yesterday,' observed Jamie.

On the drive downtown smoked-glass limousines glided beneath pristine skyscrapers. On every block there seemed to be a homeless person. Some were Cree or Ojibwa. The traffic was bad and Beagan asked a Sikh Mountie in a turban for directions to the ferry pier. He was sent to a parking lot three miles away beside the Daily Bread Food Bank, one of the 'assistance centres' which helped to feed the poor in 174 communities across the province. A recent Department of Public Health survey pinned to its front door warned that 59 per cent of the city's senior citizens were at risk of illness due to malnutrition.

It was the last day of Caravan, the city's annual cultural carnival, and the streets bustled with people in festive mood. Fifty different 'ethnic pavilions' had been set up in civic gardens and squares. In the Jamaican tent revellers bought synthetic rum-flavour cakes then bumped and ground to high-volume reggae. Across the road in the Hungarian pavilion goulash and instant Viennese coffee were on offer. Beagan tried to spot Piri in the crowd but only managed to attract the attention of a gay gypsy musician circulating among the tables and serenading all the young men. Behind the Japanese marquee a geisha girl on her lunch break listened to a Walkman and ate pot noodles.

In the Mexican tent a Rastafarian crowned by a great white stovepipe hat swallowed and laughed, 'Man, I just love tacos.' He took another mouthful of refried beans. 'That's why I come to Canada, to make me life better.'

'We're not as colourful as the Ukrainians,' explained an ex-New Yorker to Beagan while dishing out lashings of cabbage rolls and potato *ponchiks*. A brigade of draft-dodgers had come north in the sixties to avoid fighting in the Vietnam War. 'Like, we don't reminisce about the New Jersey Turnpike.'

'Thai food is crucial,' enthused an anorexic tank-topped woman over her uneaten chicken satays, 'but actually I don't eat salt.'

Entry to each pavilion was by 'passport', a ticket which was stamped at the door as proof of the visit, and the urban globe-trotters rode rickshaws between events. In an afternoon a spectator could take in a dozen pre-packaged cultures, each carefully laid out on a map, and still ride the subway home for supper.

At the foot of Bay Street Beagan caught a double-wheelhouse ferry across the harbour to the island. Under the trees where Bessie had learnt to ride a bicycle a young Malay mother with walnut skin sang to her child. 'Row row row your boat, gently down the stream . . .' Near to the place where Eden Goode had taught himself photography Cantonese students in designer T-shirts and black Bermudas took turns videoing a family picnic. On the sands where Jamie had once beached his canoe an albino Indian family, with skin of translucent silver and long almond eyes, sat in saris on an embroidered mat and nibbled at bhajis.

An amusement park had been built where bulldozers had cleared away the old island homes. A Filipino boy whooped from the Log Flume Ride ('No pregnant riders please'). His optimistic 'My Canada includes Quebec' T-shirt further distressed Beagan, knowing as he did that the English-speaking child would not be welcome in the province itself. Beagan rode the Centreville B. & B. R. miniature railway around the farmyard zoo and through Kermit's Frog Bog. He was not surprised by the scarcity of northern European faces but rather by the dearth of mixed groups. It seemed to him that Caravan and the island fun fair were Toronto's earnest, superficial response to its own dynamic metamorphosis; an ethnic Plato's Cave where residents preferred the shadow of their city's myriad nationalities to the reality of the neighbourhood next door. He half-expected to find a Quebec pavilion full of jolly *habitants* and back-slapping voyageurs. Then a blond-haired man arrived with popsicles for his Malaysian wife and child. '. . . merrily merrily merrily merrily, life is like ice cream.' They began to play together and when their frisbee spun away Beagan retrieved it and struck up a conversation.

'We in Toronto,' said Glen, pointing across the island, 'this is something we're really proud of.' A tribe of Africans in luminous baseball caps camped around a picnic table. A bewhiskered manda-rin lounged in a deck chair reading the *Sing Tao* Chinese daily. 'When Katelynn was born our parents were pleased as pie. My mother said, "Isn't it nice that her skin is so dark."'

'My mother said, "Isn't it nice that her skin's so light,"' murmured Salbiah, his shy, diminutive wife.

'The trouble only started when I lost my job.'

Salbiah lowered her eyes. 'My mother wrote, "It's not right that you have to work. If your husband cannot provide for you then you should come home. You are losing your culture and you're not even getting rich."'

'But can you see her back in Malaysia now?' gloated Glen. 'There's no way that she'll sit below men at table or keep quiet all the time. No, sir.'

Beagan remembered a pair of gregarious Egyptians who had opened a corner shop in dour Halifax. They only did good business when Arab ships were in port. He asked Salbiah about the diffi-culties of assimilation.

'It's no problem,' replied Glen. 'My friends love Salbiah.' Beagan heard no trace of doubt in his voice. 'Hey, we're Can-adians. We get on.'

Little Katelynn slipped and fell and Salbiah scooped her up in her arms. She didn't answer the question but clutched her child to her breast. 'I don't talk to her in Malay but I do sing the old lullabies that I still remember.'

HECTOR, ZACHARY AND Jamie sat in a circle under a broad weeping willow and stared back across the harbour. Clean-lined sailing boats and ultra-modern gin palaces glided across the city's gilded façade. On the beach below the ghosts Beagan skipped pebbles across the water's surface.

'What a f-f-fine f-f-folly,' laughed Jamie in sad wonder at their aspiration. 'The communities that we tried to draw together in our day were diverse enough. But now,' he said with a humility that sprang from loss, 'well, I doubt that the printed word still has such power.'

'Open your eyes and look around you,' insisted Zachary with a preacher's zeal. He considered Jamie's disillusion to be out of place. 'It has been done.'

'Not with Quebec or between these neighbours,' insisted Jamie, his broad gesture trying to gather the diverse people in his arms. 'Our ideal seems f-f-fragmented; small is now beautiful.'

'The newspapers helped set in motion trends which brought these good people considerable gains in material goods, social mobility, racial and sexual equality,' persisted Zachary.

'Yes, but at what cost?' asked Hector, laying down his Bible. The absence of pious devotions in the city tormented him. He had turned to the Word for comfort. 'It is their moral well-being which distresses me.' He watched a replica paddle-wheeler splashing in the bay. 'And how is it that anyone can be going hungry in this rich land? A man with an empty stomach worries neither about feeding his neighbour nor about his soul,' he recalled from Promise.

Zachary did not want to be distracted by his father's concerns so ignored him. 'Maybe even more could have been done if you had rejoined the firm and not wasted away your time,' he told his brother. 'I offered you a generous salary.'

'And I thanked you. But I preferred to paddle my own canoe rather than ride as second officer on another's yacht.'

'That's your damnable pride.'

'My pride?' retorted Jamie. 'You forget that my success was a modest affair. When I returned from Windsor in 1910, and pried the Boy away from his boats, I owned a mere fifteen trade papers. They were designed to complement your thirty-seven titles. Don't you remember that you and I and Sandy met every week to discuss new acquisitions, to share circulation figures and to avoid our journals coming into competition? The only pride that I ever f-f-felt was for you. You made a great success of the b-b-business. You outgrew office and plant capacity f-f-four times.'

'Five times,' corrected Zachary.

'No group of publications under single control anywhere in the world surpassed Gillean for breadth of readership proportionate to population. I always admired your achievement. But wasn't expansion achieved at the expense of publishing's service obligations?'

'The growth of the Dominion made it necessary for local and regional industries to merge and form national companies. You should not have resisted the tide.' Zachary was disappointed with his younger brother. 'Your mistake was not to amalgamate your papers with mine.'

'It was your insensitivity which made that impossible,' flashed Jamie in sudden anger. 'Our history would have been very different had you just once laid your hand on my shoulder and said, "I'm sorry."'

'Sorry?' The bitter accusation startled Zachary. 'But I have nothing to be sorry about, other than being dead,' he puffed. He stabbed an ethereal finger at the willow. It passed clear through the trunk. 'This is my only regret.'

Jamie held his breath and tried to regain his composure. While he counted to ten the ferry *Sam McBride* disgorged another load of day-trippers. Young families of every colour and hue carried picnic baskets across the trim lawns to claim a patch of grass. Tupperware pots of spiced okra, trays of baklava and litre bottles of home-made chianti were laid out on their respective tartan travel rugs. 'It's a curious thing,' he observed, nodding towards Beagan. 'But in Muskoka when he went swimming did you notice his skin?'

'I can't say that I paid much attention.' Zachary had taken a pique against his brother.

'Its colour struck me,' recalled Jamie. 'Pale clay with a sheen like eggshells. And that fine tracery of life.' He paused to remember. 'I hadn't noticed before but it is just like hers.

Like Bessie's. Beagan inherited his grandmother's skin.'

'What of it?' shrugged Zachary. 'He has Father's high forehead and down-turned eyes.'

'His great-great-grandfather's eyes,' corrected Hector. 'The grey-green. It is the gestures that would be his too.'

'It is genetics, Father,' Zachary explained. 'The science of generations, the heredity and variation in plants and animals. It is fact.'

Jamie interrupted them before an argument could develop. 'The point is Zachary that you never said that you f-f-felt for me,' he accused. 'After Bessie's death. Or that of her first child.'

'Of course I did. I expressed my regrets in the proper manner.'

'No,' said Jamie firmly. 'No, you didn't. And well, I think I can say it now that we're dead, your lack of compassion never ceased to distress me.'

'You are certainly mistaken,' Zachary asserted. Hector lay his hand on Jamie's arm. Zachary ignored the gesture. 'In any event, I better expressed my compassion in the care of the living. In the early twenties I repeated my wish that on our deaths the companies should be united and control passed to Sandy. It wasn't my fault that he turned down the opportunity. You never thanked me for that generosity.'

'But by then outsiders had begun to slip the wedge between us. They brought two of our papers into conflict knowing that Sandy was too f-f-forthright for his own good and that you would defend your mission. They exploited our differences with calculated patience and our firms became estranged. The control of Gillean Publishing slipped out of family hands.'

'Hush-up-with-you, chap,' ordered Zachary. 'I don't remember it happening that way.'

'But you do remember that they circulated stories in the trade about our quarrels. We always had our differences but we never argued back then. It was those lies which widened the gulf between us. You came to see your employees as your only f-f-family. They in turn treated you as a patriarch, the venerable father who throughout his life remained true to his ambition, even as your partners came more and more to emphasise profit margins.'

'And what does it matter now?' snapped Zachary, bristling his thick, snow-white moustache. 'We were old and I was dying. It's history now. We can't affect it.' He hated the impotence of death as much as the loss of time.

'It matters because the end of our co-operation was a grave blow to me,' replied Jamie. 'Not because of any hindrance to earthly success, I didn't care two hoots that my titles would never f-f-flourish in the shadow of such powerful competition, but because of the evil of the deceit.' He shivered as if someone had walked over his grave. 'It haunted Sandy too. That's why he set up on his own. He launched the *Toronto Mirror*, Canada's first picture newspaper, in an attempt to distance himself from the iniquity. "Reflecting the truth" was his watchword. The paper was a success but too heavy a drain on our limited capital, and when he came to you for help, your partners advised you not to become involved. The enterprise collapsed. Sandy packed his bags, took F-F-Father's old globe and, like us before him, went west in search of a promised land.'

Zachary examined his watch then struck it with his knucklc. His patience had worn as thin as Jamie's tweeds. 'What is that grandson of yours doing now?' he blurted as if noticing Beagan for the first time.

Hector watched him throwing rocks for a moment, then twisted his wrist and began mimicking Beagan's movement. 'See that now,' he smiled. 'It is myself that skipped stones in that manner when I was a boy.'

'He would be better employed going back to Scotland and growing oats.'

'It is a vanity to speak of our traditions in a deprecating manner,' Hector snapped at his son.

'He's too reflective to live in a progressive country,' replied Zachary, anxious as always to move on. 'There's not been the time for looking back in the New World.'

Beagan threw a last stone towards the gilded façade then turned his back on the city. He began to walk to the ferry landing but stopped and instead stepped under the willow. He stood among them, his forefathers at his feet, and it seemed for a moment that he was going to speak. Then a breeze blew off the water and he shivered. He put his hands in his pockets and walked away.

Beagan didn't visit Gillean Communication's hi-tech editorial offices or vast new printing plant. It wasn't among the Apple Macintoshes and Quark XPress DTP software that he would find a trace of his grandfather or great-uncle. Nor did he see them on the island. He caught the ferry back to the mainland and drove west along Lakeshore Boulevard to Sunnyside Beach. He sat at the mouth of the Humber River beneath the concrete pillars of the Gardiner Expressway and felt waves of loneliness wash over him. He tried to ignore the roar of the traffic and to imagine the Huron warriors paddling down the river with Étienne Brûlé, Champlain's prime scout and the first white man to look upon Lake Ontario. Beyond the ranks of apartment blocks he tried to see John Graves Simcoe coasting along the shore, erecting Captain Cook's canvas tent and establishing a settlement. He wanted to count the bateaux and steamers as they tacked around the flat swampy island bearing the settlers who transformed the oak-covered plain into Canada's metropolis. He tried too to conjure up the boats skimming across Bras d'Or, their paddlers and rowers drawn by Reverend Hector's words, and the puffing Mosquito steamers loaded with newspapers and mailbags carrying the printed word away from Jamie. But from his noisy vantage point Beagan could not summon the past. He saw no trace of the first immigrants' arrival. There was no bay marked by a solitary Celtic cross, no landing beach scored by the keels of ships, no quarantine islet haunted by the spirits of typhus-infected travellers who had lost the battle for life. Instead he saw a history had been forgotten. It had been erased beneath public swimming pools, highway overpasses and civic incinerators.

The Western Sea

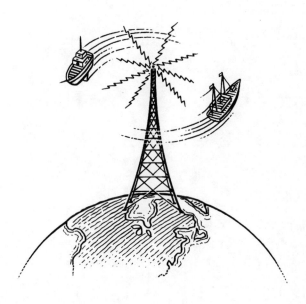

CHAPTER VIII

BACKWATERS

I COULDN'T FIND the spanner anywhere. It wasn't in the tool box, in the bilge or under either of the dogs. I looked behind the cowling and in with the charts. Under the cushions there were only old spark plugs and one squashed chocolate biscuit. It was very soggy but still lovely and sweet. The engine had fouled and I needed the spanner to blow out the carb, at least I did if the problem was with the carb. It might have been water in the fuel line. I would have flushed that out instead had I been able to put my hands on the needle-nose pliers. They seemed to be missing too. *Primary* wallowed in Lake Erie's swells off the end of the Nanticoke pier and I lay my head on the sleeping Samoyed to wait. My feet rested against Brendan, my scruffy mongrel setter. The late summer sun was warm and I found the spanner in my pocket.

I was proud of my old Dad, uncle Zach too for all his faults. They started with nothing, no contacts or friends, and made good. Two quiet, honest sons of the manse created a publishing empire that in their time was maybe the biggest in the Commonwealth. They devoted themselves to encouraging home industry and reducing the dependence on imported goods. The legacy that they left was a knowledge, a confidence in the achievement and potential of Canada and her people. That optimism could never have taken root had the country been served only by English periodicals and American magazines. Without it we would have remained a colonial appendage or even sooner become the fifty-first state of the United States.

It's funny though, the brothers who worked to bring people together lived so much apart. In the tangled web of memory I retain the clear picture of a single Muskoka morning. Dad was inside the cottage. He had arrived the evening before on one of his rare visits. I had readied my boat to take him for a ride around Bohemia Island. Nan was at the dock, insisting that the *Mink*'s butcher cut away the fat before weighing the chops. She and I were climbing up the pine-needle path, me chattering all the while about the Kermath's overheating gearbox, when the sound of singing echoed down to us through the trees. At first I didn't recognise the voice. I had never before heard Dad so much as whistle and his full, deep baritone startled me. He thought himself to be alone in the big empty house and in the privacy of the pine bathroom waved his straight razor like a baton and piped, 'O ye'll tak' the high road and I'll tak' the low road'. My instinct was to run to him, to bury myself in his arms and to feel the tickle of the twisting rust-red moustache but instead I let go of Nan's hand, turned away and slipped back to the boat. For I knew then that he was singing to Bessie.

Only my mother ever found the key to his heart and it went with her to the grave. Dad stayed away from home for months on end but his letters to me arrived every week. He wrote from Atlantic liners and lake steamers and grand hotels on richly embossed stationery.

'My room is on the seventh floor,' he enthused on his first trip to New York. I was eighteen months old at the time. 'When going up to my room a gentleman asked the elevator boy to let him off at the <u>seventeenth</u> floor.' He had underlined the word twice. 'You can quite imagine what a high building this is.'

The envelopes were postmarked Edinburgh, Assiniboia and Bermuda. They were filled with reports on the growth of western trade and the operation of his Muskoka fleet. He wrote as if to an adult, noting the cost of taxis in Naples (two lire from the customs wharf to the Hotel Bristol) and describing his ship's wait in Halifax for the trans-continental train that brought the China mail.

'This is the country of the crocodile,' explained his letter from the Royal Poinciana in Palm Beach, then the world's most expensive hotel at fifteen dollars per day. 'The negroes do a thriving business in catching the young ones and taming them. If it is not too cold I will bring one home for you.' Nan sat by my bedside and read his words aloud.

'Hundreds of people were on the wharf to see friends off,' he had written aboard the Dominion Line's SS *Vancouver* while *en route* to Southampton. 'I seemed to be about the only passenger without a friend to say *"bon voyage"* and I felt decidedly blue.' Nan's tears pattered on the waxy leaves like the first drops of autumn rain. 'Oh how I miss your mother, my boy.'

He understood my loss too. His letters reached out to me year after year in Muskoka, at Upper Canada College and aboard HMS *Chatham* in the Mediterranean during the Great War. In them he scolded me for my shoddily-written replies and reminded me of duty. 'You are a privileged boy. In your short life not only have you never known hunger, not only have you had a large share of good things, but you have never had any real wish ungratified.' His script was simple, bold and sincere. 'Do you realise that in return for these gifts you must give something back to the world? It is you, and boys like you with the advantage of education and background, who must maintain the standards of speech and manners, of integrity, in personal and public life. If you are satisfied with the second-rate, if you let money, material pleasures and superficialities become all-important, then you forsake all that we have worked for, you betray me and break your mother's heart.'

As the waves rocked *Primary* I remembered his letters that had tried to fill the void left by death, the words which my son Beagan carried with him in the family trunk. 'When you grow to be a man I want you to know her. I want you to read all her letters and the papers which I have put away for you. They will give you a faint idea of her sweet life and dear love. Then after they have planted me away in a bone-yard you will have them – and these words which I write from time to time – to guide you.'

THE PICK-UP TRUCK writhed down Slag Pot Captive Road and cut behind No. 1 Blowdown Treatment Plant. 'I come. You come. He comes.' Carlo, a young uniformed security guard with ink-black curls, conjugated verbs as he steered around the coke oven and ore piles. 'I will come. You will come. They will come. Is good, no? Super good.' Beagan nodded in agreement. He sat in the passenger seat, the trunk rattling behind him in the back, and watched Stelco Steel's Lake Erie Works flash by the window. Pavarotti sang *Tosca* on the radio. Carlo glanced at his watch and turned right at the hot-strip mill. 'I have language class now.' He quoted from memory, 'English skill help you communicate at work, better your career opportunity and ensure an open line of communication with younger generation growing up in Canada.' Most of the employees at the hundred-acre works were Italian or Portuguese. Some were newcomers, other families had been with Stelco for two or three generations, all spoke their mother tongue both to co-workers and at home. 'The union and company they offer teach English.' The pick-up skirted coal heaps and followed the mile-long conveyor belt towards the lake. Along it swept twenty-six thousand metric tons of iron pellets, each the size of a blueberry, from a ship's hold to the mill's furnaces. 'You go during regular shift and company pay for all classroom time.' Carlo crunched to a stop and kicked up a cloud of grit. 'I lift. You lift. We both lift.' They heaved the trunk out of the back and on to the pier. 'I go. You go. We all go. *Buon viaggio*,' he chanted and drove back towards the training centre.

The MV *Tadoussac*, a blunt-nosed, self-loading laker, had the look of a vast aquatic caterpillar. Her slinky body stretched from the raised head of the forward bridge to the steaming engine-room tail. Like all Great Lakes bulk carriers she had been built to move not through the waves as an ocean-going ship but with them, and her passage over swells could be traced by the ripple down her deck; the wheelhouse rose on a roller, amidships she arched while the after-house dropped away into the curl of a trough. The lanky proportions enabled her to crawl through the narrow Seaway locks.

The pier was coated in iron dust and Beagan dragged the trunk around the auburn pools of rusty rainwater. 'Fore!' A golf ball shot by his left ear, ricocheted off the hull and splashed into the lake. 'Bloody hell, sorry about that, mate.' The *Tadoussac*'s chief engineer, his eyes crinkled by light and laughter, appeared from behind a coal heap. He wore Bermuda shorts, white socks, sandals and carried a golf bag on his shoulder. 'I was practising my chipping.'

'Here?' asked Beagan, looking back at the black acres of coal.

'Nowhere better. There's loads of space and you just can't lose your balls.' He glanced into the water and added, 'Most of the time.' He held out his hand. 'William Wellfit's the name. You must be our passenger; welcome aboard.' Wellfit took hold of a trunk handle, pointed at the ship's twin stacks and said, 'Do you like my smoke?'

'*Mensch*, Bill,' cried his wife from the forward deck. Gabi Wellfit was as round as a Prussian prune pudding. 'The last time you asked someone that it got you into real trouble.' Wellfit smiled and rolled his eyes. 'You will excuse my husband please,' she shouted, lifting the drooping brim of her sunhat. 'This is his last trip and he's gone soft in the head.'

Beagan and Wellfit carried the trunk over the gangway and Beagan asked if, like the *Global Trader*, the ship had a foreign company. 'The *Tadoussac* has a hyphenated-Canadian crew,' explained Wellfit. 'I'm English-Canadian from Hartlepool and my junior engineer is Kazakhi-Canadian. Dai, the third officer up there on the bridge, he's a Welsh–Canadian. The cook Eddie Palladini is Italian–Canadian and Ruby over there is Jamaican–Canadian.' A bosomy black woman leaned on the starboard rail dreaming of the Caribbean. 'We used to employ cheap labour on board, Poles and Russians who had jumped ship in Halifax, but no more. Now all the foreigners have become Canadians and earn four times their old pay.' He took a swing with an imaginary club. 'That's why the line is in trouble.'

Wellfit paused at one of the open hatches. In the cavernous belly four crewmen used shovels to ease the last few tons of pellets off the saddlebacks and through the chute gates. Three conveyor belts running between the hulls carried the load aft and up the boom to spill into the pier-side hopper. 'Our only Canadian-Canadians are Buddy, Mark and Luke there. They joined us when the fishing died out in Newfoundland. Barry too. He's from Cape Breton and came on when the Sydney steelmills were closed.' Here and there the sooty hold was daubed with flecks of green. Grains of wheat from a previous cargo had taken root between the bulkheads and begun to grow. The *Tadoussac* had been designed to carry iron ore, a million bushels of grain or enough coal to feed a power station for a week but on this trip up to the head of the lakes she was sailing empty.

'Not much goes up the lakes anymore, at least on this ship, and only wheat comes down, most of which is sent to Russia.' Wellfit led Beagan up a flight of steps and into the forward super-structure. 'And when the Ukraine starts feeding Russia again there will be nowhere to sell that wheat.' He shook his head. 'Shipping on the Great Lakes will be dead for us in ten years. We've had the good days and, I tell you, I'm glad my time's up.'

The cabin, grandly named the First Stateroom, had a double bed, shower and porthole view over the bow. Ruby ambled in with a stainless steel mixing bowl overflowing with fresh fruit. A handful of kumquats rolled away under the video recorder. Wellfit pointed out the well-stocked larder and second galley. 'Come and join us aft for dinner when we're underway.'

A vermilion sun dropped beneath the surface and cast a band

of copper across the horizon. A passing laker smeared a smoky smudge along the mauve American shore. As dusk gathered the *Tadoussac* eased astern and swung west around the black silhouette of Long Point. The trip into the heart of the continent would take her across three of the Great Lakes and reach 2,260 miles inland from the Atlantic. A breeze blew up, fretting Erie's surface with a fine pattern of fish scales, while the clear night sky filled with constellations of aircraft landing lights making for Detroit, Toledo and Toronto. The half-moon lay on its back and smiled like a Cheshire cat.

'You look like a ten-pounder,' said Ed. The *Tadoussac*'s cook had mischievous chocolate-brown eyes, fingers the size of Somerset sausages and a deep yearning to satiate appetite. His chins wobbled as he nodded, 'Yup, ten pounds minimum.'

'Ten pounds of what?' asked Beagan.

'Every time someone new comes aboard,' replied Wellfit from across the table, 'Eddie sizes up how much weight he can put on them.' He thumbed a well-worn copy of *Golf Illustrated*.

'But it only takes three days to reach Thunder Bay.'

'Ten pounds,' repeated Ed. He rolled up his sleeves to reveal leg-of-mutton forearms. 'Tonight you can have chicken cacciatore, steak and mushrooms, chilli con carne with cheese or a home-made sausage submarine sandwich.'

'*Ja*, the steak is delicious,' said Gabi, who ate with a determination that would make her a fifteen-pounder.

'It's all delicious,' corrected Ed. 'If you can't find something to eat on this ship you're not hungry. So what's it to be?' Beagan felt spoilt for choice. 'Tell you what,' the cook suggested. 'I'll give you a sample taste of everything, then you can decide.' Before Beagan could object Ed had slipped back in his galley like a whale into a fjord.

'On some ships the crew wouldn't eat if the cook lost his can-opener,' joked Gabi through a mouthful of prime beef. 'Eddie is not a can-opener cook.'

'So what brings you onboard?' asked Wellfit. 'We don't get many passengers.'

'I'm trying to travel to Vancouver by water,' replied Beagan. 'I'm following the family history and my father lived there.'

'Vancouver?' he said in disbelief. 'You know the lakes stop at Thunder Bay? After that it's just prairies and mountains.'

'And rivers all the way to the Pacific. The waterways used to be the only route west.'

'Wouldn't it have been easier to buy a bus ticket?'

Gabi groaned as she put down her knife and fork. '*Ach, das war lecker.* Delicious.'

Ed reappeared at the doorway with a plate in his hand. 'Another helping, Gabi?'

'Well, maybe just a little taste.' He placed a second porterhouse steak before her. 'Eddie, are you crazy? I can't eat all this.'

'Now don't disappoint me.'

'Oh what the hell. I enjoy a challenge,' said Gabi picking up her utensils with renewed gusto. Her enthusiasm for supper revealed a great joy for life. 'Do you know why I eat so much?' she asked Beagan. 'It's the same reason that I came to Canada.'

'I wouldn't encourage her if I were you,' advised her husband, retreating behind his magazine.

'For crying out loud, honey, I was just trying to tell him a story.' Gabi turned back to Beagan. 'At the end of that *furchtbarer Krieg*' – she never used the noun 'war' without the adjective 'terrible' – 'I weighed eighty-six pounds. *Ja*, I know it's hard to believe now that I'm a little *pummelig*, that's chubby, but there was nothing to eat in Berlin. We lost our vegetable patch during an air raid. I had to jump into the Spree to avoid the phosphorus bombs and the last turnips just floated away. My girlfriends in the *Landarmee* were shot by the Russians for stealing food and I watched my mother die of typhoid. In Germany there was no future for me and, *mein Gott*, everyone was so hungry.'

Gabi paused to dab a little mustard on her plate. The aroma of frying onions wafted in from the galley. 'I started walking west on wooden-soled shoes with only the clothes on my back and one extra pair of panties. I washed them every day but in the camp in Bremen someone stole one pair from the line. It was terrible but they had nothing and, *Mensch*, I was lucky. I spoke some English and Canada offered me a job and passage.'

In the galley Ruby crashed between sink and cooker, dropped pots and pans and called on the good Lord for strength. Some crewmen came in for coffee while others took submarine sandwiches back to their cabins and watched television.

'Everything was organised and I was due to sail on a ship called the *Samaria* but it was changed at the last moment,' Gabi continued. 'I cried and cried but that was my fate you see.' She looked at Wellfit concentrating on his magazine. 'Come on honey, tell him.'

'Gabi, he's not interested in ancient history.' Beagan said that he wanted to hear their story, it had already begun to counter the bitter after-taste of Toronto, and when Wellfit relented Gabi returned to her steak. 'I spent the war in the merchant navy, stepping into dead men's shoes. Ten ships were torpedoed out from under me in six years. In 1949 I was engineering officer on the *Scythia*, a twin-screw geared turbine built for five hundred passengers. We were going home to Liverpool when we were diverted to Bremen to take on a thousand DPs, displaced persons, bound for Canada.

'There were only two huge cabins,' interrupted Gabi, 'one for men and one for women, with bunks on top of bunks and no air conditioning and everyone being sick.'

'Everyone except you.

'*Mensch*, no. I never stayed below decks. I was up in the dining room. There was so much food that I stuffed myself like a goose. A steward taught me how to eat grapefruit and I learnt right away. I also rediscovered ice cream. I just couldn't get enough of it and after every meal I would sit out on deck taking deep breaths and feeling sick.' Gabi re-enacted each stage of her story: she puffed up her cheeks with imaginary ice cream, distended her stomach and even tried to turn a bilious shade of green. She didn't so much recount events as relive them. 'One day when I was especially full a sailor approached me and I told him to leave me alone. They weren't supposed to fraternise with the passengers but, you know,

I felt bad for sending him away. He was just trying to be friendly. So when an officer came up behind me and said . . . and said . . .' Gabi paused until Wellfit looked up and met her eye. 'Come on honey, are you going to help me tell the story or not?'

'I said,' sighed Wellfit, '"Are you feeling unwell, miss?"'

'*Ja*, and I was, from the ice cream or the motion I don't know, and I told him so. He gave me some pills. Then he pointed up at the chimney and asked . . .'

'"Do you like my smoke?"' Wellfit blushed then explained, 'The *Scythia* was steam powered and she made that lovely rushing sound of wind and water. Nothing like the rattle from these modern, metallic diesels.'

Gabi did not let technicalities divert her from the story. 'The next day during lifeboat drill Bill made a special point of checking my lifejacket. He inspected the straps two or three times then asked if I would meet him. I agreed and we sat together on the boat deck beneath the half-painted funnel.'

'The *Scythia* was still battleship grey. The lads had just started painting her back in the Cunard colours, the old red and black.'

'I was a displaced person. Do you think I was in the mood to fall in love?'

'You were only in the mood to eat ice cream.'

'*Ach, ich kann nicht mehr.* I'm stuffed.' Gabi pushed the steak away from her. 'Falling in love put me off my food. I couldn't even eat my lovely ice cream. And Bill, his friends told me later, was off his beer. Then all of a sudden we arrived in Quebec and I had to catch a train to my job in Hamilton. For crying out loud we only had an hour together, one hour. Bill threw me to the ground and kissed me and kissed me and promised to write and gave me a dollar bill.'

'I wouldn't have given you a whole dollar,' he teased.

'A dollar was a lot of money. It was my only money. I remember oranges cost four cents apiece. Two months later his letter arrived, thrown off the ship to the dock crew with money tied to it for postage, and Bill had written, "If we follow our hearts with our hands and heads we can make it."'

'I handed in my ration cards at the pierhead in Liverpool, bought my passage to Canada and we were married in Toronto.'

'In a Lutheran church . . .'

'I didn't mind. I like Martin Luther.'

'. . . with organ music because my father had played the organ at church in Germany. We had ice cream at the reception and I got back my appetite.'

'We bought a caravan and a plot of land on the outskirts of the city. I found a job on lakers. Then over the winters and on my weeks off we built our house together; the walls, the roof, even the plumbing and the electrics. No time for playing golf then.'

'We made it with our hands and our heads. We've earned our retirement.'

'It's the only house we've ever owned, and now that the city has grown up around us it's worth a bomb. Ontario has been good to us but it's time to sell up and move on.'

'Where will you go?' asked Beagan, his hope restored by their faith.

'West. End of this season I'll collect my gold Rolex, put an oar on my shoulder and we'll walk inland. First place someone asks me what I'm carrying that's where we'll stay.'

'That will be the day.' Gabi shook her head in disbelief as Beagan thought of Pike and Rosa paddling away from their sawdust hotel. 'Bill, you'll never leave boats behind you.'

Ruby appeared bearing a platter of food. Instead of serving up a small sample of each dish Ed had arranged four full entrées on the plate. The meal would set Beagan well on the way to becoming a ten-pounder. 'And the Word became flesh,' said Ruby.

'*Guten Appetit*,' chirped Gabi.

Beagan awoke at dawn to the low of a foghorn. Along the misty channel the rising sun gilded navigation buoys with golden light. The Detroit River looked like the Nile lined by white picket fences. It was broad, flat and calm but instead of feluccas plying between dusty docks, flotillas of open outboards lay off leafy islands. Yawning sportsmen lounged in deck chairs fishing for perch and bass. A Chris-Craft flying the Italian *tricolore* bounced across the wake. Grebes and coots fed in the shallows. Red-winged blackbirds clucked among the willows. The river narrowed and the *Tadoussac*'s shadow fell across the immaculate lawns of grand Colonial estates. Along backyard canals the luxurious cruisers of the car-making élite lay moored beside the fibreglass pleasure boats of their employees. The five Great Lakes contain 20 per cent of the world's fresh water but past Grosse Île the morning haze took on a tarnished hue. A whiff of sulphur wafted on the breeze. The clouds became fetid and stained as the chimneys of the Great Lakes Steel Mill loomed out of the smog. A line of grimy lakers disgorged black hillocks of coal to feed the furnaces of the Allied Chemical Corporation. The River Rouge ran russet, its waters discoloured by the Ford Motor Company's effluent. The bulk carrier *Algowest* made ten knots downstream *en route* to papermills on the Cuyahoga. Not long ago the river had caught fire. A spill of hot slag had ignited a stream more awash with oil, chemicals and debris than water. Buddy, the Newfoundland mechanic, appeared on deck wearing a T-shirt: 'Detroit: where the weak are killed and eaten', and Beagan's heart sank like a drum of toxic waste. The forty million people who lived along the Great Lakes, including one in three of all Canadians, were exposed to more poisonous chemicals than those inhabiting any comparable area of North America. Pregnant women and nursing mothers were warned not to eat the fish that their husbands and brothers caught downriver.

As well as being a shared transportation network the world's largest inland waterway also delineated the border. Across from Detroit's belching smokestacks and neo-Gothic Renaissance Center lay a sleepy provincial town of wooden buildings and low-rise office blocks. On Saturday morning Windsor's residents, when not driving over the Ambassador Bridge to do a little trans-border shopping, strolled along the river walk watching the bustle on the American side. Their unpretentious houses occupied large gardens, in contrast to the imposing Michigan homes squeezed on to small lots. Life on the Canadian shore appeared to be comfortable, self-satisfied and safe, revealing a people of lazy ambition who settled for half of that to which their materialistic southern neighbours aspired.

At Sarnia the land fell astern and Huron, the second-largest Great Lake, spread her waters before the ship. Ed rustled up a simple breakfast of grilled ham, fried eggs and pancakes as the wheelman adjusted the heading for true north. Only routine maintenance occupied the crew so Mark and Luke relaxed in the sun. Wellfit also took a break from the engine room and strolled on to the deck with his golf bag. He was determined to practise his swing. 'This is how I'm spending the rest of my days,' he announced. An Algerian grain carrier passed to starboard on its way to the sea. 'Did you know that in the first decade of this century the value of this country's wheat production doubled?' he asked.

'And the population grew by a third. Everyone thought that it would be Canada's century,' nodded Beagan. He had been reading back-issues of the Gillean trade journals. 'It started out to be that way too. The country was so optimistic. People believed in possibilities. They had faith in their potential.'

Wellfit admired his ship's fine lines. 'The men who started this company dreamed of creating the largest inland shipping line in the world. And they did it. Up until twenty years ago there were three hundred ships on the lakes. But today there are less than one hundred.'

'What went wrong?'

'I don't know for sure,' said Wellfit as he selected a club from his bag, 'but, well, do you know what I earn?' Beagan shook his head. 'Sixty dollars.'

'A day?'

'An hour. And on top of that there's what we call the Newfie lottery: work on ships for twenty weeks, collect welfare for the other thirty-two. It makes for an easy life all right, but it doesn't seem right.'

'There was no unemployment benefit when we started out,' said Gabi from under the brim of her sunhat. On her lap rested a plate of home-made brownies to tide her over until lunch. '*Mensch*, we didn't want government hand-outs, we didn't want to be a burden on anyone.'

Wellfit pointed at the Algerian *Nea Tyhi*. 'The chief aboard that saltie will bless his lucky stars if he gets a dollar a day. It costs ten times more to run a laker with a Canadian crew than it does to run a foreign ocean-going ship three times the size.'

The red-hulled bulk of an American ore carrier heaved into view. Wellfit fished out a tethered ball and tied it to a hatchway. 'And there are still too many ships on the lakes today.' He took a few practice swings aimed at the leviathan. 'Just watch, some day soon lakers will start having accidents. The *Tadoussac* cost three million dollars to build in 1969. She's insured for her replacement cost; that's sixty million dollars.' Wellfit swung at the ball and missed. 'They had a dream, you know, and something or somebody shattered it.' He tried again and managed to hit the ball but the elastic snapped. It struck the railing, bounced back and almost knocked off his head. 'Golf is a dangerous game,' he declared.

For the rest of the day the *Tadoussac* ran north beyond the sight of land and Beagan walked the deck trying to digest his tortellini Piedmontese and two bowlfuls of tiramisù. There was no doubt that he was gaining weight. Ed promised to serve only a light supper but the fresh blueberry pie was too tempting for anyone on board to resist. Beagan eased his down with two scoops of ice cream.

The following morning found the ship in a timbered archipelago. Retired lakers with sheared propellers or cracked hulls were laid up behind rugged headlands in the De Tour Passage. Across from Frying Pan Island the bleached wooden ribs of an old passenger paddle-wheeler rose out of the shallows. Beyond Manitoulin the *Tadoussac* zigzagged up channels and down narrows, between low, pine-clad islands uninhabited but for the odd isolated cabin tucked into a settler's clearing. The stern swung left then right as the ship rounded buoys and markers. A lofty orange navigation range erected beside an oversize church guided her past Sailor's Encampment, the deserted waystation where west-bound ships of an earlier age had pooled to await a tug tow up Lake Nicolet's fast waters. Nothing remained of the once bustling piers, hotels and mariners' bars. The church looked locked. In the bay where fleets of steamers had laid at anchor a lone Cree fisherman cast for king salmon.

In the wheelhouse the radar reflected the orderly column of lakers queued along the shipping lane. A faint blip caught the eye of Dai, the third officer. It suggested that a small motorboat hugged the ship's stern. He glanced aft over his shoulder and, seeing nothing, adjusted the sensitivity control until the ghostly echo vanished from the screen.

The *Tadoussac* turned into the Saint Mary's River and was thrust out of the wilds into downtown Sault Ste Marie. At the height of the last war more tonnage went through 'the Soo' than through the Suez and Panama canals combined. Now the International Bridge reached across the waterway between the twin American and Canadian cities. Townsfolk dawdled in shops and wandered around Republic Steel's graceful *Valley Camp* floating museum. The ship sailed along West Portage Avenue, close enough to shore for Beagan to watch the flickering television screens in the Seven Seas Motel and to read the take-away menu at the drive-in Dairy Queen. Three crewmen abseiled down the freeboard on to the dock to guide the ship into the lock. The great five-hundred-ton doors closed behind her and, with the beam leaving only a foot of clearance, the ship was eased seven metres up above Lake Huron.

Ed noticed a farmer selling bushels of sweetcorn off the back of a truck and sent out for three dozen ears. Beagan asked him about the wire mesh suspended over the grassy banks. 'The lock-keepers used to get downstream lakers to donate a bag of grain to give to the migrating Canada geese,' he explained. 'But the birds got to be real well fed and stopped flying south, settled down on the islands and became pests. So the authorities decided to introduce pigs on to the lawns to eat their eggs. The scheme worked a treat until someone stole the pigs.'

'Sounds to me a bit like an allegory,' jested Wellfit.

'My pork's all raised on barley-meal,' retorted Ed. He had misheard 'allegation'. 'I never touched those pigs.' The western lock opened and the ship slipped out into the largest freshwater lake in the world.

SUPERIOR SHONE LIKE burnished silver, possibly from the mercury that had been pumped into it by the pulp mills and chlor-alkali plants. I tucked *Primary* in behind the laker, using her bulk as a windbreak and riding in the smooth waters of her slip-stream. A breeze blew up from the south and flicked frothy tufts off the wave tops. The Kermath ticked over well enough but, as she only made ten miles per hour at full throttle, it needed all my imagination to keep up with the *Tadoussac*.

Like grand-dad Hector before me I have always liked to take the measure of a place from the water, and nowhere in Canada is one further from land than on Superior. The lake is shaped liked a giant wolf's head biting into the country's geographic centre. Its volume is so great, some 2,900 cubic miles, that if God took umbrage against America and poured out its waters they would cover the whole continent to a depth of ten feet. It is so long that the *Tadoussac*, even with her Sulzer 9600 supercharged diesel, would take more than a day and night to cross its length. It was no wonder then that the first explorers had mistaken it for the legendary Sea of the West.

Long before our time Étienne Brûlé became the first white man to see the lake which the Ojibwa called *Gitche Gumee*, Big-Sea-Water. His discovery so convinced Champlain's scouts of their proximity to the lantern-lit cities of Cathay that Jean Nicolet, who followed Brûlé in 1634, stepped ashore near Green Bay in ceremonial damask robes. He fired a salute with his pistols and advanced upon a band of astonished Native Winnebagos. It was a disappointment that they didn't welcome him in Chinese. Although Lakes Michigan and Superior proved not to be the explorers' fabled sea, their cartographers did note the hundreds of rivers that led still further west. In 1671 the French crown claimed 'all the countries, streams, lakes and rivers contiguous and adjacent, discovered and undiscovered'. Louis Jolliet and Father Jacques Marquette, a Jesuit missionary, then pushed on beyond the Great Lakes to reach the upper Mississippi. The belief that 'the great river of Canada' flowed like Herodotus' Nile in two directions from its source and across the continent persisted for more than another century. As late as 1782 Janvier's map of North America illustrated a vast '*Mer ou Baye de l'Ouest*', a great body of ocean which gouged deep into the Pacific mainland.

The first voyageurs may not have discovered the North-West Passage but they did find that there were fortunes to be made in the *pays d'en haut*. The 'up country' was filled with beaver and the felt hats which could be made from their fur were enormously fashionable in the seventeenth and eighteenth centuries. 'The Honourable Company of Adventurers of England Trading into Hudson's Bay' was established to acquire pelts in the north. Its rival the North West Company fused French zest with Scots loyalty to reach west up the Saint Lawrence. Every spring the Nor'Westers' big birchbark *canots de maître* raced from Montreal to the western tip of Superior. They followed the barren north shore, traversed wild bays and paddled in close line astern under pitch-pine torches when fog blanketed the lake. Their destination was a summer rendezvous with the beaver-laden *canots du nord* from the interior. It was a trade so valuable that without it, without this whim of fashion, Canada would have been ditched by Europe and absorbed into the United

States. The forty-ninth parallel, the border which stretches almost two thousand miles west from the Great Lakes to the Pacific, was only surveyed to stop American traders poaching Canadian pelts. It was the beaver that created Canada.

I had told all this to my boys, Beagan and Alex, tucked into their cots in the Pacific house, and the stories had carried them out over the dusky waters to sleep. If he remembered his history then Beagan would know that to continue west he had to travel as the voyageurs. No ship could navigate the rapids and shallows of the western rivers. A canoe might be slow but it would speed him on his interior journey faster than any speedboat. It would be easier too for me to keep up with him. I had grown tired of staring up the *Tadoussac*'s backside.

'BEAR PAWS, ROAST porcupine and moose's muzzle were their delicacies,' noted Beagan. Ed had proposed preparing him a farewell voyageur feast and Beagan had reached back to claim the bequest. 'Though out in the bush they tended to survive on strips of dried pemmican.'

'I'm fresh out of buffalo,' said Ed as they leafed through a dusty French tome unearthed from the depths of the box trunk, 'but I figure I can rustle up something tasty.'

That evening the galley was bathed in candlelight. Beagan asked the Wellfits to imagine that they were in a great banqueting room and that outside four hundred *hommes du nord*, the élite voyageurs who paddled the northern waterways, were camped with their Native wives.

'*Ja, ja,*' enthused Gabi. 'I can hear them shouting. *Mensch*, what a racket.'

'That must be the *mangeurs de lard*, the pork-eaters,' suggested Beagan. The sound of shouting in fact came from Buddy's television set. 'The Northmen taunted them for leading a soft life. They only canoed up from Montreal.'

'That's hardly a thousand miles,' said Wellfit in his wry, gentle humour. 'No wonder you didn't bother catching a bus.'

In his excitement Beagan reached for his great-grandfather's globe. He traced the waterways west, then felt sadness that modern, secessionist Quebec might cut itself off from its nationwide legacy. He pointed out the fictitious western sea. 'A Frenchman named Bonne drew a map in 1781 which not only records this fancy but puts a town on its south-east shore, a place he called Quivira.'

'That sounds like Spanish, eh honey?' Gabi said to Wellfit. '*Quivira*. Maybe it means "Who has seen?"'

'Or "Who will see?"'

'I don't know about that,' answered Beagan, wondering for a moment if the separatists like their voyageur forebears were still striving for a fictional destination. 'But according to Indian tales Quivira contained fabulous wealth in gold and silver. A Spanish explorer called Coronado is said to have reached it, God knows how, considering it lay on an imaginary sea, but he found there only rich black soil.'

'Then again, maybe it means "What truth?"' speculated Gabi.

Ruby stood in for a mixed-blood *Métis* serving girl and ladled out soup of beef. Ed followed the appetiser with hotch-potch, or salmagundi, a dish of chopped meat, eggs, onions and seasoning. As an alternative to beaver tails he produced a haunch of venison. Its taste was rich and gamy.

'It's larded with fat salt-pork, marinated in cognac and rolled in powdered herbs,' he explained. 'One of my secret recipes.'

Gabi risked a taste of every dish but in the end asked Ed for a steak. Retirement meant not having to eat buffalo tongues. She and her husband raised their goblets, which contained Dr Pepper instead of claret, to wish Beagan a safe journey.

'May you find your *Mer de l'Ouest*,' said Wellfit.

'*Ja*, but watch out for bears in the woods,' advised Gabi. 'And wild Indians too.'

*   *   *

Beagan smelt Thunder Bay before he saw it. The winds, which had blown heady wafts of pine resin twenty miles out into the lake, brought with them the acrid stench of pulp. It was pungent enough to bring tears to his eyes. The ripe odour of fermenting prairie wheat followed as the slender grain silos sprouted above the horizon. The *Tadoussac* eased herself into the Keefer Terminal and made fast beside the Saskatchewan Wheat Pool elevators. Beagan had not finished repacking the trunk, wrapping the family papers in waterproof plastic, before the loading pipes had been dropped over the open hatches and durum wheat poured into the hold.

Freight trains shunted back and forth along cat's-cradle rail lines spilling iron-ore pellets and potash. Grain took root between the ties. Beagan stepped ashore feeling restored, well fed by the Wellfits and, thanks to Ed, at least ten pounds heavier. He rented a room overlooking the port in a ubiquitous Mariner's Motel. The window had been welded shut to lock out the screech of the hopper cars' steel wheels. He didn't visit the site of the old trading post, which now lay under a railway marshalling yard, or catch the tourist ship *Welcome* to the replica Fort William at Pointe de Meuron. Instead he bought a six-pack of Miller Lite and watched a western on television. Outside the motel a trio of drunken Indians crumpled on to a park bench as if shot by a Hollywood cowboy. At the restaurant the waitress wore an off-the-shoulder dress with wired-hoop skirt and took orders for over-easy eggs. French fries were served with a tiny paper cup of ketchup. In the morning when he opened the bedroom curtains the *Tadoussac* had gone.

Beagan didn't stay long in the world's largest grain-handling port, but travelled the few miles south to the American border and Grand Portage. It was over this Great Carrying Place that Pierre Gaultier, the Sieur de la Vérendye, had climbed in 1731 in search of the Sea of the West. The thousands of voyageurs who had followed in his wake, hauling pelts and trade goods between the Great Lakes and the rivers of the western watershed, made Grand Portage the Nor'Westers' most thriving trading post. In contrast modern travellers tended to venture no further than the screens of the audio-visual presentation. They idled around the rebuilt stockade before driving up the hill to the Grand Portage Lodge. There they played slot machines and tried their hands at blackjack. The thriving casino had been built by the Chippewa and, being on their reservation, was exempt from state gambling laws. Big Bucks Bingo offered a $500,000 grand prize. Every morning a hopeful queue formed outside the gleaming glass doors. It was an opportunistic use of the white man's world to reclaim a subjugated culture. The profit enabled the Indian band to build Native schools and buy back the ancestral lands expropriated from their forefathers.

The climb was steep and the path overgrown but Beagan followed the snaking nine-mile portage past the Lodge, across Highway 61 and around the rapids to reach the lowest navigable section of the Pigeon River. There the wilderness outfitter met him and they slid the aluminium canoe into the waters of *Le Beau Pays*. They lowered the family trunk between the gunwales. As the pick-up drove back up the trail Beagan felt for a moment deserted, the silence he misconstrued as emptiness, the peace as paucity, but then the spirit of the woods gathered around him and he sensed that he was no longer alone.

THE WATER'S DARK mirror, oily black and polished bright, reflected earth and sky, drawing together the jack pine lands and the reeds of the riverbed. A flush of wood ducks fused into a shoal of fish. Clouds merged with polished rocks. Copper spruce boughs sighed in the breeze like a mermaid's hair adrift on the current. The canoe slipped across the burnished glass, paired with its reflection and became two dancers moving through intricate steps. Beagan knelt at the curved stern, rolled on the gentle swells, paddled with an inside flick of the blade and left with every stroke a trail of twisting whirlpools behind him. Waterbeetles skated across the surface like minute balls of mercury. A crow's caw echoed through a valley of wild blue iris. Around a curve of crimson waterlilies my son waded the sparkling shallows and lined along rapids. At a portage, marked in autumn by the conspicuous yellow leaves of the black ash, he hauled his canoe up on to the beach. The carrying trails often followed the small streams that ran between lakes and ash, red maple and white elm grew in the rich soil. He hiked along the tunnels through the woods, making three trips back and forth for canoe, pack and trunk, at ten places in the fifty miles between Superior and the Divide. At the Height of Land Portage Beagan crossed between North and South Lakes, from the Great Lakes to the Hudson's Bay watershed, and let the current draw him downstream towards the western sea.

It was water not earth which was the dominant element between Superior and muddy Lake Winnipeg. From the divide an intricate labyrinth of interconnected waterways flowed east to the Atlantic, west and north to the Arctic, south down the Mississippi to the Gulf of Mexico. The ridge-pole of the continent rose at an 1800-square-mile wilderness park of six hundred lakes, a thousand tangled rivers and countless unnamed streams. Quetico was an unchanging sanctuary of deep quiet, a place where angels flew overhead and the past could be easily felt.

'Its name,' stuttered my dad Jamie, 'is said to be an old Cree word.' He dug his paddle into the water and lifted up a splash of spray. 'It describes a benevolent spirit who dwelt in a place of great beauty.' He and the others had caught up with us after dawdling behind in Toronto to watch the caber-tossing finals at Caravan's Scottish pavilion. The contest had been won by a Pole named MacTier.

'I think you will find that it is an acronym for the Quebec Timber Company, James,' asserted uncle Zachary, his paddle lying across his lap. He sat in the bow of grand-dad

Hector's slender birchbark canoe dabbing the water off his evening dress. The apparel appeared somewhat incongruous against a mossy hillside of old firs.

The Reverend sat bolt upright at the stern, his legs folded beneath him Indian-style, collar tightly fastened and tartan cloak around his shoulders in spite of the heat. 'Quetico,' he said in his soft Gaelic accent, 'is a kind of Native pidgin for the French phrase *la quête de la côte*, the search for the coast. It is true enough that along these channels passed nearly every explorer looking for China.'

'Whatever the word means, the number one thing that I think about is its people,' I said, bringing up the rear in a rowing boat. The pulling of an oar was better suited to the bush than the putter of mechanical propulsion, so I had left *Primary* tied up to a mirage in Thunder Bay. 'Those Northmen for example, wiry little men dressed in breech-cloth and moccasins with a belted shirt and beaded tobacco pipe, ran all but the most dangerous rapids. What did they feel as their canoes plunged down some thundering shoot?'

'F-F-Fearful,' answered Jamie as we slipped into single file behind Beagan. 'Any jagged edge could tear the thin birchbark skin and suck the voyageurs into a watery grave. No fewer than thirty wooden crosses stood beside some rapids where their *camarades* had drowned.'

'Faithful,' pronounced Hector. 'Every Sabbath-day Alexander Mackenzie, the Scot who first crossed the continent by water, assembled his voyageurs beside their upturned canoes to listen to the Scriptures. In the most extraordinarily pronounced French he would convey three chapters out of the Old Testament and as many out of the New, adding explanation as seemed to him suitable. I read that over Beagan's shoulder, right enough.'

'If you will forgive me, Father, what they were most thankful for was their salary,' contested Zachary. 'It was the thought of money which sustained them through the eighteen-hour days and along the portages when each man carried a 180-pound load of trade goods with tump line and broad leather harness.'

'The devil has beguiled you, Zachary,' scolded Hector.

'They sang *chansons* as they paddled too,' volunteered Jamie, anxious as always to smooth over disagreement. 'Each verse was launched in solo then repeated in chorus North West f-f-fashion, timed to the rhythm of fifty strokes every minute. Somewhat faster than our pace today.'

'Their route was guided by memory and lob pines, tall spruces on high promontories which had been stripped of lower branches.' I pointed up to the evenly pinnacled tree-line. 'Back then the bristly tops stood out like destination signs along a highway. Next exit Lac la Croix, this lane only Lake of the Woods, turn left for the Rockies via the Saskatchewan River.'

'Isn't it grand to feel the world about you from a canoe, to hear the wind in the trees, to notice the shape of islands?' laughed Jamie as we sailed over silver spouts of white horses in the isolated and empty land.

'It is hard to believe now that the volume of early-nineteenth-century canoe traffic made Quetico one of the busiest regions of interior North America,' I said.

'Would that be true?' asked Hector without breaking his stroke.

'Quite true,' I replied. 'I used to tell Beagan and Alex that in 1821, after decades of vicious rivalry, the Nor'Westers amalgamated with the Hudson's Bay Company to create a fur trade empire which encompassed nearly three million square miles of territory.'

'It was a mercantile colony that spanned the continent from Labrador to Nootka Sound,' confirmed Zachary.

'There were trading posts as far south as San Francisco and above the Arctic Circle,' I added. 'And the vast empire was under the mastery of one man.'

'Sir George Simpson,' noted Zachary with a hint of envy

in his voice. 'He had been born in a manse on the Moray Firth and rose to become "head of the most extended Dominions in the known world – the Emperor of Russia, the Queen of England and the President of the United States excepted".'

'Didn't he inspect his domain in the f-f-finest canoe paddled by the most stalwart voyageurs?' asked Dad as we passed beneath glaciated humpback hills. 'I seem to recall that was one of your stories, Sandy. And that he was accompanied by a Scotch piper to herald his arrival at the scattered posts?'

'He was called "the little emperor", a shrewd, despotic, avaricious master of an almost uninhabited land,' I answered. 'But his monopoly over the waterways and beaver swamps ended with a change in fashion. Canada had been opened in a failed attempt to find a route to the Orient. It was a paradox that when the object of that quest reached Europe two centuries later it killed the enthusiasm for pelts.'

'I may say that I preferred the silk topper to a fur hat,' opined Uncle Zach.

'The trade collapsed and the beaver, which had been adopted as the national emblem, was replaced by the maple leaf.'

OF THE THOUSANDS of explorers and voyageurs who had paddled along Quetico's waterways, pausing to gum their canoes and breakfast on a sandy beach, only memory remained. The crosses and lob pines had gone. But it was said that ghosts stalked the portages and phantom brigades still moved across the lakes. In the slap of waves against a rocky shore Beagan heard the splash of paddles. A jay's cry became a voice in the next bay. The wind carried mellow voices singing *La Belle Rosier*. He made camp on a ledge scarred by the last ice age and shaped like the bow of a ship. He scrambled eggs, boiled up a pouch of freeze-dried scalloped potatoes and, after hoisting the food pack into a tree to deter inquisitive bears, opened the trunk to read by the firelight.

'They were hurled down with surprising velocity through three successive cascades,' the Nor'Wester Duncan McGillivray had written in his log-book. 'The canoe was several times overwhelmed with water and threatened every moment with being dashed to pieces in the windings of the rocks.' The words helped Beagan grasp at the past. 'It remained a considerable time under water. At length however the current drove it toward shore, with the men still hanging on after it, and though they at first seemed insensible, yet they recovered their strength and before night renewed their labours with as much alacrity as if nothing had happened to them.'

The intricate labyrinth of the waterway twisted through Crooked Lake, skipped across Thursday, Friday and Saturday Bays then wound into Lac la Croix. Its crystal waters reflected a shoreline of brooding spruce and silvery birch. Beagan met no other travellers along the looking-glass route so to keep himself company he tried to imagine that his mirror image was a fellow canoeist. But it wasn't Champlain or Brûlé whom he saw paddling beside him, it was the Reverend Hector. After a long moment of synchronous movement his great-grandfather turned towards him and bowed his head. Beagan nodded in return. With a great splash of spray the Peterborough lapstrake sprinted between them. Jamie wore his striped cap and britches and stretched forward with each stroke, splashing great showers of spray in his wake. 'Come on, you old men,' Beagan imagined him shouting from the next riverbend. 'Put a little effort into it.'

Beagan's picture of me was conjured up from an old photograph that he had found in the trunk. I was a boy under a folded paper hat, in sopping wet dockside shoes, with blisters on palm and inside fingers. My light cedar skiff was steered by rudder and tiller ropes rigged up with three electric bells to order the 'engine' ahead, astern or stopped. The two dogs rode with me; the mongrel at the bow and the snoozing Samoyed astern. My shirtsleeves were rolled up and my tie was splattered with grease. It always insisted on dangling in the bilges.

We fell into a line behind Beagan and rode the Namakan's first rapid of long, easy riffles then descended the froth of white water to the lower river. At High Falls and Lady Rapids, where sturgeon lay in the shallow bays, he turned around as if to check that we had not fallen behind or capsized in the swells, but we never strayed far from his trail. In fact the canoes seemed to be tethered to Beagan's stern as Zachary had lain back to read a newspaper and Reverend Hector had lost interest in the passing scene and began to study his Bible.

'Look F-F-Father, there's a moose,' called Jamie as an ungainly brown male raised its broad muzzle from a waterlily-root feed. 'Its name means "twig eater" in Algonquin.'

'"*Alces alces*" in the Latin,' said Hector.

'I shot one on Lake Temagami,' added Zachary, turning to the financial page.

A hen merganser with her chicks on her back shuttled across placid Rainy River, the misnomer for the old voyageur name *la Reine des Rivières*, Queen of Rivers. Our family flotilla eased down its broad brown waters, slipping between tall stands of bulrushes and golden rows of wild rice. Fat black ducks, heavy and sluggish from their gorging, rose reluctantly as we slid past. Their wings whispered over the boats.

'What did Canada promise you?' Beagan asked aloud. He had become accustomed to talking to himself but was unprepared to hear a response.

'In my day it was a promised land that we dreamed of building,' replied the Reverend without looking up from his reading.

Zachary put down his paper and shook his head. 'With all due respect, Father, you still speak as if the world were what you would have it to be, as if the ideal were real. Canada never promised a star-spangled dream.'

'But it was an admirable society, Zachary,' insisted Jamie. 'Why, any immigrant could buy a plot of land and become a home-owner within a generation.'

'It offered a place to work, no more no less,' continued Zachary. 'Any fool could succeed here.' He met my eye then raised the newspaper again to cut me out. 'Almost any fool.'

Beagan knew these thoughts. He had read them in our diaries and letters, yet it surprised him how loudly the words now echoed in his head.

'Hector is right: it *was* a promised land for the newcomer,' he heard me say, 'though only because emigration was for most a matter of necessity. A settler takes what he can get.'

'And thanks the good Lord for it.'

'The country provided a sanctuary, Sandy, and the value of that cannot be underestimated,' emphasised Jamie.

'I don't deny that, but what about her subsequent generations? How does the settled descendant fit into a place that changes to accommodate every newcomer, that becomes a land of the displaced?' I hoped that Beagan didn't detect the cynicism in my voice. 'I became a stranger in my own country.'

'Canada offered the same opportunities to one and all,' stuttered Jamie. 'And everyone came here f-f-for that same reason.'

'Everyone except the Scots,' interrupted Hector.

'What then brought the Scots?' hazarded Beagan. He was convinced that he was dreaming.

'We came looking for something more,' Hector answered. 'This was to be the land that Scotland could have been.'

'But this is no new Scotland,' I said.

'We dreamt of promised lands in a land which promised nothing.'

Beagan stared at us as if he didn't believe his own imagination, then turned and without another word paddled away.

It rained so heavily in the night that at dawn Beagan expected to see a dove fly past the tent, a maple leaf clamped in its beak, but instead swarms of mosquitoes rose up from the rockpools. A heavy mist veiled the far shore in half-colours. Columns of vapour rose out of the forest like the smoke from bonfires. Blue holes pierced the grey clouds as if poked out by divine fingers. He tried to make a pot of tea but there were no dry pine-needles to start a fire. The camping gas wouldn't light either. He sat on a stump and listened to the sough of the wind through the trees. As the mist lifted off the lake and extended our horizon beyond the edge of the island Beagan pushed away from shore.

We kept our distance over the next few days, lagging behind as he navigated through the maze of the Lake of the Woods, dragged his canoe over sandbars and made the short, easy carry from Portage Bay on to the Winnipeg. Once the river had been the grandest and most spectacular on the voyageurs' route to the west. Its waters had surged through tortured rock and dropped fast over roaring falls. But beyond the protective boundary of Quetico modern man had harnessed the wild grandeur and built six hydro-electric dams along the river's length. At Whitedog new channels had been blasted out and the old watercourse was a forlorn and stony emptiness. The Seven Sisters Dam had reduced tumbling rapids and green whirlpools to an idle narrows. Turbines whined within Pointe du Bois's concrete curtain and high-voltage pylons marched away to the city. The dancing river had been drowned beneath headponds and reservoirs and only beyond Pine Falls' reeking pulp mills did Nature reassert itself.

It was there at the edge between two worlds that we realised something too had changed in Beagan. Dad saw it first in his paddling. He dug the blade into the water, thrust the canoe forward and finished each stroke with a strong inside flick. Even Zachary noticed the new confidence, and complained at having to paddle harder to keep up with his great-nephew. After the power and material luxuries of his prosperous life he found the levelling nature of immortality to be a bit of a comedown. 'At least,' he puffed, 'he's no longer wasting time.'

It seemed that in the solitude of the woods Beagan had realised that he was not alone. He might not have felt a sense of belonging but he had understood the value of the journey. He had found the renewed strength too in knowing that we travelled beside him. We closed in upon him and he wrapped us around his shoulders as one would a coat in winter. The river broadened out and at the low misty line of Elk Island spilt into the coffee-coloured lake that the Cree called *Winnipee*.

IN THE OPEN prairie towns of arrow-straight streets and wind-swept bungalows visitors were welcomed with a wary question. 'You going any further?'

'I'm heading for the Pacific,' Beagan answered.

'Oh, you'll love the mountains,' the locals sighed, relieved that their town was not someone's final destination.

Everyone in Manitoba was on the way to somewhere else. Winnipeg had always been a place through which travellers passed. The Native people had long paused to trade at the junction of the Red and Assiniboine rivers. The French explorers had paddled through the Forks *en route* to *le Mer de l'Ouest*. The Scots were the first migrants mad enough to try to settle the wide, sleepy banks. They endured plagues of locusts and winter starvation in hipped-roof houses of rigid symmetry. When the trans-continental railway passed by in 1881 it brought with it an illusion of permanence. A million settlers poured through Union Station, agriculture became the backbone of the economy and citizens bragged that Winnipeg was destined to be 'the Chicago of the Prairies'. At the turn of the century no other Canadian city boasted a greater value of building permits. The Electric Railway Chambers glittered above the skyline, its Italianate exterior columns illuminated by six thousand lightbulbs. The lofty Lindsay Building was decorated with bulging cornucopias of English roses, Scotch thistles and Irish shamrocks. On Portage Avenue the elegant Paris Tower soared eleven stories high to elaborate cornice motifs of teeming immigrant galleons. But Winnipeg's fleeting fortune ended with the First World War. Newcomers stopped homesteading on the plains. The Panama Canal enabled eastern goods to bypass the railway and reach western markets by sea. The crash of 1929 preceded an intense drought which ruined farmers. The grounds of the neo-classical Legislative Building were ploughed for vegetable gardens to feed the city's poor. After forty optimistic years winsome Winnipeg returned to being a stopping place; people came, stayed for a while then moved on.

'I never knew a Kristjanson who wasn't a fisherman,' shouted Marvin Kristjanson above the hiss of his diesel. He gestured at the dozen blond children playing on the deck of the *Hekla*. 'They'll all be fishermen too if there are any fish left.' Across Lake Winnipeg's horizon the peaks of whitecaps looked like the furls of distant sails. The broad-beamed, steel-plated whitefish boat churned north through the caramel swells towards a funeral.

In town that morning Beagan had freighted the canoe back to the Thunder Bay outfitter and gone looking for a boat. At first he hadn't found one. In the tourist bureau he learnt that the passenger steamers and shipping lines had been replaced by eight-wheeled tractor trailers and provincial highways. Commercial vessels no longer plied the world's twelfth-largest lake. His only option had been the sightseeing riverboat MS *Paddlewheel Queen* which ran the few miles downriver to Selkirk. It at least headed in the right direction. There, at the end of the line and behind a giant 'Chuck the Channel Catfish' statue, he had found the Marine Museum of Manitoba. Five beached ships lay on the grass beside a parking lot. None of them would be puffing him up the lake to Grand Rapids. Beagan had bought a hot dog from the A&W on Main Street and eaten it in the shade of the SS *Keenora*. As he considered his next move a blond boy with hooded sky-blue eyes appeared beside him bearing a slice of *vinaterta*, a rich multi-layered Icelandic prune cake. 'Grandpa's gone to heaven,' he announced by way of introduction. 'And now we're sailing there too in his old boat.'

Towards the end of the last century a series of severe earthquakes and volcanic eruptions laid waste parts of Iceland. Hundreds of refugees were forced to leave the island and look for a better life in the New World. On the western shore of Lake Winnipeg they founded Gimli, or heavenly abode. The site offered an abundance of heavy timber, good farmland and, most importantly, fish. The Native people taught them how to set nets under the ice and in summer they built fishing stations around the lake. In 1878 'New Iceland' was officially established and for twenty years no other nationality was permitted to settle within the reserve. The community thrived, until there were more people of Icelandic descent living around Winnipeg than in Reykjavik. But overfishing depleted the stocks on which their prosperity had been built. Mercury pollution poisoned the waters. Wall-eye and pickerel no longer enriched the heavenly abode.

The slice of *vinaterta* drew Beagan to a picnic wake. On his father's death Marvin Kristjanson had gathered together his scattered siblings and their children. At the Marine Museum they ate peanut butter and jelly sandwiches and then clambered over the old man's boat. Little Inga, her hair tied into plaits, tugged at her uncle's hand. 'You said that Opa's gone to heaven.' Kristjanson had been trying to explain death to the children. 'Is heaven near Gimli?'

He introduced Beagan to his family. 'This here is Inga and those are her brothers Thor, Gusti and Stefan. Gusti's the one who brought you the cake. Magnus and Johanna are in the wheelhouse. Over there are my three: Dayna, Brett and Tom. Bjorgvin has gone to the little boys' room and Geiri has as usual disappeared.'

Kristjanson's sister was attempting to rub a grape-jelly stain out of Thor's shirt.

'And will Gusti die?' the five-year-old asked his mother.

'Yes, dear,' she replied, dabbing the cloth in water.

'And will Johanna die?'

'Yes, she will too.'

'Will I die, Mummy?'

'Yes, Thor.'

'When?'

'In about sixty or seventy years.'

Thor knotted his brow. 'Will you die, Mummy?'

'Yes, me too.'

'When?' he persisted.

'In about forty or fifty years.'

'Is that a longer time?'

'No, shorter.'

'But when we've all died who will sail in Opa's boat?'

The hull was well suited to the lake's fickle weather. It was deep and long and reminded Beagan of his own father's last boat and the final, fiery journey aboard her. 'Going together to the funeral by boat is to honour him,' Kristjanson explained as they stowed the box trunk in the hold among the children's sleeping bags. There were no old lottery tickets pinned to the cabin wall. 'I'm sure he'd be happy if we took you along with us to Grand Rapids too.'

The *Hekla* cruised up the low-lying shore past Hnausa, Calder's Dock and Fisher Bay. Anvil-headed kingfishers perched above driftwood beaches and sandy coves. Crows as big as Christmas turkeys cast great black cloaks high on their backs. On board the children drew crayon pictures of a lake filled with fish. Johanna felt sick and Bjorgvin asked if grandfather was alone in heaven.

'No, Oma is with him,' answered his mother.

'My father used to say, "If he's a good fisherman, he's a good man."' Kristjanson gestured away to the north-east and told Beagan, 'He and his brothers came this way every May. They'd spend the summer at their station on George Island, living in a bunkhouse, gill-netting from catboats. The *Lady of the Lake* called in every other week to freight the fish back to Gimli. Now the few of us that are left don't go out for more than a day at a time.'

From his wallet Kristjanson produced a frayed photograph of a bright-eyed old man wrapped in a hooded snowsuit. His thick moustache was silvered by frost. On his feet he wore ice creepers, galoshes inset with steel blades which enabled walking during a winter gale. 'My father made the best damn ice jiggers on the lake. An Indian taught him. You lever the jigger under the ice then set the net. He and his brothers would haul the catch on sleighs to Riverton – 225 boxes in a load, each box with 140 pounds of fish. It was hard work but he loved it. He loved what he could make. "If you want your dreams to come true," he used to say to me, "first you have to wake up." Most folks now just stay asleep.' Kristjanson laughed and waved his hand over the sea of blond heads. 'But look at us. He made us all.'

Brett wanted to know where Opa had gone. 'Well,' said Kristjanson, 'he's moved on. He's gone to the next room.' Brett looked confused. Kristjanson tried to explain. 'You know that you and Dayna and Tom live in a big apartment block with people on the floors above and below.' The child nodded. 'Let's pretend that you have magic powers and can see through the walls and floors and ceilings. You can see me in the kitchen, Tom playing in his bedroom . . .'

'Mummy on the toilet?' said Brett and giggled.

'Old Mr Sigurdson upstairs and Oma . . .'

'But Oma's dead.'

'Yes, that's right Brett,' said Kristjanson, 'but with your magic powers you can see her – and Opa too – in the next room.'

'Telling stories?'

'Probably.' He smiled. 'Now can you imagine that all our family, everyone here and everyone who has died, lives there in our building?'

'Someone flushed the toilet last night and I thought it might be Opa,' said Tom.

'Well, it might have been. And just because we can't really see through walls doesn't mean that it wasn't Opa, does it? He's probably in the next room now, talking to Oma and *his* Opa, watching you, making sure that you're good and waiting to come and help you whenever you need him.' A hint of a smile played on Beagan's lips.

North of Dancing Point sheer rockfaces rose up from the water-line. Spires of pine stretched away beyond the horizon. *Hekla* tramped past isolated villages that clung to the shore, strung together by freight canoes. Telephones were so few and far between that they were marked on provincial maps. Beagan turned on his portable radio but heard only static. Beneath the high blue sky he felt again the immensity of the vast northland where a thousand miles can lie between settlements and there are tracts of tundra on which no man will ever stand.

'Most days the lake's like a spoiled child in tantrums,' said Kristjanson, casting his eye over the placid waters. 'We're lucky, the weather's good today. Winnipeg's shallow, which makes for steep-fronted, choppy waves, and there're almost no islands to break the prairie winds.'

Beagan had noticed that the few small islands along their route were uninhabited, yet were spanned by wide gravel highways. The roads appeared to come up out of the water, strike straight across to the far shore then plunge back beneath the waves. It was as if the world had been flooded and only the highest mac-adamed hilltops showed above the surface. Kristjanson explained that as no roads penetrated the lake's wild eastern shore many communities had been cut off after the demise of shipping. To supply them the government had decided to build winter highways across the ice. Every December huge graders, great roaring Cyclopses with single flashing blue eyes, ploughed aside cascades of snow like a northern Moses dividing the frozen waters of a white sea. In their wake sped oil tankers and heavy transports laden with a year's provisions. In the spring break-up the ice roads melted away and left only the traversed islands.

Two great rivers meet at the head of Lake Winnipeg: the wild

Nelson flowing north-east into Hudson's Bay and the now sedate Saskatchewan which meanders down from the Rockies, across three prairie provinces and drains a watershed twice the size of Britain. The *Hekla* tacked into her wide, smiling mouth and disturbed a regal procession of waterbirds. A dozen cormorants took off as one, lifting themselves up on to the surface then running into flight. The pelicans followed, their black wingtips beating out semaphore signals as they lumbered into an elegant glide.

The whitefish boat came ashore at Lover's Point Park, once Hudson's Bay Wharf, the lower terminal of the derelict Grand Rapids tramway. The first railway in western Canada had been built around the gorge in 1877 to carry passengers and freight in horse-drawn cars between the lake steamers and Saskatchewan paddle-wheelers. But modern travellers preferred the southern highways and the thundering river had been silenced by a great curtain of broken stone and concrete. The rapids over which canoes and fur-traders' cumbersome York boats had been dragged hummed at sixty cycles per second. Manitoba Hydro's dam had rendered meaningless the waterway's original Cree name *Kis-is-ska-tche-wan*, 'the river which flows swiftly'.

In the tail-race terns and shags, their wings dipping below their bodies, swooped into the froth to scoop up beakfuls of fish. Gulls paddled on the surface, lifted now and again by the swells washed out from the generators. Kristjanson cut his engine and the parents who had driven north caught hold of the lines. The children jumped on to the dock, excited by the memory of holidays with Grandfather. Every summer vacation he had led them down moose-track trails, over shining white sands and built match-stick Viking longboats. He had tied to their waists two-quart jars which they filled with raspberries, blueberries and sweet pear Saskatoons. But their laughter stilled to a hush at the sight of the old man laid out in a tired, shuttered bungalow.

'Death is not an end,' Kristjanson reassured Beagan. 'We have split life into two parts far too drastically. It is important that the children understand that the dead don't leave us, they precede us.'

'When I die,' Bjorgvin asked his uncle, 'can I be buried with Hoppy?' The boy clutched his one-eared, fluffy toy rabbit to his chest.

Beagan left the family to their mourning and followed the sound of digging to the small cemetery. Two young Crees had opened up a new plot for the old fisherman but had left the graveyard grass uncut. Beagan sat on a boulder dislodged during the blasting of the power station and saw the boys' high cheekbones, crescent-moon eyes and small pointed chins. To his shame he realised that apart from Gogo, whose compassion lived on in the pages of Hector's journal, the only Native people whom he knew were the primped squaw adorning summer-blue packs of Land o' Lakes unsalted butter and the befeathered chief logo of the Red Indian Mini-Cab Company ('We're no cowboys'). The painted names on the wooden crosses told him too of his arrival at a new frontier. Beneath the willows rested Cyril Mamageesick, Angus Ducharme, Donty Holowachuk and Rusty Vigfusson, names part-immigrant, part-indigenous in a borderland where European influence waned. Away to the north and west lay an ancient land with traditions and customs which stretched back thousands of years. The modern nation-state that had been threaded over it was like a tenuous spider's web through which the wind whispered.

CHAPTER IX

———•———

WHERE ANGELS BATHE

'CALL ME AL,' said Corporal Alan Sutherland and let go of the patrol boat's wheel to shake Beagan's hand. He was a slender, soft-spoken Mounted Policeman from The Pas detachment a hundred miles upstream. 'I'm glad I could help out.' His curls, so red that they would clash with the cochineal RCMP dress uniform, were flattened by the breeze. 'Grand Rapids is outside our division but I had to come down to look for Harold Finn – again.' He gestured at the black Avon inflatable raft tugging at the end of a tow rope. Its intoxicated owner lay asleep on the patrol boat's deck with his head craned over the trunk. 'Third time he's got lost this season, but, hey,' Al confided with a boyish smile, 'anything's better than office paperwork.'

The lip of the dam dropped away behind them as the outboard sped west across the headpond. Silver driftwood from the drowned forest cluttered the swampy shore. Rotting branches reached above the surface. Cedar Lake was a shallow, man-made reservoir of dead-end channels and switchback passages but Al knew the route and followed the Saskatchewan's current as it wound beneath the surface.

Beagan had recognised the Scottish surname and asked if Al knew his family's history.

'We go way back,' enthused the Mountie. 'My grandmother came out from Leeds to run the school and teach the Indians how to use a knife and fork. It was my father's people who came from Scotland,' he confirmed. 'You heard about the Red River Settlement?'

'Yes,' answered Beagan. 'In 1811 the Scottish peer Lord Selkirk was granted land to establish the North-West's first colony. About ninety people, mostly Highland crofters from Sutherland and some emigrants from the west of Ireland, were sent here by way of Hudson's Bay.'

'My folks came over on the second ship. They took one look at the blue swamp, the spruce and tamarack and decided to head south before freeze-up. They weren't going to spend the winter in log tents at York Factory.' Al eased back on the throttle to skirt a deadhead. The drunk groaned in his sleep. 'So they just started walking, pulling their boats up the Nelson, hauling their freight over the thirty-four portages and going near on seven hundred miles. Well sir, it was one cruel journey. They lost most of the old people. Then, just north of here at Cross Lake, they turned right instead of left and got lost. The snows came, their food ran out and they started to starve. If it hadn't been for the Moose Lake Indians they would all have died. The tribe's hunters heard the weeping of the women and children and helped them to survive the winter.' Al swung the boat out of the marshland and into the river. A flush of teals scattered out of its path. A beaver slapped his tail and vanished into the swirling water. 'I went up one weekend to the place where they were found. They still call it Crying Island.'

Nine years after the Highlanders' arrival John West, the newly-appointed Hudson's Bay Company chaplain, had followed to establish the Church of England in Rupert's Land, the richest fur region in the Empire. 'Thousands are involved in worse than Egyptian darkness around me, wandering in ignorance and per-ishing through lack of knowledge,' he had written. 'When will this wide waste of howling wilderness blossom as the rose in the desert and become a fruitful field?' West had prayed for his strug-gling colony of Kildonan settlers and dispossessed fur traders who, while living on pemmican and hope, aspired to establish a farming community. 'May a gracious God hear their cry and raise them up as heralds of His salvation in this truly benighted and barbarous part of the world.'

Beagan glanced astern and tried to catch sight of Hector's canoe.

He could imagine him pausing to wrap his Bible in oilcloth, reflecting for a moment on similar histories.

'They were terrible years,' confessed Al. 'But having lived through them is something we're real proud of.'

'But didn't you want to move on?' asked Beagan, shivering at the memory of the bucket of live coals that had warmed his great-grandfather's pulpit.

'Nope. The experience taught my family to respect the land, and even to learn to love it.'

Ashen trunks clung to white dolomite cliffs. In places forest fires had charred the shore and toppled copses of hoary trees like a giant's spillikins. The patrol boat glided over the silty waters, described a wide arc and slid under the metal-grid bridge into The Pas. The town had grown up at the confluence of the Sas-katchewan and Pasquia rivers where migrating geese had paused to feed and travellers found a sheltered berth. The birds still came every autumn, filling the delta with their cackle and hiss, but Beagan was the first stranger to arrive by water in a year. There were no vessels to be seen, nothing to carry him further up the Saskatchewan, unless the flat-bottomed riverboat *Skippy L* could be unbolted from its concrete plinth in Kelsey Park and relaunched.

A good policeman can sense people's thoughts and as Al eased up to the dock he nodded at the drunk. 'Harold here came down the river a few years ago. He's the only person I know who's done it.' He secured the painter then pulled the inflatable up on the shore. 'You should discuss your trip with him – when he's sober. Rise and shine, Mr Finn,' said the Mountie, shaking Harold's shoulder. 'You're back home.'

A single bloodshot eye strained open and gazed over the gun-wale. 'As sure as there's shit in a dead cat that ain't Fortune.' The eye snapped shut. The accent sounded like Irish that had been soaked by four centuries of bad weather. Harold Finn was from Newfoundland.

'No, Harold, it's The Pas. You're home in The Pas.'

'Oh Lord jeez, will I never get off this damn prairie?' His eyes sprung open and started at Beagan. 'I've been here so long looks like I'm becoming a tourist attraction,' he moaned. 'What you doing here, b'y? You lost?' Al explained that the two men had a journey in common, all be it back to front, and asked Harold to help put Beagan on the right track. The drunk heaved himself up on to his feet and swayed to port. 'Anybody who don't listen to Al here is three sandwiches short of a picnic.' Beagan looked at the wizened face, the scruff of hair and the beef-red nose swollen like a dory's bow and concluded that all he would learn from the whiplash-thin Newfie were the directions to the nearest liquor store. 'You'd better come home with me then, b'y. We'll talk while Lily rustles us up some supper.'

As they carried the trunk along Fischer Avenue Beagan asked if any craft still went up the Saskatchewan. 'Upstream?' exclaimed Harold, talking at the speed of a force-nine gale. 'You can't go upstream no more.' They turned into a side street and veered through a back gate. 'There used to be one heck of a lot of boats on the river – packets, tubs, queen and tramp steamers that sailed all the way to Edmonton – but only local fishers use the river now. They run their outboards up aways to a favourite fishing hole then hurry back home for supper. Natives use it for sure, but only on social visits to nearby reserves. Hydro went and built a dam on every babbling brook and the old ships, hell, they been dragged around to the far side of the island and dynamited. Anybody wants to go upriver nowadays he gets in a car and drives.'

The back door was open but the bungalow felt empty. Harold breezed along the corridor, called out a woman's name and pulled two bottles of Labatt's from the cooler. 'Forget about going west, b'y,' he advised, leaning so close that Beagan could smell stale breath. 'Come down east with me. It's clear sailing all the way to the Bay and home to Newfoundland.'

'Isn't it a bit late in the year to cross Hudson's Bay?' asked Beagan. Churchill, the country's main northern port, and Polar Bear Capital of the World, was frozen in for all but the few months of high summer.

'Got to get back soon, eh? I got no passport. So if Quebec up and separates I'll be stuck here for good, and I don't belong here in this dustbowl. B'y, when we get down home we'll put into a cove with a flat of beer, jig a fish and drop it in a boiler with some potatoes.' He leaned back in his chair and sighed. 'That's where I was heading just now, until I went and got lost in the Cedar delta. Third damn time this year.'

The mention of food reminded Harold that he was hungry. He set to work making Jiggs dinner, pulling foil-wrapped salt and roast beef from the refrigerator, peeling turnip, carrot, cabbage and potatoes, throwing the lot into a cast-iron pot.

'I been trying to get back to Fortune Harbour for as long as I can remember. I'm a plumber, eh? There weren't no work in Newfoundland so I got a job up in the Arctic. I was the only plumber in a thousand miles but, I tell you, it was some cold. Eskimos say that there are only two seasons in the north: winter and the first of July. Houses up there, they got two big tanks: one for water, the other for waste. If the heating packs in the sewer tank freezes up, and where do you go for a crap in the tundra? Ain't no trees to hide behind.' Harold grabbed two more beers from the fridge. 'One time I got a call to fix this leaking bath in an Inuit house. The government built them new housing and there were always an odd nut wanting tightening, eh? Well, I turned up to find that this Eskimo had killed a caribou and while chopping it up in the tub had axed clean through the fibreglass.' Harold laughed as the house filled with the rich aroma of cooking. He enjoyed the sound of his own stories. 'The money was good but it weren't home, so I hitched a ride to Hay River, bought the inflatable and started to work my way back. When I reached The Pas I met Lily. She was as welcome as a flower in May and, b'y, I got her some pregnant. So now it seems the good Lord won't let me leave.' Harold emptied his bottle in one swallow and reached for another. 'Don't get me wrong, this is a nice town. The people are friendly and I like to watch them bringing in the wheat, but most mornings when I come out and look up at the sky I think, "Another grey day." I sort of wish my cake was still dough.'

It took a dozen beers for Beagan to convince Harold of his need to continue the westward journey. 'Maybe it's too late to go east this year anyways,' Harold admitted. 'For sure I'd end up getting frozen in at Churchill.' He wandered away for a moment, blew open the other doors in his bungalow, dawdled outside the bedroom, then returned. 'Tell you what, b'y. Seems Lily has gone off to her folks' place, not that I can blame her. If you buy gas and the beer I'll run you upriver in the inflatable. It won't take no time to get to Edmonton, and I could do some shopping.' As Harold warmed to his theme his voice began to boom. 'We'll drink lots of brew and tell a few yarns. It'll be great crack.' It was an offer that Beagan could hardly refuse. Six hundred long, wet, ferry-free miles lay between him and the city at the edge of the Rockies. 'But there's one condition, eh?' added Harold.

'What's that?'

'No wisecracks.' Newfoundlanders were to other North Americans what the Irish were to the English and the people of Kerry to other Irishmen. 'Except this one: what's black and blue and floats in the bay?' Beagan shook his head. 'A mainlander after telling a Newfie joke.'

At dawn iron stormclouds weighed on the horizon. The sky was a cold, thin winter blue. A skein of geese rippled south calling to each other as they flew. Harold and Beagan carried the supplies down to the dock and smelt frost in the air. They bolted the Evinrude on to the Avon. A gaudy bumper sticker dangling from its stern read, 'Don't follow me – I'm going to Hell.' Harold yanked the cord but the outboard refused to start. 'This damn motor's two days older than God,' he complained then hit it with a boot. It still wouldn't start. Harold checked that the fuel line was clear and the plugs were clean. He pulled on the starting cord until he broke into a sweat. The Newfoundlander paused to catch his breath then embraced the Evinrude and whispered endearments into its carburettor. It started first pull. 'Just like a woman,' Harold confided to Beagan. 'You got to treat her right.'

The Saskatchewan cut a broad arc across the northern prairies, twisting and turning through the rich alluvial soil. Its brown current babbled over sandy shoals, shifted gravel bars overnight and washed away muddy islands in a season. A red-tailed hawk peered from a lazy willow. Wood ducks nested in old woodpecker holes. For the first hundred miles there were no houses along the shore, apart from the odd cluster of tarpaper shacks used by passing moose hunters, and the inflatable ran easily alongside the secluded banks of aspen and blood-red sumach. Jamie will have to raise a spread of sail above the Peterborough to keep up, thought Beagan, anxious that his imagined companions not fall too far behind. But across the unmarked provincial border the silty river opened into the marshland of Cumberland Lake and the Avon's swift progress faultered.

'Hey b'y,' Harold shouted above the drone of the motor, 'Why is Canada like Christopher Columbus?' The blustery Newfoundlander had stopped singing shanties to concentrate on navigating between the weed beds. 'Because he didn't know where he was going, didn't know where he was when he got there, didn't know where he'd been when he got home, and all the time he was paid by the government.' Harold roared at his joke. 'That's us for sure, except you're not collecting unemployment.' The outboard screamed. 'Well sod me rigid,' he yelled. 'This Evinrude is as useless as tits on a nun.' Every few moments he had to tilt his outboard. 'The big trouble is that box of yours,' Harold complained as he cleared off the propeller. 'Makes us too low in the water and we snare all these frigging weeds. What's in the damn thing? Gold bars?'

'Papers,' said Beagan. He snapped open the trunk and after digging among the plastic sacks extracted his father's naval tin hat and a box of fold-back clips. 'Family papers.'

'Can you tip any of them out? We'd sure make some good speed then.'

'If they go, I go,' replied Beagan. He attached the clips around the edge of the helmet to fashion a sort of bomb-proof colander. 'There,' he said handing it to Harold.

'You expecting trouble, b'y?' Harold scanned the sky for a stray Messerschmidt.

'It's a prop guard,' explained Beagan. 'Tie it in front of the propeller. It should deflect the grasses.'

Through the long afternoon the Avon twisted and turned around the dense fields of reeds. In places they grew as tall as walls and divided the waters into channels like unmarked streets. The shadows began to lengthen and Harold's humour sank with the sun. Beagan too was quiet, listening to the rustle of the grasses. 'Are we lost?' he asked.

'Hell no,' chirped Harold. 'There'll be a bus along any minute.' His bravado sounded hollow.

A narrow passage opened up between the beds and the reeds whispered in the breeze. 'I think we should turn left here.'

'You been down this way before, b'y?' cracked Harold as he cruised past the entrance. 'The main channel goes straight on.'

'My great-grandfather was handy with a sextant,' said Beagan. 'And I have a hunch.'

'Maybe he went and left us a compass in the box too?' Harold had left his charts on top of the refrigerator in The Pas, and they had been forced to navigate from a voyageur canoe map which Beagan had found in the bottom of the trunk. 'At least it'd be newer than this old thing.' He steered on in silence for a moment, then turned the outboard so suddenly that the propeller broke the surface and lifted a rainbow of spray over the boat. 'Oh Lord jeez,' cursed Harold as he doubled back and slipped into the passage. 'What I wouldn't give now to drown myself in a beery bucket of brew.' A minute later a line of low buildings rose up beyond the flats. 'For sure that's Cumberland House,' he declared, his spirits restored by the thought of a drink. 'It's been here since Noah was an oakum picker.'

Cumberland House, the oldest permanent settlement in the west, had been the Hudson's Bay Company's first inland trading post. Established on Pine Island in 1774 it lay at the crossroads of the fur-trade waterways; to the east ran the routes to York Factory and Montreal, from the north down the Churchill came the fine pelts of Athabasca and to the west out along the Saskatchewan were the great plains which supplied the dried bison meat on which the voyageurs depended for their subsistence. Tribes were drawn in from the surrounding lands to live around the post which at its peak stored and distributed furs and food for half a continent. But with the collapse of the trade and the departure of the white man the outside world forgot Cumberland House. Until 1945 the Natives had no permanent government representative, other than a nurse. It was 1967 before a road reached the village. The first telephone wasn't installed until 1971.

Beagan and Harold came ashore on a boggy marsh and walked inland past the old wharf. With the construction of the E. B. Campbell Dam the lake level had dropped and boats had to be moored away from the village in the myriad of shifting channels. On the dusty main street the windowless brick blockhouse Northern store sold silk plants and shotgun shells, plastic picnic sets and double leg-hold muskrat traps, fluorescent bingo markers and Deep Woods insect repellent. Two boys tried to choose a birthday card. Should it be the Indian Heritage series or Teenage Mutant Ninja Turtle? At the counter the manager and a slight, dark man in a baseball cap bartered a few steaks for a load of gravel. Outside the shop the town's residents perched on benches in the sun. Most were *Métis*, the offspring of Cree women and the original white traders who had been joined in *mariage à la façon du pays*.

'My name's McKay,' said a tawny-skinned red-haired fisherman, introducing himself to Beagan. 'My cousin over there he's a Macaulay, and that's Hilyard McKenzie who operates the cable ferry over the river. There are a lot of McKenzies in Cumberland.' The explorer Alexander Mackenzie had passed through the post in 1793 on his way to the Pacific. 'We don't know exactly what he got up to here, but we can guess,' added McKay. A chuckle rolled down the benches like a wave along a beach.

One would have expected the years of isolation to have made Cumberland House a desolate place adrift in the weed beds but it wasn't the case. The children emerged from Charlebois School filling the street with bustle and games. Jessie McKenzie led Harold through the throng to buy fuel at the Hems and McKenzie Gas Bar. Beagan was passed on to Virginia McKay, the town's amateur historian. She and the recreation director, Cyril Goulet, talked in Cree and laughed softly as they led him down a path in the bush to a clearing among the birches.

'The experts in Regina wouldn't believe me,' she said, recalling her discovery of the site of the original fort. 'They said I had only found a church and that it was not important. So I filled a pail full of old glass and china to send to them, you know, but my husband left it in the office and the janitor threw it out thinking it was junk.' Nevertheless Virginia had hounded the archaeologists until they agreed to examine the compound. Beneath the mounds of mossy stones they had found the old stockade, crumbled fire-places, moose bones and Hudson's Bay Company buttons. 'Not only didn't they thank us but they took all the artefacts away with them for dating. They only left our museum a barrel of bullets and a snowshoe needle. Maybe I should have just kept quiet about the fort.' On the walk back to Cyril's pick-up Beagan asked Virginia what the Native people had called the land before the arrival of the white man. 'Ours,' she replied.

In town they stopped to collect Harold and their supplies. The Newfoundlander looked crestfallen. 'There's no beer in town, b'y,' he whispered to Beagan during the drive out to the boat. 'Not even Molson's.'

'THE NEW ELDORADO, that's what they called it,' I said as we slipped through dawn's will-o'-the-wisp. 'Do you remember? "The Last Best West".'

'"This is your opportunity, why not embrace it?" is what the old immigration posters used to say,' added Jamie. He was tucked out of the wind beside Beagan, his hand on his shoulder, reading my book on the early homesteaders. The Peterborough tugged behind us on a fanciful towline. Hector stood on the bow and threw up his sextant for sights while Uncle Zach wrestled with the lunar tables. Harold Finn sat astern at the engine scratching a mosquito bite and humming 'Hurrah for Our Own Native Isle', a near-forgotten Newfoundland anti-confederation song.

The night had been dry not only because of the lack of alcohol. The volume of water released by the Campbell Dam varied considerably and travellers had been known to wake in the morning to find that their canoe had been carried away by a rising river. So Harold had pitched the tent well up the shore but the precaution hadn't given Beagan any extra sleep. My son had been awoken long before daybreak by the screech of fervent singing. Like his forefathers he preferred mornings when the Newfie had a hangover. They tended to be quieter.

'Do you remember the fear that America would seize the western provinces?' I asked Dad. The inflatable spun the rising river mist into a twisting, conical funnel. 'They called it their Manifest Destiny, the God-given right to occupy the whole continent.'

'Yes, that was in my day,' recalled Jamie. 'The prime minister John A. Macdonald said of the Prairies, "I would be quite willing to leave that whole country a wilderness for the next half-century, but I f-f-fear that if English men do not go there, Yankees will."'

'Sir John A. Yes; I met him in Ottawa,' said Zachary. 'An energetic man.' He laid down the tables then leaned against the inflatable's rubber freeboard, letting grains of sand slip through his fingers. With his other hand he tried to catch them before they fell into the water. 'He would have preferred to develop the east first, building up industry there, concentration being Emerson's secret of strength in politics and trade.'

Along the shore the vast undernourished forest resembled

the stubble on an old man's chin. As the sun rose above the treetops it burned through the haze and Harold stopped humming and began to sing.

'Ye brave Newfoundlanders who plough the salt sea
With hearts like the eagle so bold and so free,
The time is at hand when you'll all have to say
If Con-fed-eration will carry the day.'

'It was the Americans who least relished a united Canada,' I said, raising my voice to be heard above the din, 'even less than the insular Newfoundlanders.'

'It would have been f-f-far simpler for the Yanks to annex the disunited parts one by one.'

'Sir John and his ministers, the Fathers of Confederation as they call them now, saw the need to people the uninhabited interior. They led the call for the "stalwart peasant in a sheepskin coat with a stout wife and a half-dozen chickens". Quite right too; the need was urgent, even if the drive west did dilute our resources.'

'Listen to this, Harold,' said Beagan, interrupting both his great-uncle's reminiscences and the Newfie's singing. 'The government gave every homesteader who came west a quarter section – that's 160 acres – for only ten dollars.'

'B'y, you can't buy a sixpack of cold ones for that these days. Hand me that rope there, will you? I think I'll go hang myself.'

'That's how the river came to be opened up, so the settlers could reach the virgin prairie.' Beagan stabbed at the book that he had found in the trunk. 'That's why they built the river-boats.'

'Jeez,' blustered Harold, 'there's a thought.'

'In the decade before the completion of the promised trans-continental railroad,' Beagan read aloud, 'a fleet of spark-belching, twin-stacked paddle-wheelers plied the Saskatchewan. This would fascinate my father.'

'And his f-f-father too.'

'They were lovely puffing leviathans,' I agreed with Jamie, indulging our shared enthusiasm. 'Swirling steam and wood smoke, ferrying settlers, forges and church organs upriver.'

'And bringing down wheat, timber and furs for trade,' added Zachary. 'They established the essential commercial infrastructure of the west.'

'They blew the whistle so loud that they made the very cattle rear up their heels and take to full gallop.' Beagan recited the observations of the Reverend Henry Budd, missionary at The Pas, which had been written in 1874 on the maiden voyage of the *Northcote*. 'Not only the cattle but people of all ages and sexes were no less excited by the sight of the boat, the first boat of the kind to be seen by them all their life; in fact, the first steamboat going in this river since the Creation.'

'Aye, true enough,' said Hector, not lowering his eye from the sextant. 'There were none before it.'

'The Native people called them *Ku . . . Kuska Pah . . . ,*' struggled Beagan.

'*Kuska Pahtewoosi*,' corrected Harold. 'It means fire canoes, b'y. Lily taught me the word, eh?' He chuckled a raunchy rumble. 'Along with a few others that would make your hair curl. If you had more that is.'

'To what is this sea-dog sinner referring?' asked Hector, his worst suspicions aroused.

'To the tortuous route up from Grand Rapids to the Rocky Mountain foothills,' I suggested as Harold narrowly avoided a shifting bank, his mind distracted by tender thoughts of Lily. 'There were twenty separate sets of rapids, dozens of sandbars and innumerable horseshoe bends. Each boat was equipped with hawsers to winch it up stubborn currents and stout crutch-like spars to lever it through shallows.'

'I may say that they weren't particularly reliable,' affirmed Zachary. 'You couldn't set your watch by them.'

'Time?' barked Hector, taking his sight and consulting

the almanac. 'Come along, Zachary, it is difficult enough without having a rotator log towed astern.'

Zachary shook his pocket watch. 'Two minutes past six,' answered Jamie, peeking at Beagan's wristwatch.

'During spring run-off the *Northcote* could carry fifty passengers and 150 tons of cargo up to Fort Edmonton in two weeks. But at drier times,' I conceded, 'the schedule did tend to be irregular. On some journeys wing dams had to be built on the spot to raise the water level and passengers were ordered overboard to push the vessel around hairpin turns. To lighten the load cargo might be left behind. It wouldn't then be delivered until the following year.'

'What an extraordinary way to travel,' said Beagan as his celestial entourage rocked over the waves. 'It says here that the elegant *Marquette* was loved for her shallow draft. Her captain bragged that she could "navigate on a light dew". The steel-hulled *Lilly* was built on the Clyde and the plush *North West* boasted a strolling deck, two bridal suites and a $5,000 piano.'

'The fleet lasted only twelve years,' I lamented. 'The year after the railway was finished they laid them up and let them rot away.'

Zachary was intolerant of excessive sensibility. 'They served their purpose, Sandy. They – and the overland trails to the south – prevented America from seizing the land at that time. The boats were instruments of economic development, not something to put your heart into.'

'In any event the Americans didn't need to seize the country,' said Jamie. 'It was surrendered to them later, without a f-f-fight.'

'James,' snapped the elder brother, 'I am disappointed in your continued confusion of matters economic and emotional.' He dropped the handful of sand into the river. The splash distracted Harold. 'The nations' convergence is simply a matter of shared values and objectives, a process of maturing realism.'

Before I could form my reply the inflatable lurched up

on its side, sailed into the air then slapped back down on the water.

'In the name of Providence, what was that?'

'Shall I take over for a bit?' offered Beagan, picking himself up from the deck. As Harold's attention had wandered the Avon had grazed a sandbar.

'That's some kind of you, b'y, but you don't know the river, eh?' replied the Newfoundlander. The outboard had stalled during his aerobatic manoeuvre. He reprimed and balanced the fuel tanks then pulled the starter cord. The engine coughed back into life. 'These waters can be trickier than a single woman turning thirty. You stick to your books, I'll handle the boat.'

'Thanks to the blessings of the Good One above us we are on course,' Hector acknowledged with a stern eye on Harold. The rising sun had given him his reading. He could have conjured up the position in his imagination but he preferred to do things the old way. 'Only this Arcadian is not to be thinking that he's brought the ship into harbour yet.'

'There's a town round the next bend. We'll take a break there and get in some beer and grub,' proposed Harold. As the boat regained its speed, he resumed his singing.

'Cheap tea and molasses they say they will give,
All taxes take off that the old man may live;
Cheap nails and cheap lumber our coffins to make,
And homespun to mend our old clothes when they break.'

West of the Campbell Dam the river looped south and the scenery changed. The unshaven Land of Little Sticks fell away and opened on to a bright, clean prairie of primary hues. Yellow wheat fields soared towards blue horizons which red railside grain elevators anchored to the earth. As the inflatable raced across the Tobin Lake reservoir Beagan imagined Polish and Ruthenian immigrants standing on the *Marquette*'s hurricane deck looking out over the golden virgin land, dreaming of a home in the promised west. Mennonites had settled on the river's south bank between French farmers and a German Catholic colony. Every Sunday the district's dusty roads filled with spade-bearded men driving horse-drawn buggies to church. On the north shore the Doukhobors cultivated broad acres of barley and flax. The pacifist sect had fled Tsarist Russia in the company of Tolstoy's son in their search for religious tolerance. They had arrived with neither money nor oxen and in their early communal villages the women had been yoked to ploughs while the men worked away from home on the railroad. As their farms prospered they abandoned the communes but never strayed far from the community. Behind a single windbreak of trees Beagan saw a grandfather's collapsed sod dugout, a father's first cabin of mud and wattle and the son's proud clapboard frame-house.

'Down home,' announced Harold, 'no one pays much attention to the wind until they see whitecaps in their bathwater.' A cool breeze had blown up, plucking autumn orange leaves from the trees and scattering them on the choppy waves. Beagan had retrieved his father's tin hat from under the outboard and jammed it over a thick woolly scarf which he wrapped around his head. Harold had tired of steering around the sandbars and rather than slow down he now tended to accelerate through the shallows and plough over any obstacle. It made for a faster passage but more than once they had had to step into the cold stream after the inflatable had run aground. 'Never seen anything like it,' Harold exclaimed after avoiding one deep trench by grabbing on to Beagan's scarf. 'If Moses had been here he'd have gone in right up to his tits.'

All too soon Harold decided that his seamanship enabled him to ignore rocky shoals too. He was singing above the whine of the Evinrude, a robust song about the squid-jiggin' ground, when the boat hit the outcrop. The force of the impact punctured the starboard flotation bladder and the jet of escaping air spun the Avon around like a hysterical merry-go-round. The trunk sailed out over the deflating side and Beagan splashed into the water after it.

'Save the Labatt's first,' instructed Harold as the cardboard case fell open and the brown beer-bottles bobbed away in the current.

But Beagan was more concerned with rescuing his papers. He swam hard and managed to catch the trunk at the head of a small set of rapids. It hit a log, turned over on itself and struck him on the head. Both Beagan and the box trunk were sucked under by the cross-current.

'How you getting on there, b'y?' yelled Harold from the shrinking vessel. 'Quit horsing around, eh?

The trunk broke surface below the rapids with Beagan astride it like Arion on his dolphin. He sailed across the whirlpool using the helmet as a rudder and guided himself towards the shore.

Harold ran down the bank and helped pull the unlikely ark ashore. 'Jeez, you all right? You had me worried there.' Beagan managed a damp smile then displayed half a dozen rescued bottles of beer. 'Oh Lord, couldn't you do no better than that? There were a full twenty-four in that case.'

A hundred yards upriver there sprouted from behind a copse of autumn trees the onion domes and slanting crosses of a Ukrainian Greek Orthodox church. 'Did I ever tell you about the time I was called out to fix the plumbing at a church?' Harold asked Beagan as they dragged the deflated inflatable towards the town. The story had already been told . . . three times. ' "Hello Father," I says to the priest, "Is it the holy water again?" ' Harold cackled at his wit then sneezed. 'You know there are three faucets in a church: hot, cold and holy.'

A broad-beamed petrol attendant in an embroidered blouse laughed as she sold Harold a puncture repair kit. While he mended the hole Beagan checked the box trunk's contents. The plastic bags had kept the papers dry and none of the glass negatives seemed to have been broken. Even Hector's globe had survived the dunking intact.

Beagan changed his clothes in a lace-curtained rest room and accepted the woman's generous invitation to lunch. Over the century three great waves of Ukrainians had descended on the province and their colony had grown to be twice the size of the Native Indian population. Her *borshch* was rich and hot and he asked her what had brought her family to the Prairies. 'Why did we choose Canada?' she answered, fluttering her blonde bovine eyelashes like the Blue Ribbon winner at the Royal Winter Fair. 'Because it is a safe, pure country. Because we could work hard, save money, buy an encyclopedia for boys and a piano for girls.' Her solid frame was filled with pride and *pyrohy*. 'All my children are now university graduates.'

The town's general store where they replenished their supplies was owned by a Slovak. 'When in 1968 Soviet tanks invade our country I escape to Austria,' he explained while slicing thick wedges of fatty sausage. 'From refugee camp I apply to come to Canada and they fly me and others twelve hours through the night. The airplane, it land in a blizzard. The doors opened and big men in fur coats step on board. The men, they speak Russian not English and we all know immediately that we are tricked, that we have never leave Czechoslovakia, that the KGB have fly us to Siberia. The women cry, the men not leave aircraft, we all frightened until a Mountie in a red coat come and tell us, "This is Edmonton. Russians emigrated here after the war. Look at me, my name is Shavrov. You are in Canada."'

The Saskatchewan swung north-west to run through an undulating grassland. The earth was the colour of burnt umber and dotted with beehives. Cattle grazed on the crests of wooded knolls and picked their way down the steep slopes to drink. They dislodged divots of turf which rolled off the path and slapped into the water. The dappled reflection of a woman on horseback played on the mackerel riffles. She led a damp setter and stray calf along a line of mustard-coloured oaks. On the roads beyond her, Kubota tractors towed threshing machines past signs for Livelong, Goodsoil, Paradise Hill and Jensen's Alfalfa Seed Cleaning Service.

Oil rigs began to appear over the Alberta border. Their seesaw pivots pumped the ebony crude that had transformed the province from dirt-farm poverty to petro-dollar fortune. There were seven thousand wells operating within a hundred-mile radius of Edmonton. The new wealth grew not only from oil and gas deposits but from the vast reserves of coal, silver, gold and uranium. On lawns the size of football pitches antique traction engines were displayed beside sleek modern combine harvesters. Even the wrecked cars dumped on the riverbank appeared to be newer than those rusting away in Manitoba and Saskatchewan.

The greasy waterway snaked beneath highway flyovers and powerlines, between refineries and factories into the oil capital of Canada. Under the graffiti-trimmed arches cliff swallows built their muddy nests. Beagan had hoped to arrive in time to watch the Kiwanis Club Duck Challenge when rubber ducks were raced between the city's bridges but the shore was deserted. There were no boats on the river or wall-eye fishermen at Whitemud Park. 'They'll all be at the mall, eh?' explained Harold, skirting a gravel bar and running the inflatable on to the Laurier Park launch site. 'So what do you say you and me do a little shopping too?'

Beagan had no desire to visit a store. He was anxious to get on to the Pacific. 'I'm due to meet my brother in Vancouver in less than a week.'

'Hey, it's no ordinary shopping centre,' Harold stressed, itching for some conspicuous consumption. 'The West Edmonton Mall is the biggest damn retail complex in all Creation.' Beagan stared upriver and couldn't make up his mind. 'Come on, b'y, fish or cut bait. Listen, we'll do some shopping, play a little roulette, knock back a two-four of Labatt's and be back on the river in twenty-four hours. Then we'll swim like a dog up to Rocky Mountain House in no time flat. And hey, if you're crossing Canada by boat for sure you got to go some of the way by submarine.'

'Submarine?'

The mall looked like a monstrous moon-base colony dropped on to suburbia. It straddled the equivalent of forty-eight city blocks. Beneath its glass domes and illuminated cupolas were crammed eight hundred stores, 110 restaurants, a children's zoo and an amusement park with a thirteen-storey high 'Drop of Doom' rollercoaster ride. At the Ice Palace the Edmonton Oilers held their hockey practices while four Atlantic bottle-nose dolphins performed throughout the day in a 300,000-gallon tropical lagoon. In the five-acre indoor Waterpark shoppers donned bikinis or trunks to bask on the Caribbean blue beach, to body surf on five-foot waves and to learn how to scuba dive. Throughout summer and winter the Waterpark temperature was maintained at a constant 86° fahrenheit.

The taxi dropped Harold and Beagan outside the Fantasyland Hotel. There was a seven-foot-high carved ivory pagoda in the gilded foyer. Harold wanted to rent a theme room but couldn't decide between Roman and Hollywood. 'The Victorian Coach Suite is real popular, sir,' advised the blonde receptionist. She wore thick blue eyeliner and had perfectly aligned teeth. Harold went upstairs to have a look. The bed was an ornamented carriage driven by a plaster coachman and drawn by two fibreglass steeds.

'I don't like the idea of sleeping behind some horse's arse,' he told the woman. 'You got an Arabian room left? We've got kind of used to sleeping in tents.'

'I'm sorry; the Arabian, the Truck and the Canadian Rail suites are all occupied. But I do have one Polynesian still available.'

The bellhop lay the trunk under a plastic palm tree at the foot of the catamaran-shaped bed. Beagan asked for his roll-away to be made up on the other side of the waterfall whirlpool bath. In Edmonton it was said that one could stand on a sardine can and see the Rockies. Further west still, they said, one didn't need the can. Looking out the window Beagan believed that he could discern snowy peaks. Harold was studying a mall map. 'So what's it to be first?' he said, clapping his hands. 'A round of golf at Pebble Beach, a brew on Bourbon Street or a ride in a sub?'

Harold led the way past Lady Evelyne Lingerie, Cookies by George and the full-scale replica of Columbus's *Santa Maria*, its aquarium hull containing two hundred species of tropical fish. Outside Dawn's House of Fashion he shouted over his shoulder, 'They got four submarines here; that's more than the whole

Canadian Navy.' A broad, rocky lido stretched along the length of the atrium. Suspension bridges reached between the shores and stores. Harold bustled around the coconut trees and down a walkway to the Deep Sea Adventure departure deck. As he and Beagan followed twenty-two other shopping-mall submariners past the yellow conning tower and down the metallic hatch the Newfoundlander yelled, 'Never had any of these back in Fortune Harbour.' The captain secured the hatch, the ballast tanks blew and the submarine dived beneath Ikea and the Body Shop. 'Holy jeez, b'y, it's a shark.' Through portholes and on television monitors the passengers followed their voyage past stingrays, barracudas and around a dwarf replica of the Great Barrier Reef to discover a sunken shipwreck. Lights flashed, whistles blew, the sonar pinged and when it was all over Harold wanted to go again. 'I sure wish Lily was here to see this. She'd be as chuffed as a clam in chowder.'

In between mugs of beer Harold tried to take in all the mall's attractions. He rode the bumper cars, admired the replica Crown Jewels, ate a chilli dog in the mouth of a bronze whale and tried his luck at Caesar's Bingo. 'I'm busier than a one-armed coat-hanger with crabs,' he told Beagan over a plate of Café Orleans oysters. 'You got a lady friend, b'y?' he asked with the arrival of the third frosty jug of Labatt's.

'No; something – or someone – always gets in the way.'

'Well my Lily, she's a big girl,' continued the Newfoundlander. His expansive gesture brought to mind the Abominable Snowman's sister. 'She turns over in the night and the whole damn bed shakes. You wake up from a dream holding on to the headboard thinking that your dinghy's going down in a storm.' Harold laughed at the memory and sloshed beer all over the table. 'Loving her is sort of like docking an ocean liner – the various bits have to be eased into position, eh?'

In the late afternoon Harold decided to buy Lily a pair of dancing shoes but as he didn't know her size the matter became rather complicated. At Sole Comfort a compliant clerk let him hold her foot and they agreed that Lily was about size six. 'Better make it a seven so she can grow into it,' he hollered into the storeroom, then added to Beagan, 'She can always wear a second pair of socks.' Later in the Carlos O'Grady saloon he told Beagan, 'You know, when Lily and me are really close, like all excited, eh?, I like to lick her neck. Yes sir, the saltiness makes me think of the sea.'

They couldn't decide which film to see in the mall's nineteen cinemas so settled instead for a few frames of billiards at the Master's Club. After steak and kidney pie with French fries and a couple of more pints at the Elephant and Castle Olde English Pub Harold and Beagan stumbled back to the hotel. In the Jacuzzi Beagan's headache and nightmare visions of shoe stores receded until Harold found a dubbed version of *Grease* playing on the Univision Spanish cable channel. Although he didn't understand the dialogue the songs unfortunately remained in English, and Harold sang along at the top of his voice until the night manager hammered on the door and Beagan passed out beneath the Kon-Tiki bed.

'B'y, your face would stop an eight-day clock.' It was not long after dawn. Harold was packed and ready to go. 'Better let go a shotgun in here to wake you up. Come on, the day's awasting.' Another taxi ran them back to the inflatable. The morning was cold. As soon as they were underway Beagan was sick over the side. He was surprised by Harold's strong constitution and asked if he felt all right. 'If I was any better I'd be too good,' replied the Newfoundlander, taking in a deep breath of the crisp autumnal air. 'In a day or two I'll be dropping you off and heading home to Lily. I was stunned as me arse leaving her alone in The Pas. And, no offence, but you snore. Kept me awake half the damn night.'

Above Edmonton the water grew clearer and the current strengthened. Harold ran his boat up the inside of bends, avoiding rollers and haystack waves, skirting sandy islands and the low gravel shore. Around a corner the soft pumice-grey horizon of clouds found sharp contours and the mountains defined themselves. They rose at the end of the prairie, beyond the last chocolate-box grain elevator, silhouetted by the morning's apricot sky. A calm backwater mirrored the peaks until a single ripple broke them into spots and tones like a pointillist painting.

'You know, Lily makes the best bannock bread this side of the Rockies,' reminisced Harold above the whine of the motor. 'Serves it up hot with bakeapple jam, just like I had when I was a kid.' He licked his lips. 'I could do with a slice now for sure.'

Above Buck Creek the glacier-fed river flowed two-tone. The crystal-clear waters of the Brazeau ran alongside the Saskatchewan's familiar silty brown. Dense stands of aspen with bark like tarnished silver huddled along the banks. Their saffron canopy was pierced by the blue tips of spruce and the occasional bald sandstone cliff. The last fairy-skirted harebells flirted around unbowed bull thistles. Iron-red buffalo rye and foxtail barley swayed in the clearings. The inflatable cut across the current, avoided a white eddy and at the Clearwater confluence found Rocky Mountain House.

The town had once been the last fur-trading post before the Rockies. At the start of the nineteenth century the Scots cartographer David Thompson had made the post his base while searching for the western sea. Later, mining and logging camps had thrived in the surrounding Clearwater district. Finns and Swedes had cut trees in Nordegg. Welsh miners had been settled in a hamlet called Harlech. Every Friday night the lumberjacks, coal-miners and men from an unnamed railhead mill had ridden into Rocky for weekend relaxation. Often they failed to return to work before Tuesday or Wednesday, so to improve productivity the owners decided to bring Rocky's pleasures to the mill. A hotel was built, a bar was opened and certain compliant ladies were invited to take up residence. The settlement had grown into a town known as Horburg. But when the mills and mines closed the whores had departed and Rocky had become a forgotten gateway ringed by ghost towns at the edge of the mountains.

Harold ran his Avon ashore below the railway bridge. 'All

change for the Pacific. This is the end of the line, b'y.' Upriver the
white water appeared to run colder and wilder. Beagan thought he
could hear the roar of rapids. 'The Continental Divide's just a
gunshot away.'

'How far is a gunshot?'

'Oh, about a city block.'

It was in fact about a hundred miles to the Height of Land,
but between Rocky Mountain House and the Saskatchewan Glacier lay eighteen sets of rapids up which no boat had been tracked
in over a hundred years. 'Them canoeists may shoot downstream
singing a merry ditty but a man'd be crazy to try going up them,'
Harold explained as they carried the trunk in to town. Beagan
took a room in 'Rocky's Finer Place To Be', the Walking Eagle
Motor Inn. In the parking lot a wrinkled old man snored under
his cap in the cab of a Dodge Ram pick-up truck. An elegant
cast-iron bathtub was lashed on to its flat-bed back.

Harold dawdled in town only long enough to refuel. Beagan
bought him three cases of beer and a waterproof compass. At the
landing Harold pumped his hand. 'Got to get back to my Lily
before freeze-up.' His eyes glistened at the thought of docking
his ocean liner. Beagan asked if he had decided not to return to
Newfoundland. 'No man should spend the winter alone. It gets
too damn cold.' He laughed as they slipped the Avon into the
river. 'But come spring, for sure I don't know. You just might
find me looking for that channel out of the Cedar again.'

'I hope you won't need that passport.'

'Too right by a half, b'y.' The Evinrude started on the first pull
and with a wave Harold was gone.

Beagan saw no Peterborough lapstrake or cedar skiff along the
shore so dragged his feet back to the motel. He felt in need of a
long hot bath and an even longer sleep. Tomorrow he could
decide how to reach the Divide. Over a Denver sandwich in the
Eagle's Nest Lounge he fell into conversation with a young
woman. Her thick hair brought to mind a beaver pelt, a rich
warm fur pulled across her forehead and over her ears. The bathtub
and pick-up, she explained in a soothing voice, were hers. 'I'm

a marine biologist,' said Elsie Faithful with quiet confidence. A puppy dozed at her feet. 'I work over on Vancouver Island netting and tagging sturgeon.' Her crescent-moon eyes were coloured tawny lion yellow.

'I don't know much about sturgeon.'

'Do you know that they have been all but exterminated within the lifetime of a single fish?'

'But how long do they live?' asked Beagan, grateful that he hadn't ordered fishcakes.

'On average 135 years. It takes them eighteen years to reach sexual maturity. That's longer than you and me.' He offered to buy her a drink. She shook her head. 'I'm pregnant.' He hadn't noticed. 'And anyway, sturgeon are the only creature that I'd leave my boyfriend for. That's him in the cab.' Beagan thought of the fossil asleep in the Dodge. 'The love and burden of my life. The bath is my luxury.'

BEAGAN LAY BACK in his tub and tried to relax. Even nominal Canadians felt morally reprehensible if more than three days passed between baths. After so long afloat he retained the sensation of movement. The whine of the outboard still buzzed in his ears. The vessel seemed to rock and sway and he half-expected to see whitecaps blow across the bathwater. We settled ourselves down around him in the dim, pine-clad room. Dad dozed under a mildewed map of mountain trails and passes. Hector lacked the strength to read, the mayhem of the mall and the raw consumerism having sapped his celestial concentration. 'I never wish to ride a roller-coaster again,' he groaned. Even Zachary was quiet after the long, weary trip.

The last hundred miles up over the Rockies had always been the most difficult section of the waterway. The mountains had defeated the early French explorers. Alexander

Mackenzie had tried to skirt them by paddling north along the Peace and Parsnip rivers yet even then he still had to line his canoes down the Blackwater and trek over the Rainbow Range to Bella Coola on the other side. But David Thompson, the Nor'Westers' map-maker, had been told by the Natives of a great southern river which led to the Lake of Salt. In 1801 he had followed their trails to the head-waters of the Saskatchewan, only to choose the wrong fork. For over a month he had battled up the Ram, dragging the canoes through black shale canyons, wading in fast glacial water so cold that it 'was known to give the goitres'. When he had given up and turned downstream the savage current had hurled him back to Rocky in six hours. It would take six more years for Thompson to find the Howse Pass through the mountains and follow the Blaeberry River down to the Columbia and the sea. The Blackfoot named him *Koo-Koo-Sint*, 'the man who looked at the stars', after the sextant with which he had charted 1½ million acres of wilderness. His surveys remained the basis for all cartography of the north-west until the 1940s.

'To the Westward Hills and Rocks rose to our view covered with snow, here rising, there subsiding, but their Tops nearly of an equal height everywhere,' Thompson had written on first sighting the Rockies. 'Never before did I behold so just, so perfect a resemblance to the waves of the Ocean in the wintry storm. When looking upon them and attentively considering their wild order and appearance, the imagination is apt to say, these must once have been Liquid, and in that state when swelled to its greatest agitation, suddenly congealed and made Solid by Power Omnipotent.'

Beagan had fallen asleep in the bath and in his dreams the rocking tub began to skim up the Saskatchewan. It swept over the flurries of Fisher's Rapid and skirted the Old Stoney boulder. At Devil's Elbow, an inverted U-bend downstream of Horburg, it surfed around the inside curve and sloshed some suds over the side. Beagan grabbed the rim as the bath picked up speed. It ran past the mouth of Thompson's Ram and up the narrow braided channel above Deep Creek. His face-cloth blew away into the frothing wake. He dropped the soap. Above Dutch Creek the Saskatchewan swirled in a whirlpool and the Bighorn Dam towered above him. Beagan ducked beneath the surface as the bath lifted clear of the sluice-way and sailed up on to Abraham Lake. In his dream passing cars stopped and drivers stared as the tub aquaplaned beneath Mount Mitchener.

On the Kootenay Plain the spruce were iced with snow. Criss-crossed branches gave the tamaracks a crazed look. Eroded sandstone arches and drumlins fretted the shore. Beyond the fold of a charcoal cliff a moose stepped out of Beagan's way while a fearless grey jay chattered and chased off the water-borne intruder. The balneary projectile skimmed over eddies and chutes, skipped alongside the broad stone pebble banks and shot like a cast-iron bullet under the highway bridge at Saskatchewan Crossing.

As the bath climbed up into the mountains the temperature dropped. The river ran dove-grey and peacock, the colour of icebergs, and Beagan began to shiver. He looked for a towel but found none. The force of the wind prevented him from sitting up so he tried instead to turn on the hot tap with his toes. He succeeded only in releasing a cloud of steam. A lofty stream cascaded tears down the Weeping Wall. Streaks of morraine ran stone fingers across snow-shrouded slopes. Above Rampart Creek the river split into a maze of channels. The course became shallow and sinuous, in places all but running dry, and the tub's feet scraped along the riverbed, scattering stones dusted grey with glacial silt and knocking rotted logs up on to the gravel banks.

The turquoise tongue of the Saskatchewan Glacier slipped between mountains, licked their peaks and scarred the rock face with countless time lines. Immense icicles hung from the exposed ledges. The river whispered like voices heard in half-sleep. With a shudder the bath lifted above the frozen fount and flew up over the Columbia Icefield. The great glacier's melt ran to three oceans: back along the North Saskatchewan into Hudson's Bay and the Atlantic, down the Athabasca, the Slave and Mackenzie to the Arctic, and out the Columbia into the Pacific.

Soapy water spilt over the rim, splashed down on the icy surface that was wrinkled like an albino elephant's hide, rained on to the rental cars and tour buses motoring in the furrows. A soaked Austrian tourist wearing the badge 'Hallo I am Klaus!' shook his fist at the airborne tub. A Japanese holiday-maker switched on her video. A frill of material tickled Beagan's nose. He looked up to see Reverend Hector, his cape flapping wildly in the breeze, carrying the bath. His sons Zachary and Jamie were on the other side balancing the load, flying their descendant over the Height of Land. Zachary was dressed in tails. Jamie wore a shabby suit with a gravy stain on its cuff. He whistled as the wind swept back his thin red hair. Beagan felt like laughing but it was too cold and he sneezed instead.

It was then that he felt a presence on his right. He turned and fixed his eyes on me. Below us the mountains fell away and the Pacific rivers plunged down to the western sea. My son lifted a frozen arm from the bathwater, reached out his hand to touch me and heard a sharp knock at the motel room door.

CHAPTER X

WAVES' END

BEAGAN OPENED THE door on to the white morning and Elsie. Her Labrador puppy barked at the snowflakes which settled on his nose. 'I thought you might like a ride, what with the storm coming,' she said. The pick-up was running with its heater on. Hotel guests were scraping ice off their car windshields.

'Yes,' Beagan smiled, pulling the towel around him. 'Yes, please.' He was blue with cold and shivering. 'But I've got a trunk.'

Elsie looked past him into the room. 'You must have been a tortoise in a previous life.' She nodded. 'That's okay. It can go in the back. I'll wait in the truck.' The fresh snow crunched underfoot as she walked to the cab. 'Are you all right?' she asked, looking back at his wild grin.

'I fell asleep in the bath.'

As he tried to work his icy fingers to dress himself Beagan could not stop chuckling. The night's encounter had left him elated, and with his trousers half on he stumbled against the trunk, rolled on to the floor and laughed until tears filled his eyes. He almost kissed the chambermaid when he checked out of the room.

A braided ring of sweet grass, its ends burnt as a palliative smudge, hung on the rear-view mirror. Beagan sat with the dog on his lap between Elsie and her still sleeping boyfriend. The old man hadn't washed and his breath was stale with alcohol. An empty rye bottle rolled back and forth under the seat. 'So where's your car?' asked Elsie.

'I don't have one,' said Beagan through chattering teeth. He had drunk two cups of scalding tea but they had not warmed him. 'I've been travelling to Vancouver by water. It's sort of a homecoming. I grew up on the Pacific.'

'You got relatives there?'

'Just my brother. The rest of the family are riding in the back,' he said, pointing over his shoulder. Elsie took a long look in her rear-view mirror. 'My past is in the trunk.'

The advancing blizzard obscured the valley behind and hurried the Dodge up the David Thompson Highway. 'I guess travelling across Canada you get to thinking that it's a young country,' she said, and Beagan leaned closer to hear her soft voice above the sound of the engine. 'The Maritimes have been settled for, what, nine generations. Ontario for six. Pioneers only reached the Prairies late last century and it's not much more than a single lifetime since the Pacific was the frontier.' Along the autumn amber riverbank the spruce were crowned with astrakhan crows' nests. 'On the radio the other day someone asked if Canada had any history,' she remembered. 'It made me so mad. It assumed that time only began when the white man arrived.'

Beagan's smile ebbed away like a wave back into the sea. 'Faithful doesn't sound much like a Native name,' he said.

'It's not. It used to be government policy to adopt First Nations children off the reserves into white families,' Elsie explained. 'Some tribes had eight out of ten of their kids taken away from them. There were no restrictions, even a single man could adopt a child. Me — and Noah —' she gestured to her boyfriend, 'we were given away when we were real small to a couple in a place called Peachland. We didn't even know that we were Native until after Ma Faithful died. Her sister told us the truth.'

'I'm sorry,' said Beagan, sensing himself culpable.

Elsie shrugged her shoulders. 'It must be kind of nice for you knowing your folks.'

'Yes, it's a strength, as long as they don't try to run your life.' The boyfriend began to snore until Elsie asked Beagan his surname. 'Gillean,' he replied. 'It's Scottish.'

She took another look in her mirror. 'Can you trace them far back?'

'About four generations.' In Elsie's curiosity he sensed a compassionate, if not kindred, spirit, and he told her about his journey from the Hebrides and across Canada, about his search for the displaced Reverend Hector, about the publishing brothers and the betrayal of the dream of his ever-optimistic father. 'It's not even two hundred years of history but, well, beginning to know them teaches me something about myself and about this country.' They drove on in a silence broken only by the sound of snoring. 'You know in Gaelic one doesn't say to a stranger, "Where are you from?" One asks, "To what place do you belong?"' He grabbed an imaginary fistful of earth in his hand. 'I guess your ancestry must give you a sense of belonging. Like, this is me. I am of this place.'

'In theory, but when I tried to trace my family all I found was that the adoption papers had been lost. There are over seven hundred tribes in Canada, you know.' She cast him a sad smile. 'It's funny; I might be Squamish or Shuswap, Haida or Nuu'chah'nulth. The North-West Coast tribes have the world's longest tradition of handing down names and I don't know what mine is.'

As they climbed up on to the continent's spine they left the storm behind them on the plains. The mountains rose solid, silent, from the mantle of close dark pine. 'The Blackfoot call them Backbone-of-the-World,' said Elsie. At Saskatchewan Crossing the pick-up turned away from the river up which the bathtub had flown and headed south down the narrow canyon of Bow Pass.

'It seems extraordinary that Thompson should have stumbled on any pass through here,' said Beagan.

'The Kootenais showed him the way,' she replied, looking straight ahead, her eyes on the road. 'The Kootenay Plain was a trading place, the neutral ground where the Peigan, Blackfoot and other northern plains tribes met every autumn. The rivers and passes over the mountains had been known for a hundred generations before Europeans "discovered" them.'

Craggy cliffs crowded and jostled up against the frosty highway.

Beagan tried to imagine the centuries of unchanging migration across the cedar-green plateau. The Sarcee had arrived by canoe. The Blood had dragged their trade goods up the ancient trails by pony and travois. Dressed in buffalo skin, the Blackfoot had smoked pipes of sage over the packs of bark and rawhide and bartered maple sugar for smoked trout. But with the coming of the voyageurs the pelts and pemmican had instead been traded for blankets, knives and guns. Men had no longer hunted for what they needed but for all they could sell. Beyond the steamy window Beagan pictured a Peigan warrior flaunting a prized umbrella. His wife paraded her gleaming copper pot. The first tribes to trade for European weaponry had defeated their enemies and driven the survivors into others' territories. Smallpox had beaten victor and vanquished alike, decimating three-quarters of the Blackfoot nation in one winter alone. When Cabot and Columbus landed in the New World there had been maybe ten million Native Americans on the continent. Today only 360,000 remained, their nations decimated by the disease and famine, alcohol and guns imported by Europeans.

Noah groaned and Beagan asked Elsie if he was unwell. 'He got into a fight yesterday,' she replied. 'It happens every time some wiseguy calls him Chief. He hates that.'

'The Native people who I've seen these past months,' hazarded Beagan, 'have been in a terrible state.'

'And it surprises you?' She spoke with such venom that he had to turn away to watch Noah sleep. 'We gave away our lands, our valleys full of game and herds of buffalo, and what did we receive in return? Rum and trinkets and a grave.'

Elsie stopped abruptly for a lone big-horn sheep and a flock of tourists at Lake Louise. Tour buses paused for a shutter's snap beside glacial lagoons, beneath dogtooth mountains, between a 'Snocoach' icefield adventure and Devil's Gap boat cruise.

'I'm sorry,' Beagan repeated, feeling remorse as a white person for what had happened to the first Canadians.

'I heard somewhere that history is the study of lost alternatives. You know, the "What if . . . ?" school of thought.'

'Like, what if Columbus hadn't reached the West Indies?' he suggested.

Elsie nodded, sensing his discomfort. 'Sure. Or, what if American diseases had been more virulent than the European ones, and those first encounters had killed settlers, not Natives? Or, what if the early immigrants had recognised the culture that they were entering?'

'My great-grandfather's life was saved by a Micmac named Gogo.'

'What if he hadn't bothered?' she asked, understanding then that she too could help.

'I wouldn't be here,' he replied, and considered the dispossessed nurturing the displaced, one tragedy of Canada's terrible becoming. 'I wouldn't be.'

'Nor me, I suppose,' stuttered Jamie, the thought having never before occurred to him. He sat beside Hector on the cast-iron bath as the pick-up ran west out of Banff National Park, over the Great Divide and into British Columbia.

'There's a clipping somewhere here from the *Bismarck Tribune*,' I said, leafing through a file marked 'Intolerance (Examples of)'. A dusty copy of a treaty was snatched from my hand by the wind. 'Here it is. "This is God's country,"' I read aloud from the century-old newspaper. '"He peopled it with red men, and planted it with wild grasses, but as the wild grasses disappear, so the Indians disappear before the advances of the white men. Their prayers, their entreaties, cannot arrest the causes which are carrying them on to their ultimate destiny – extinction."'

'That does vex me, right enough,' admitted Hector.

'Few societies have ever grown at the pace of BC,' Zachary announced while enjoying the view. He sat at the head of the bath and hadn't been listening either to us or to Beagan and Elsie's conversation. His head was too full of facts. 'Why, in 1856 on the whole of the Pacific mainland there lived only 150 men.'

'White men,' I corrected. I sat on the trunk with my

back against the cab and the globe in my lap. My feet were balanced on the rim of the tub.

'Who else?' asked Zachary.

'The Native inhabitants,' replied Hector.

'I chose not to include them because no census did so, Father. It was a different matter once Christian values and Protestant thrift had been impressed upon them. Even if that attempt to make them responsible citizens didn't, I may say, pass muster.'

'It was another opportunity lost, Uncle Zach; a whole race locked away out of sight and out of mind on reservations.' For a generation or more the Native people hadn't existed for other Canadians.

'Forget about them,' said Zachary, his impatience directed at me. 'We are trying to concentrate on the year that gold was discovered on the Fraser.'

'What matters in life doesn't have much to do with money, Uncle Zach.'

'Oh no? If it wasn't for the gold your west coast might still be Indian territory, and then where would you be?'

'Building boats in Muskoka?'

'Don't be sassy with me, chap,' answered Zachary, then continued, 'One sunny Sunday afternoon in 1856 a ship out of San Francisco, the SS *Commodore*, put in to Vancouver Island and doubled the region's population. By the end of that same summer twenty thousand prospectors had sailed north from California. Gold fever drove them up the canyons and opened the interior of the province. It heralded the start of a period of remarkable growth.'

'One successful miner called William Smith changed his name to Amor De Cosmos and was elected premier,' added Jamie. He had been watching a mule deer with oversized ears, white rump and black-tip tail vanish behind a line of rowan trees.

'The Overlanders came across the plains from eastern Canada and down the Thompson, the province's second river, in cedar rafts and cottonwood dug-outs,' recounted Zachary, ignoring his brother. 'Golden City was built at the head of the third river, the Columbia, to serve them, the miners, loggers and traders. Gillean Publishing began distributing its periodicals as soon as the road and rail lines opened the country to business.'

'There were f-f-fine boats to get the news through,' recalled Jamie. 'Lovely, flat-bottomed river-steamers with blunt foredecks that tramped through the locks at Canal Flats. Why, the highest shipyard in the Americas was built just up the road here at Nakusp.'

'But the geology ensured that it was always a place apart, Dad,' I pointed out. 'The Rockies not only impeded easy access to and from the rest of the continent but also between its own communities.' The Dodge ran through a sedimentary pass where shells and fossils littered the roadside. The province had been shaped by its majestic and insular terrain. 'So there was a better medium than newspapers for holding the place together, for fostering a common spirit.'

'The province's isolation did breed an independent cast of mind,' admitted Zachary. 'But I'll have you know that my publications did very well here, very well indeed. In fact if you can stir yourself I'll show you. The figures are here in the trunk, assuming your Beagan hasn't mislaid them.' I swung myself into the bath as he began to leaf through the papers. 'They were filed alongside the company's annual reports. What the blazes is that racket?'

In the cab Elsie had turned on the radio. A brassy signature tune introduced the local evening news. The lead item was about fishing rights. The province's streams frothed with red Kokanee salmon battling upriver to spawn. She changed to a country station and then a religious programme. When the preacher called the faithful to prayer Hector knelt down in the tub.

'Bless our boatmen and our boat,' he recited for Native and newcomer alike, 'bless our anchors and our oars, each stay and halyard and traveller, our mainsail to a tall mast keep, oh King of the Elements, in its place so we may reach our haven in peace.'

On another band the commercials were all in Chinese. In years gone by Elsie might have spun the dial and found one of my stations but instead, today, she tuned to an impassioned report on Quebec.

'It's the referendum on Monday, isn't it?' said Beagan, listening to three French-Canadians debate the possible birth of one country and the break-up of another. The east coast felt a long way away.

'But why should we part?' demanded a lawyer from Lachine. 'This beautiful land was entrusted to us by our ancestors.'

'Because of those ancestors,' argued a university lecturer from Quebec City, his voice choked with feeling. 'Because this wintry cold federalism cannot be maintained. We have to have the guts to fend for ourselves.'

The third, undecided, speaker was dissatisfied with both camps. 'Do we really need to split to be separate?'

'Yes,' insisted the lecturer. His nationalism was an affair of the heart. 'This dysfunctional Canada belittles our identity, allies us with neighbours with whom we have no affinity. We can only truly pursue our destiny alone.'

'The referendum seems to have become a focus for all manner of discontent,' said Beagan, shaken by the debate.

'Many people feel out of control of their lives,' suggested Elsie.

'But I wonder how much this outpouring of emotion is due to real political grievances.'

She shook her head. 'Very little. Separatism is a persuasive placebo.'

'They used to say that BC stands for Beyond Canada,' I sighed, turning the old globe on its axis and running my finger from sea to sea. 'Maybe that's why I moved here, to a new world, for the chance to begin again.'

*   *   *

For me, hard work would make dreams a reality. I trusted in the triumph of good faith. A love of radio took hold of me at the Muskoka cottage. Dad was so often away from the island on business that I filled the empty summer days by stretching a telegraphy line from cottage to boathouse. I wired it up to an oscillating electromagnet, a queer anvil and the best fifty-cent outfit ever produced. On a cloudless July afternoon I touched the key and sent a message out from my bedroom, across the lawn, over the dogs and down to the shore. In an instant a signal came back to me. I didn't understand a word of it but it was a response, a lovely, loud, clear click. At first I thought that my lack of comprehension was the fault of the apparatus but soon realised that the problem lay in my correspondent. Nan had little enthusiasm for idling time away at the boathouse and in any event refused to study Morse. Dad bought her a Codegraph code-learning device but the only message she ever managed to send was 'Brush your hair it's time for church.'

I graduated to wireless with a crystal set. Copper wire was wrapped around an old salt container and the radio tuned with a 'cat whisker' probe on the galena crystal. I rigged one end of a long aerial to the top of a jack pine and trailed the other from *Primary*'s stern out over the lake. The line went taut and music crackled into the headphones from XWA of Montreal and KDKA in Pittsburgh. Brendan the mongrel setter howled like a high-pitched heterodyne. The Samoyed jumped overboard and swam ashore. In my excitement I stopped working the oars, let the antenna dip in the water and the line went dead.

The world touched my lake and I reached back out to it. I taught myself to speed transmit Morse messages with a Ford spark coil and an old boat windshield wrapped in tin foil as the capacitor. The spark gap was made from battery zinc rods. I established regular contact with amateur stations in nearby Bracebridge and Burke's Falls. I even tried to persuade my father to install a set in his Toronto office so we could send each other messages at the end of the day: Did you have chocolate pudding for lunch again? When are you coming home, Dad? Although he understood the principle of telegraphy, radio mystified him. He examined my spark transmitter and crystal receiver and shook his head in wonder. I tried to explain. 'If you have a dachshund long enough to reach from Bent River to Bala and pinch his tail in Bent River he'll bark in Bala. That's the telegraph,' I said. 'If you take away the dog that's wireless.'

Radio transformed the mundane and brought magic to my life. At school I slipped an antenna between the bars of the boarding house window, disguised it as a clothesline and slung it across the headmaster's garden. Through the squeaks and static a voice far-off in the distance said, 'Good evening from KPO San Francisco.' In those days the airwaves were all but empty and on a clear night stations from across the continent could be heard. One midnight in April the duty master found me under my bed listening to a London amateur reporting the *Titanic* disaster. He confiscated the Audion valve set and caned me with 'six of the best'. Two years later as a Leading Telegraphist in the Great War my day on HMS *Chatham* was determined by orders flashed from the Admiralty, across Europe to the Dardanelles. Aboard the SS *Victorian* sailing home from Southampton I danced to the music of an orchestra playing a thousand miles away. The ship was carrying the British delegation to the 1920 Imperial Press Conference and to mark the occasion the Marconi Company had fitted onboard their most powerful marine wireless. We marvelled at the wonder of singing 'God Save the King' together with a choir in Essex. Jamie used the ship's radio-telephone to call Zachary at the office and we laughed together through the ether. He told him that the onboard edition of the *North Atlantic Times* had more current Maritimes news than the Toronto papers. Zachary was not amused.

The novelty captured the public imagination and by the

end of the decade every home in North America seemed to have a wireless. There were four-tube sets in woodwork consoles, Radiolas, Parlophones and high-fidelity Atwater-Kents. On hot Muskoka summer days when the screen doors were on and the windows open I often walked through Gravenhurst following a concert, not missing a single note, the receivers in every house being tuned to the only station. Many of the country's few transmitters had been set up by hardware stores. For them radio was no more than a means of promoting the sale of their receivers by playing the latest dance bands. The manufacturers themselves, RCA and Westinghouse, went on air too to expand the market for their product. As listeners came to talk more of the Creole Jazz Band and *Amos 'n' Andy* than they did about their neighbours, the influence of radio became apparent. *Fibber McGee* and *The Fireside Hour* may have provided a popular diversion but they did little else.

Wireless had the potential both to bring people together and to enlarge the world. Its magic could do good by stealth, raising the consciousness of the listener, pushing back the boundaries of ignorance and intolerance. I came to believe that a broadcaster's responsibility was not simply to supply his listeners with music and baseball, the limited role of entertainment utility as espoused across the border, but to provide a public service. While the Charleston and the World Series might bind together Americans, Canada would be united by the spoken word.

'Crannag,' announced Hector, laying down his letter tiles one by one. 'C-r-a-n-n-a-g. You will remember that it means pulpit in the Gaelic.' Zachary hadn't been able to find the circulation figures in the trunk but Jamie, who had only been trying to be helpful, had happened upon a box of Scrabble. He had suggested playing a match even though our games tended to descend into argument as Hector used Gaelic words, Zachary technical terms and my spelling wasn't up to much.

'You told me before that it translates as ship,' said Jamie, with his letter rack suspended before him.

'Aye and it does. Pulpit and ship, the same word.'

'That's one bit of Gaelic that Sandy understands,' cracked Zachary while tallying the score. 'Radio was his pulpit.' His temper, short at the best of times, had been taxed by drawing seven consonants from the letter bag. 'I imagine you thought you were fulfilling a popular demand?'

'There is no point in trying to satisfy the public,' I replied. 'Few of us know what we want and even fewer what we need. I never presumed to preach but I did make a habit of overestimating the listeners' mentality. How else can man's reach exceed his grasp?'

'I must admit, Sandy, I hadn't seen the pedagogue in you,' stammered Jamie.

'And from whom did I inherit it?'

'Don't look at me,' answered Hector.

'What's bred in the bone will come out,' added Jamie with half a proverb. 'Whose go is it anyway?'

'It's time enough for Sandy to have his turn.'

'Well, I came out here after the collapse of the *Mirror*,' I explained while juggling my letter tiles. 'Toronto had become too stale, too restrictive for me. Muskoka would have been a good place to set up my first station . . .'

'It is a fine part of the country, right enough. With the finest boats, too.'

'. . . but it was sparsely populated,' I told Hector. 'The west, on the other hand, was young and unformed and hadn't succumbed to the moneyed prejudice of the east. And I thought, well, to be honest, I thought that here I had a better chance of doing something worthwhile.'

A great hissing Continental had pulled the train of upholstered sleepers, silver-service dining cars and immigrant

coaches with boards for beds and iron stoves for cooking.
Over seven days and nights the locomotive had strained
around Superior's north shore, darted arrow-straight across
the prairies and snaked through the Rockies to carry me
down to the sea. 'Direct and Quickest Route to all Points
East, West and South,' the line's publicity had boasted. At
Kicking Horse Pass Swiss engineers, hundreds of Chinese
coolies and seventy-five carloads of dynamite had built a
pair of spiral tunnels that twisted down through the mountains. The drivers of long freights could emerge from one
end and look back up the Big Hill to see their caboose vanish
into the other.

'Vancouver in the early thirties was little more than the
place where the rails ended,' I recalled, 'an isolated, fleshpot
port of timber mills and trader houses hankering for respect-
ability. Well, the morning after my train arrived I found
an office on Water Street. I bought a licence, settled on my
call-sign, CUAN, strung a flat-top antenna between two
poles on the roof and started broadcasting. It was that easy,'
I laughed then laid out seven letters on the Scrabble board.
'Look, I'm on a double-letter square.'

'What might the word be, Sandy?' asked Dad.

'Spinaker. Our studio was in the loft,' I continued with
a smile. 'We had a piano, two music stands and three micro-
phones, one of which was a telephone mouthpiece. I'd built
the breadboard transmitter myself on the kitchen table following the instructions of the Amateur Radio Relay League
handbook.'

'Do you mean spinnaker?' asked Zachary. 'A racing sail?'
I nodded, too excited to be distracted from my story. 'Spinnaker is spelt with two "n"s.'

'I don't have a second "n".'

'You'll recall, Zachary, that Sandy went in for the spoken
and not the written word,' said Jamie with a smile.

'Our hundred-watt signal covered the whole Lower Mainland,' I remembered, 'reached ships in the Straits and on

good nights was picked up right across Vancouver Island. It was all live, there were no devices to pre-record programmes back then, so every voice and sound had to be brought into the office. I invited in teachers, experts, anyone who held a strong belief for on-air discussions. The presenters, singers, actors and George the newsreader – who wore tweeds and a snap-brimmed trilby – all squeezed in with them in the single studio.' The memory of the early days delighted me. 'A river of words flowed out from our loft-room.'

Hector looked up from his letters and recalled the alphabet unravelling over the floor in Promise. Zachary remembered it too and shivered. 'Can we get on with the game, please Sandy?'

'I could do spinach but I don't have an "h" either,' I said, examining the letter rack. 'Tell you what, I'll put down the second "n" next time round.' I turned back to Hector and Jamie. 'So we broadcast farming news and school lessons in the morning, women's talks in the afternoon and Continental concerts in the evening. We played records too, of course, slipping educational programmes in between the popular series. But the area I concentrated on was the news. There's a tendency to favour local events, especially in a place separated from the rest of the world. You may remember the Scottish newspaper which reported the sinking of the *Titanic* with the headline "Aberdeen Man Lost at Sea"? Well, we tried to bring our listeners a broader outlook. Items were not just clipped from the Vancouver papers but gathered from various sources and presented in unbiased, balanced reports.'

'But it made no money,' said Zachary, nudging the floating board away from him. 'Wireless was not accepted as an advertising medium. Merchants preferred to put ads in newspapers which they could read when they came home from work. They didn't want to pay for announcements that went out while they were busy in their shops.'

'A minute spot earned at best five dollars and every thermionic valve which blew out cost me fifty to replace.'

'Cost *me* f-f-fifty dollars,' corrected Jamie, slipping the missing "n" into "spinnaker". He and Hector had grown tired of waiting and began spelling words out of turn.

'But radio grew nevertheless; CKFC formed their own orchestra, CRCV introduced domestic situation comedy and CNRV tied up with stations across the country to transmit to trans-continental trains. By 1939 Vancouver had more radio stations than any other Canadian city. CUAN – thanks to Dad – increased its power to twelve amps.' I chortled, thinking of the night when blue sparks crackled off the antenna and the building's metal railing gave passers-by an electric shock. 'The new signal was a little too strong. The frequency transformed all the cookers in a nearby apartment block into receivers. Their metal frames acted as aerials, the leaves of boiling cabbages rectified the signal and the saucepans amplified it.'

'I dare say that might have put some husbands off their wives' cooking.'

'When the war came, news became even more important. There were brothers, husbands, fathers and sons at sea, in the air, dug into trenches risking their lives. It was our responsibility to bring word of them home to their families. A million Canadians joined up, forty-two thousand never came back. During the Normandy landings one soldier from West Vancouver was reported missing, presumed dead but then, a few weeks later, his wife heard him on the radio. We often relayed reports from the BBC, recorded on lacquer disks at the front, and in one the correspondent had interviewed the injured at a field hospital. The wife, almost five thousand miles away from France, heard her husband's voice and knew that he was alive.'

'War transformed the country,' noted Zachary. He had lost interest in the game when Hector began adding abbreviated psalms in Latin. 'Canada entered it as a producer of raw materials and came out as a manufacturer. We built the world's third-largest navy.'

'In 1945 no country was more optimistic,' added Jamie, emptying the last letters around the board, 'or had better cause to be.'

'There was such confidence then and, it seemed, infinite abundance and promise. So we expanded into bigger premises. I loved watching the construction of the station's acoustic studios and control rooms. The newsroom was equipped with both Trans-Radio News and Canadian Press wire services. We bought record player turntables, RCA wire recorders and Model 'Y' acetate machines for field work. Cables were laid to relay stations in the Interior.' I turned the sphere on my lap. 'On the desk in my new office I had Grand-dad's globe . . .'

'On which your Vancouver is not marked,' Hector observed. 'Of it no man had dreamt when I was a boy.'

'. . . and I set beside it a framed saying: "According to the laws of aerodynamics a bumblebee cannot fly but a bumblebee . . ."' Jamie joined with me to finish the maxim: '". . . being unaware of this fact goes ahead and flies anyway."'

'It's in the trunk,' he said and we chuckled together.

'When we went on air the signal radiated from Salmon Arm to Scotch Creek, Telegraph Cove to Desolation Sound. Our low-powered rebroadcast transmitters reached out to the valleys, the far harbours, bringing the world into every living room.'

'And you stayed true to the Word?' asked Hector. He had used all his letters except for a single 'Q'.

'Yes,' I replied. 'Speech remained the core of our programming, although we did concede something towards the postwar enthusiasm for swing music. A *Jitterbug Hour* was introduced and listeners requested their favourite dance tune in exchange for a donation to charity. The songs were often dedicated to relatives or friends. I remember once the presenter misread an announcement. "And congratulations to Vernon Chipchase who is 111 years old today," he enthused, and started to play "Knees up, Mother Brown". After only a few bars the music faded and the presenter apologised. "I'm sorry but I've just reread the dedication and Mr Chipchase is not 111, he is ill." An embarrassed silence followed. "Get well soon, Vern."'

"I enjoyed the swing era dances,' recalled Jamie, roaring with laughter. 'The Lindy Hop, Pecking and the Suzy-Q; a bit too energetic for me at that age but great f-f-fun.'

'Suzy-Q?' asked Hector in sudden interest. 'Is that a proper word?'

'I don't see why that should bother you now,' complained Zachary. He still had five tiles in his letter rack and the flouting of the rules had annoyed him.

'That same energy built an underground railway in Toronto, the Saint Lawrence Seaway, new ref-f-fineries, aluminium smelters and nickel mines.'

'Few of which were financed by Canadians,' said Zachary. 'All that the war generation wanted were secure jobs, big cars and suburban bungalows with picture windows and basement recreation rooms. They stepped out of uniform and into bed, produced six million baby-boomers in fifteen years and deposited their savings in the bank. It was the Americans who had the foresight to invest in our economy.'

'You and I didn't f-f-fight in the war, Zachary. Those who did, well they felt that they had earned the right to a good life.'

'I am not belittling their sacrifice, not for one second,' snapped Zachary, 'or the value of the ensuing economic boom. But something, somewhere fostered a new complacency. Somehow I . . . I . . .' As he strained to find the words his confidence faltered. For a moment the only sound was the hum of tyres on asphalt. 'I only know that duties lost their value and everyone began to question and contest.'

'Would it be that after this war the demand for rights

became separated from the performance of duties?' asked Hector, rearranging a prayer for deliverance to spell 'Suzy Q'. 'It's myself that has seen people begin to care more and more for what they can take from society and less for what they give to it.'

'Not at the station,' I replied. 'At least, not at first.'

'It is a thousand pities but I fear that the Church may be to blame. It was our mission to maintain the vocabulary of morality.'

'No, F-F-Father,' said Jamie, inadvertently knocking over the Scrabble board and sending the letters spinning above the Dodge. Zachary's doubt had astonished him. 'We took on that responsibility. The press tried to inform and empower through words.'

'And I worked to foster that common spirit too,' I insisted. 'I shared the company stock with all senior staff. I tried to hear every voice at board meetings.'

'That is fine, right enough, but did it work, Sandy?' asked Hector, sadness in his voice.

'The commitment to high standards increased our costs but not our audience share,' I admitted. 'Commercial stations which played only music grew in popularity and, as advertisers turned to them to reach more listeners, our income suffered. My staff began to worry that our public service obligations put the company at risk. Less talk and more music, they said, would increase revenue and secure our future. I demonstrated my faith in the company by investing my inheritance in programming. Our fortunes improved for a time, we wooed listeners away from CKLC's *Dance Favourites* and *Hockey Night in Canada* with our *World Report*, but then . . .'

'Then, *a bhalaich*?'

'Then it was 1954, the year when the change came which none of us had foreseen.'

*   *   *

RADIO WAVES HAD washed over the waters and wound across the land. The spoken word had rippled over the high river terraces, surged across the pine plateaux and curled through arid valleys of mauve and pollen yellow. Elsie's pick-up truck rolled down from the mountains alongside the last miles of the Thompson River and in the whirr of the wheels Beagan heard voices.

'Did you know your father well?' asked Elsie, turning their collective sorrow to thoughts of individual loss.

'No, not really,' replied Beagan, clicking off the radio. Hereford cattle dozed beside juniper bushes. A rancher yawned under his stetson. 'I grew up too shy to ask questions and then, when I realised that I needed to, it was too late. He died when I was twelve.'

'One time an elder who I met told me I have the look of the Senijextee, something to do with my gait and cheekbones.' The puppy pawed its way across Beagan's lap and settled itself on Elsie. 'They were a modest tribe who used to fish round here from sturgeon-nosed canoes.' She picked up the dog and placed it on Noah. 'They're extinct now.'

Beagan winced before he answered, his slow deliberation not escaping Elsie's attention. 'I have my father's forehead. I've seen it in the photographs,' he said, nodding back at the trunk. 'But not his body. I remember that he was rather . . . roly-poly.'

'You mean fat?'

'He had an ample belly and long spindly legs,' Beagan admitted, 'but was too light on his feet to be considered heavy. He always seemed about to break into a jig, especially in boatyards.' Above the roadside a hand-painted billboard offered relaxed country living on the Golden Age River Estate. 'You see, his other great love was the water. He wanted to sail my family away across the Pacific.' A wistful smile crossed his lips. 'He threatened to have his ear pierced and wear a gold earring like a plump pirate.'

'Fat often means happy. Pa Faithful was thin as a rake and it made him mean. I only once remember him laughing. I'd wanted to learn how to ride and saved up for the lessons, without his help. But the first time I tried it I fell off. He rolled around on

the ground laughing his guts out. It made me climb right back
on the horse.'

Beagan felt the anger rise in her voice but detected no trace of
bitterness. 'Heaven blessed my father with a happier spirit, lighter
even than his step. It lifted him above day-to-day worries. He
owned a couple of radio stations,' he volunteered, 'but he was a
poor businessman.'

'They closed down, did they?'

'Not exactly, no. But he was too trusting and maybe too much
of a dreamer. And too kind as well. I grew up in the Gulf Islands
just off Vancouver. Once my father refused to burn a log because
there was a woodworm in it. The stump sat by the fireplace all
winter and he grew as fond of the beetle's tapping call as if it
were a pet dog's bark. Of course the larvae got into the house
timbers and infested the building. My mother wasn't amused when
we had to call in the exterminators.'

Beyond the sweet resin smell of the Savona sawmill the hills
crowded together and the drowsy river awoke in the twists and
turns of the narrowed channel. It swelled over stones and elbowed
at sandbanks. By Spences Bridge the river fumed across rapids,
grabbed at an inflatable raftload of revellers and tossed it down
the white water between wet black boulders. Pink rock scars rose
up out of the torrent at Goldpan and tumbledown wooden cabins
rotted away where Cariboo prospectors had lost their faith. The
Thompson churned into the Fraser's deep-wooded gorge and the
lines of rail, road and power jostled for footholds along the
canyon's sheer cliffs. The khaki current boiled between crags and
outcrops, frothed against mossy banks and gushed into a livid
whirlpool.

'I've come home to see what killed him,' Beagan confessed
suddenly as hundreds of bats descended from shaggy Great Pacific
cedars to skim the waters and feed on moths. 'To see how he
was betrayed.'

'This country broke a lot of promises.'

'I've always believed that Canada killed my father,' he said, and
Elsie didn't add a word.

After Hope the mountains slumped back into the earth and the waters calmed. In the Upper Fraser Valley logs moved in booms and Native fishermen cast for salmon. Ochre autumn leaves blew across a placid delta and the gentle rain which washed their faces tasted of the sea.

Dragon banners fluttered from maple-leaf lamp-posts. A cruise liner's whistle echoed off glass office towers. Russian seamen dragged shopping bags stuffed with digital watches back to their freighters. At the continent's edge high-rise buildings stepped down from the wooded mountains to working wharves in a protected harbour. Vancouver, the largest Pacific port in all the Americas, was reminiscent less of other Canadian cities than of Hong Kong. Its street signs were written in Chinese. Its Star Ferry-like Seabus linked the downtown core with the Kowloon-side north shore. Its markets smelt of durian and its cafés click-clacked with the snap of *mah-jong* tiles. Yet beneath all the superficial similarities Hongcouver, as the locals called it, was unique.

A pristine white Rolls-Royce cruised past the Balmoral Hotel and turned into Keefer Street to spill a tittering Chinese family into the On On Tea Garden. Along East Hastings petite Thai prostitutes lounged on stretched silver Lincolns. Japanese tourists bowed to one another and snapped photographs of totem poles. At the Royal Vancouver Yacht Club the forest of masts rose from boats with Haida names. There were seaplanes and salmon seiners moored to the piers. The Oriental busker outside the Marine Building played 'Scotland the Brave' on the bagpipes.

Beagan recognised the sturdy mansions in Shaughnessy, the strip joints on Granville Street, the busy quays of Saskatchewan potash and prairie grain. He remembered summer Sundays with his father watching the ocean-bound container ships sail past the Stanley Park cricket pitch. Sometimes if a good batsman was at the wicket the ships were hit by sixes. Behind him he saw the Rockies enfold the city, before him its waters ran out into the oceans of the world. Tokyo, Sydney, Shanghai and San Francisco were just a boat ride away.

'A hundred or so years ago this was all coastal cedar forest,' said Elsie as the Dodge rolled along the Grandview Highway. Across from a 7–11 convenience store a homeowner trimmed his corner of paradise with a lawnmower. 'The Tsleilwaututh hunted white-tailed deer around where the airport is now.' A hoarding announced the development of dream apartments on False Creek's prime real estate. Above the sign Mohawk construction workers bolted together high-rise girders, as they had done on skyscrapers throughout North America, while at its foot a Musqueam brave slept, crumpled and drunk. 'His grandfather would have steamed mussels in their shells at the mouth of the Fraser.'

'Maybe yours and Noah's too.'

'Sure,' acknowledged Elsie.

'It's different now,' observed Beagan, her pain now his own, the country's own. 'For us both.'

'For us all.'

Vancouver's population had quadrupled in fifty years, Pacific Rim business-immigrants bought citizenship in exchange for government-approved investment and half the city's children now spoke a language other than English at home. Elementary schools offered Mandarin immersion courses aimed at making the anglophones bilingual. Local estate agents boasted resident geomancers, experts in the Chinese art of *feng shui* which predicates a building's design and orientation.

'But cross the Lions Gate Bridge and beyond Capilano,' Elsie gestured out over the yachts and bulk carriers in English Bay, 'a man can still walk all the way to the North Pole and not meet another human being.'

She dropped Beagan and the trunk by a hedged garden at the end of his brother's drive. She and Noah had a ferry to catch and she asked Beagan to visit them when he reached Vancouver Island. 'Come over for a meal, for a bath too if you fancy another ride,' she added without a smile. 'Mind you, the tub'll be plumbed in by then.' They shook hands and Noah slept on. Beagan watched the pick-up drive away until it disappeared out of sight.

He carried the trunk down to the beach-house of wooden shingles. Its weathered shutters glistened silver-grey in the autumn sunshine. The windows looked out over the sound and had no curtains. Alex had left him a note on the table. It read, 'The kayak is on the lawn and crabmeat's in the fridge. Meet me at North Shore at six.' Beagan's brother was at the studio. On the kitchen wall Bartlett's *Timber Slides on the Ottawa* hung beside a map of canoe routes through Nouvelle France. Etched steamers crossed Toronto harbour above a wooden model of a Scottish *bàta*. Captain Lecky's *Wrinkles of Practical Navigation* was shelved with *Cook's Voyages*. In crisp monochrome gentle Doris Pilch wore a flapper hat and stood by Sandy on the *Kipper*'s hurricane deck. The building was unfamiliar to Beagan but the family possessions welcomed him as an old friend's embrace. He made a sandwich then carried the kayak over the rocks to the shore. Shells crunched under his feet and he slipped on a mane of seaweed. The salt from a splash of cold water tightened on his skin. He launched the canoe away from the beach, out into the bay and felt the surface swell beneath him with the incoming tide.

The ghosts sensed it too. No bathtub was as comfortable as a boat and it felt good to be back on the sea. '*Sàl is bùrn*,' twinkled Hector. Salt water and fresh water. Chalk and cheese. He dipped his hand in the brine then, for the sake of a little devilment, splashed Beagan. His great-grandson hardly reacted to the soaking; he had grown used to the presence of his forefathers and trailed them behind him like a cloud of argumentative midges.

Sandy was laughing, lying on his back at the kayak's bow, recounting a radio story to Jamie. 'During the war we hired a new studio manager. It was hard to get good people then as the finest men had gone overseas. Well, one evening while we were on air this fellow telephoned his mother for a chat. "I'm sorry dear, I can't hear you," she said. In the background he heard the sound of our programme. "I'll just turn down the radio."

'"Don't worry, Mother," volunteered the manager. "I'll do it from here." So he lowered the studio's main output control and shut us down right across the province.'

Father and son chortled together but Zachary, who had been admiring the slick yachts in the bay, sighed and asked, 'So what happened?'

'Pardon, Uncle?' chuckled Sandy.

'What was the change that you failed to foresee?'

Sandy stopped laughing and sat up on his haunches. The kayak shivered with a passing wave. 'Television,' he said.

'Television?' scoffed Zachary.

'In 1954 CBUT-TV Vancouver came on air,' nodded Sandy. 'Almost overnight all the Lower Mainland's radio listeners became television viewers. Their Bakelite wirelesses were stowed away and new General Electric receivers with veneer cabinets stood in place of honour by family sofas. Fathers settled into their easy chairs, mothers put down their knitting and children stopped chattering. Within two years the whole nation was sitting bug-eyed and passive in front of a million sets.'

'I f-f-found television to be very educational,' recalled Jamie. 'Every time someone turned it on I went into the next room to read a good book.'

'And missed the opportunity, chap,' exclaimed Zachary. 'It was the start of a revolution, the electronic age. I can tell you, Gillean Publishing was prepared for it.'

'It was quite a novelty. Audiences watched anything: Don Messer and his Islanders, Bob Hope, Jack Benny, even the test pattern. Hypnotic, it was.'

'Radio had to search for a new role and most stations found it in easing the monotony of household chores and soothing the drive to work,' lamented Sandy. 'It no longer aspired to stimulate thought but instead numbed the listener with non-stop music, local news flashes and the phone-in chat-show. The scenery might well be better on radio but it took less imagination to picture it on TV.'

'So much changed after the war.'

'I died,' reported Zachary.

'We all did, but there was something else,' mused Jamie. 'This, the finest of countries, prosperous and at peace, lost faith in its potential. The blessèd good people f-f-forsook their resources, their inventiveness, their bounty of land and water. And I don't know why.'

'People like moral absolutes. They like to be told what to do and to ignore it,' said Zachary. 'It is a matter of self-assertion.'

'It is a selfishness that I see,' observed Hector, pointing towards the shore, 'behind this mild-mannered exterior. A spoiled people are unlikely to work for the common good.'

'F-F-Fewer cared about service, that's true enough. Principles changed.'

'Not all of them,' Sandy reminded his father.

Zachary dismissed the argument with a wave of his hand. 'But you cannot blame television for all these ills.'

'Well, no, of course not.'

'I'm not suggesting that,' answered Sandy. 'Television didn't close my radio network. I lost it. I resisted the call to change from speech to music output and my managers pooled their shares to vote me off the board. They maintained that our stations had to provide what the audience wanted, not what I, in their words, "ordained".'

'It is your failing then,' snapped Zachary. There was no emotion in his voice. 'You admit it.'

Sandy's laugh had a lost, hollow sound. 'Times had changed. Radio, they said, was entertainment not education. Information to them meant news flashes on traffic jams and lottery winners. There wasn't the airtime to explain issues and to put complex events into perspective.' He lay back on his son's kayak and shut his eyes. 'I gave my partners the opportunity that I expected Canada to offer me. They repaid me by asking me to empty my desk and leave the building. They didn't even have the courtesy to forward my mail.'

'I may say again that a successful man does not try to stop the tide,' advised Zachary. 'He moves with it, redirects it.'

'Is that why Gillean Publishing came to stray from the discipline of the Word?' asked Sandy.

'Yes,' replied Zachary with a sidelong glance at his father, 'but only after my death. It diversified first into local radio and then into the emerging field of cable television. A very sound financial move, you'll no doubt agree.'

'The acquisitions reshaped the firm into a multi-media conglomerate,' confirmed Sandy. 'The huge profits of the new movie and sport channels proved to be irresistible.'

'The company also established lucrative financial information services for traders on nationwide telephone line links,' added Zachary with pride. 'Yet Gillean Communications' core business remained publishing.'

'Until last year,' said Jamie. Hector had laid down his Bible to listen.

'The firm was bought out, Father,' explained Zachary. 'For many billions of dollars. We started it with what, James, a few hundred?'

'But the paradox is that the aggressive corporate raider who stalked the company wanted it for its cable assets alone.'

'He didn't play by the rules, that's quite true,' admitted Zachary, who believed in the adherence to sound business ethics. 'Stock was amassed in secret and multiple voting shares used to seize control.'

'And the new owner has already dissected the company,' said Sandy. 'He has begun overbuilding the existing copper cable system into a broadband fibre-optic digital super-highway to provide national entertainment packaging and telephony services.'

'I heard English right on the start of my existence but in

the old days I understood it better,' confessed Hector. 'It would be fine if you would please tell me what all this means?'

'It means that Canadians from sea to sea will now be served by twenty-four-hour shopping channels and inter-active advertising, that the nation will be united on quiz shows and in video games.'

'A f-f-funny thing that; as the new technology reduces distance, people want more space between themselves.'

'It means, Grand-dad, that after 150 years, this is what has become of our work.'

'The new owner has no interest in the press, F-F-Father,' added Jamie. 'The trade magazines and newspapers which accompanied the sale are of limited use to him.'

'And the fate of the Word?' asked Hector, his voice unusually quiet.

'Uncertain,' answered Sandy. 'As is that of our own. We become foreigners in our own land.'

'CUT!'

'Check the gate,' barked the assistant director.

The clapper-loader released the lens and examined the film track for dust. The actors and crew stood stock still, suspended like a celluloid image. 'Gate's clear.'

'Thank you people, that's a wrap.' The lights went out. The director embraced the lead actress and smudged stage blood on his bomber jacket. The boom operator coiled her mike cable and the make-up man checked his blusher. Everyone on the studio floor relaxed except the assistant director. 'Eight a.m. call tomorrow,' he ordered. 'Scenes 12 to 16 inclusive. That's low-loader and high-hats, grips. Wardrobe; see me before you go.'

'We got to end more upbeat. Give it more hope.' The US network co-producer strode out of the shadows. 'I told you that we can't go out on a downer.' A script-writer worried behind him, tugged at a thin lock of hair and dropped his notes. 'Can you handle it, or do we fax it to Willy?' The writer made a transparent gesture of confidence.

The sturdy figure beside them had Sandy's walk, Zachary's athletic frame and a trim version of Hector's beard. Beagan saw in his brother's face his own grey-green eyes and felt a stab of recognition, as if all the trunk's photographs had been fused into a single composite and come to life. Alex embraced him, a brawny bearhug with ursine grunt, and said, 'It's great to see you, bro. How was the trip?'

'A lot of water,' he replied with a smile.

The American co-producer introduced himself. 'Edgar Jumper Junior. How you doing?'

'Edgar's up from L.A. He's joining us for dinner,' explained Alex.

'Great,' lied Beagan.

'We'll take my car,' said Jumper.

In a black and red sushi restaurant Japanese diners were welcomed by '*Irashaimase*' and replete Westerners sung away with 'Thanyouvelimush.' Jumper ate tempura and talked deals. A weak Canadian dollar, tax concessions and the variety of locations had lured Hollywood producers north of the border. Canada, he said, was a damn good place to shoot pictures. The red postboxes were painted US blue, the street signs changed to Pennsylvania Avenue, and Vancouver made into America's second-biggest television production centre.

'Talent love working up here,' said Jumper, emphasising the point with a jab of his chopsticks. 'The crews are friendly and there's a real let's-do-a-good-show-together feeling.' Beagan asked about the necessity of disguising Vancouver as a faceless Anycity. 'Hey, if all the world's a stage then Canada is the theatre's auditorium, the safest place in a dramatic world. This is the country where anxiety's been reduced to an acceptable level. There's no drama here.'

Alex took exception to Jumper's comments, even though the American was giving him his 'big break'. He had worked for years building up a reputation as an independent producer. His small-budget pictures, all of which had been set in British Columbia, had achieved a minor success and been shortlisted for the Critics' Award at Cannes.

'Hey Alex, don't get me wrong. This is a great country if you like a quiet life. It's like Kansas with mountains. But, really, who cares what happens in Moose Jaw?' He poured out three glasses of Kirin beer. 'Come on, let's drink to free trade. We're all Americans at heart. We all share the same dream.'

'Which dream is that, Edgar?' asked Beagan.

'You have been away a long time,' said Jumper. He thought it was a dumb question. 'The pursuit of happiness, OK? What else drove those emigrants out of Europe and across America? The search for a better life. They chased it to the west coast and then, whammo, they couldn't go no further.'

'So California is the promised land?'

'Yeah, but only in the mind,' mumbled Jumper. He was gnawing on a prawn the size of a croissant. 'And that's where we come in. We're the inheritors of generations of hope. Movies are the manifestation of dreams.' Alex rolled his eyes heavenward. 'Hey, no, guys, I really believe it. Hollywood gives the audience that promised land for ninety minutes then takes it away and leaves them wanting more. It's no wonder movies are our top export. They're universal.'

'I saw their influence near Singapore,' volunteered Beagan. 'I was drifting around Asia and got a construction job with BP.' He poured from the fresh pot of green tea. 'There was a really beautiful tropical atoll on which a refinery was to be built. The island had a natural amphitheatre and on Saturday nights the company would put up a movie screen for the locals. At dusk sampans and junks came across the sea from the surrounding archipelago. The families laid out picnics under the palms and as the sun set the projector was switched on. It was free, so the films were all oldies – *Babes on Broadway*, *Stagecoach*, *The Wizard of Oz* – and the islanders loved them. Here they were living in paradise but by the end of every movie they didn't want to be there. They wanted to be in New York or Cheyenne or the Emerald City.'

'Hey, I never heard that,' responded Jumper. He gulped his miso soup and signalled at the waitress. 'It's a great scene. We could use it.'

Alex asked, 'What happened to the island?'

Beagan shook his head. 'It's a floating factory now. The refinery covered it. There are no trees, no valley, no cinema.'

'Yeah it's tough,' said Jumper, paying with his gold American Express card. 'But at least they can still rent them on video.'

It was late when the American dropped them off at his hotel. The faded script-writer, his skin colourless and hair thinner still, was asleep in a foyer armchair, the rewritten pink pages spilling off his lap and on to the marble floor. On the way home Alex stopped to buy a 6/49 lottery ticket. 'The world is full of bastards and most of them are in this Filofax,' he said, fishing in his organiser for a ten-dollar bill. 'At least if I win I won't have to do co-ventures with one of them.'

'So is this the biggest dream then?' asked Beagan, selecting his seven numbers. The slogan printed on the game card read 'Imagine the Freedom'. He shook the ticket. 'Is this what Canada has become?'

'Hey, not just Canada. And if you win you won't knock it.'

At the beach-house Beagan wanted to lay his trip out on the kitchen table, to introduce Alex to Piri, Harold and Elsie. He hoped that his brother would share the Reverend and his *Good Intent*, Jamie and the *Kipper*, Zachary and the *Canadian Vegetable*. He tried to tell him something about Quetico and his companions on the journey but Alex was too much of a pragmatist to believe in spirits. He had inherited Zachary's realism as well as his drive. So instead they opened the trunk and together looked through its contents. Beagan uncovered the papers for the inherited island. 'I thought all that land was long gone,' said Alex. 'I'd really love to see it with you but the network's got us under a lot of pressure. I can't get away this month.'

At the bottom of the trunk were buried a few of their father's dusty broadcast tapes. The brothers dug out a reel-to-reel machine and wired it into the stereo. They laughed at the old school lessons and dated women's talks then heard a play on the life and death of Mary Queen of Scots.

'Do you remember how he made the execution effects?' asked Beagan. Sandy had revelled in creating the on-air sounds, proving like Eden Prosper Goode that truth was not the facts. 'He cut a cabbage with an axe, let it fall into a wicker basket then squirted a hot-water bottle full of baked beans on to the straw – all in two seconds flat.' Alex laughed with Beagan but there was no spark in his eyes. 'Don't you remember? The crinkling cellophane that sounded like campfire? The half coconuts for horses' hooves and gossamer ladies' gloves for the wings of small birds?'

'No,' admitted Alex. 'I guess I was too young.'

Deeper still in the trunk there was a copy of *Tapestry*, CUAN's weekly programme for listeners who were not of British descent, and a Continental concert. They threaded the last tape on to the player and listened in silence. It was a recording of Sandy's obituary.

'We grow up thinking that our parents will be with us forever because they always were there,' said Alex, 'but then they're gone.'

'In a way our old man still is with us.'

'Sure, in a way,' acknowledged Alex. 'But it's difficult to ask his advice or chat about the weather.' Alex leafed through a sheaf of photographs of island cottages, lacquer disk recorders and old boats. He dwelt over a staff portrait taken six weeks before CBUT-TV came on air.

'Did I tell you that I want to go to the old station tomorrow?'

'Forget it, there's nothing there,' advised Alex. 'They tore down the building years ago. It's now a YMCA or something.' He dropped the photographs back in the trunk and closed the lid on its history. 'You know, our family had one great failing. We always looked for the best in people. We gave strangers the benefit of the doubt, at least that was the old man's downfall. All my life I've tried to fight against that instinct.'

'He didn't fail,' asserted Beagan. 'Canada failed him. It deserted him.'

'I don't buy that,' said Alex, shaking his head. 'He should have seen the place as it was, not as he wanted it to be.'

'He lost his country without ever leaving its borders.'

'Because he didn't adapt to its changes.'

'But why should he have? It was his Canada. His family, our family, had helped make it. The Scots really did believe that they could build a promised land here, that thought would restore purity and justice. The tragedy is that the country wasn't up to his faith in it.'

'Canada, for better or for worse, has always been open to all comers: Italian peasants, Jewish intellectuals, American business-men, you name it,' said Alex. 'Sure, successive immigrants have been more practical in their ambitions but what of it? Each new-comer changes the society and everyone else has to adapt.'

'It's not the newcomers that I'm talking about; new blood has always enriched the country. No, it's the balance between the old and the new. I just can't get over the feeling that there's something missing here now,' said Beagan, 'something to do with the re-sponsibility of continuity. You know, continuity keeping the possibilities open, keeping alive hope and vision. The Church used to provide that vocabulary, then it was the press and, for a time, radio too. But today, I don't know, it's as if the words have been lost.'

'I'm sorry,' yawned Alex, 'but the only vision I can deal with now is television. Can we talk this through tomorrow night? It's an early call and I'm so bushed I can't think straight.'

While his brother caught the last minutes of *Entertainment Tonight* on the bedside portable Beagan cupped Hector's old globe in his hands and squeezed it as if the force of will alone could hold together the yellowed panels and faded land marked 'Unexplored Countries'.

In the morning Beagan drove Alex's Mercedes through Stanley Park, across False Creek and south down Cambie Street. A seal sunned itself on Siwash Rock. Two Korean bankers in yellow gumboots fished off Prospect Point. Beyond the sari and spice shops of Little India he found the site of his father's station. But there was no familiar old oak tree for him to climb, no crystal-watered bay in which he could swim, no reminiscent skyline to admire. In the same way that the great stands of Douglas firs had first been supplanted by tidy rows of cabbages, that those allot-ments had then been ploughed under clapboard neighbourhoods and shopping malls mushroomed atop the swelling city, the breeze-block radio building had been replaced by a sports hall. It in turn had been converted into a modern Chinese Presbyterian church. Each episode was layered beneath another like the skins of an onion.

The Reverend 'Rocky' Poon Ho Sing was out jogging in Pacific Spirit Park so Beagan passed an hour driving around the neigh-bourhood and stopping for petrol.

'$17.89,' said the student behind the till and handed Beagan his change. 'The first Chinese were brought to BC.'

'I beg your pardon,' said Beagan. He had filled the tank and given the petrol attendant a twenty-dollar bill.

'You put in $17.89 worth of gas. 1789 was the year the first Chinese labourers were imported to Canada. They built John Meares's ship the *North American*,' explained the student. 'It's a game I play so this job doesn't drive me crazy. I'm studying Chinese-Canadian History at UBC.' His textbooks lay on the counter between the Milky Way bars and packets of automobile air-freshener. A 'Proud to be Canadian' sticker adorned the top volume.

'What if I'd spent more? Say $18.85?' asked Beagan.

'1881 to 1885.' The student swept his fine black hair off his brow. 'Seventeen thousand men from Kwantung, the Pearl River delta, are brought over to build the Canadian Pacific railway. It's they who named Vancouver *Hahm-sui-fau*, the Saltwater City.'

'How about $19.49?'

'Chinese-Canadians are given the vote.' Beagan was surprised. 'There's a long history of prejudice on the west coast. The 1923

Immigration Act excluded Asiatics from settling here. In the following twenty years only eight Chinese were admitted into Canada. Chinese immigration wasn't placed on an equal basis with other nationalities until 1967.' The student didn't smile. 'The game helps sharpen my memory.'

Beagan shook his head and took two Danishes and a coffee from the food bar. The bill came to $4.58 including sales tax. '458,' he hazarded. 'Surely nothing happened here in the year 458.'

'Oh, it certainly did. Hwui Shan, the Buddhist priest, discovered America. He and four fellow missionaries sailed a junk across the North Pacific. His narrative records the accurate distance of the journey, describes the west coast redwoods and the unwalled cities of Mexico.' The student counted out a few coins and pushed them across the counter. 'Wasn't that about the time that Rome was being pillaged by Vandals?'

'I regret that I do not know anything about your father,' said the Reverend Poon, folding his strong hands together like a muscular Manchu mandarin. He wore a clerical collar with his king-size tracksuit. 'There are sixty-five Chinese churches in Vancouver. Maybe his radio station was in one of our other buildings.'

'No,' said Beagan, hurrying to keep up with the Reverend's energetic tour of the church. 'It was definitely here.'

'One of our elders is an architect,' Poon explained, striding into the chapel. 'He adapted the sports hall's facilities to suit our needs. The gymnasium was transformed into the nave. The shower became the choir. The locker room was redressed as the vestry. This building is a living testimony to the miracle of God's will.' He twisted himself into a standing back-stretch then added, 'The Lord also ensured that we were the first church to have an underground parking garage.'

Beagan admired the vaulting-horse altar and pulpit, the donated pews and exercise-mat carpet. The cross seemed to be made up from climbing ropes and parallel bars. He thanked Poon for his time but there was disappointment in his voice. 'Coming back here after so long I thought that I'd find a sense of belonging. Instead everything is unfamiliar. I feel torn,' Beagan admitted. 'I'm pulled back towards an old country yet still reaching out for the new to the west.'

'Or to the east.' Poon lowered himself on to a bench and rolled his shoulders. Beagan expected him to do a dozen sit-ups but instead he said, 'The first Chinese felt displaced too.'

'It seems that every Canadian has two countries. Except the Native people, of course.'

'To our forefathers America had always been the Land of Fusang, an earthly paradise where everything grew to supernatural size. They called it "the Mountains of Gold". You know, that's what the modern ideograph for North America still means in the literal sense.' He sketched the characters on the back of a parish newsletter. 'Last century thousands of Chinese sailed east across the Pacific dreaming of great riches. It wasn't any wonder, in Kwantung a hundred dollars could buy a man both a wife and a house. But instead of discovering a golden mountain they only found work in salmon canneries or down the mines. They were sold like piglets into forced labour, toiled like slaves on the railway, lived above wash-houses and opium dens, tolerated racism. Most had no settlement papers and the Church took pity on them. The mission gave classes in the Bible, English and hope. The first generation is all up there,' said Poon, pointing beyond the basketball hoops and the steel-beamed roof, 'but the second, third, fourth and fifth generations participate in our fellowship and worship. Our role hasn't changed in a hundred years, except today it's Cantonese not English that is taught. We don't want the younger generation to lose their mother tongue.'

'It was the same on the Atlantic coast,' recalled Beagan. 'The Church kept the newcomers' dreams alive. It helped them cope.'

Poon stood up, flexed his hamstring and strode into the presbytery. 'I was an eighteen-year-old weakling when I heard the call to be God's servant,' he said. 'I was a tutor of marine welding in

Canton.' On a wall-map behind him Canada brought to mind a
ship sailing east. Its bow was the Saint Lawrence, Labrador looked
like a jib and the north was its mainsail. The southern border was
the water-line. 'I tried and tried but I could not ignore the call.
In secret I organised a church group disguised as the shipyard
gymnastic team.' He shook his head as if trying to dislodge a
jammed clot of memory. 'Of course the authorities saw through
it. I could no more walk on water than do a handstand then.
They arrested me and separated me from my family for a year. I
was paraded through the streets wearing a conical hat that read
"Reactionary Revolutionary". But in my humiliation was the mysterious guiding hand of God. We escaped to Hong Kong and I
enrolled both in theological college and a sports club.' A shy
woman and a serious young man stood before a running track in
the photograph by the desktop computer. 'As soon as I was fit
enough I applied to come here.'

When Reverend Poon was appointed minister the church's
membership had numbered less than one hundred souls. It was
his athletic faith coupled with the Pacific Rim's rising prosperity
which had nurtured the congregation's confidence. 'You cannot
just sit back and pray to God for a new church,' he had preached
in fund-raising sermons. 'You each have to push yourself hard so
that we may achieve this goal together.' Over the century since
the arrival of the first Chinese their community had swelled to
comprise 20 per cent of Vancouver's population. Its sons had
grown wealthier than the men who had imported their fathers as
labourers. Its studious daughters challenged white children for
the limited university places. Chinese had become Canada's third
most-spoken language.

'There are those who say that there is no God. But without God
where does the widow go for comfort? Without God where do the
weak find strength? Without God man has only himself to blame
for his woes and lacking the courage to do so blames everyone else.
It creates a selfish, lonely society. The mission tried to help by giving
its parishioners a sense both of place and continuity.'

'My great-grandfather shared that ambition,' said Beagan,

looking away from Poon's Cantonese Bible. 'But maybe what is important is not His existence but people's belief in His existence. Having faith in possibilities.'

'I want to fill our church with hope,' replied Poon, then stole a glance at the clock. 'And today is a special day.'

'Because of the referendum?' asked Beagan, aware that the vote on secession had begun in Quebec.

'No, because today my son is becoming Canadian.' Quebec seemed too distant to concern Poon. 'Maybe you would like to join me for the ceremony?' He looked at his running shoes. 'After I've changed.'

Ten minutes later Poon took his fedora from the hat-stand and led the way to the lift. 'Why is your son only now taking up citizenship?' asked Beagan. Beside an exercise bicycle hung a map of Christian missionaries in Africa: sons of China, raised in Canada, preaching the Word in Zaire. 'Was he a missionary?'

'Lord no,' laughed Poon. 'Stanley stayed behind in Hong Kong. He wanted the best of both worlds, the security of Canada and the excitement of Asia.' The elevator descended into the basement garage. 'My wife and I call him *juk-kat*. That translates as a short segment of bamboo, you know, one that doesn't reach one end of the pole or the other. He was neither here nor there, always somewhere in between.' Poon started the engine with a flourish and slammed the car into gear. It leapt up the ramp, dawdled at a stop sign then sped downtown. 'To be honest, Stanley thinks Canadians are lazy. For him every hour of the day is made for work, time used for enjoyment is wasted money.'

'I think he would have got on with my great-uncle.'

An open-top Lotus nipped passed them, its young Chinese driver and passenger both doing property deals on their portable phones. 'But when life gets hard Stanley's attitude has always been to move, to bend like bamboo. It's Hong Kong's unstable political situation that finally convinced him to settle here.'

*   *   *

'Indivisible' was embossed on the bronze-alloy maple leaf. A middle-aged woman, the sort who writes complaining letters about subway riders' feet on seats, guided Beagan, Poon and fifty other people from twenty nations into the panelled Citizenship Court. The immigrants sat in alphabetical rows and studied the words of the national anthem. Children wriggled in stiff new clothes and relatives took photographs. The clerk, who was of Taiwanese origin, introduced the RCMP officer. Corporal Marina Morazzoni wore a resplendent dress uniform. The Somalis, Colombians, Iranians and Chinese all rose as Judge Jerzy Opolski took his seat between a gold-tasselled flag and the portrait of the Queen. Stanley winked at his father.

The flash pictures stopped during the Oath of Citizenship. With right hands raised the assembly repeated their pledge line by line in English and then, with embarrassed smiles, in halting French. The clerk called out the unfamiliar surnames with equal difficulty. One by one they stepped forward to receive their certificate and shake the judge's hand. 'This is a special day for you, your family and the twenty-nine million other Canadians who welcome you,' said Opolski, maybe wondering if the country would exist the following morning. 'Canada is a diversity of various cultures woven into a harmonious whole.'

Corporal Morazzoni snapped to attention as the room swelled with optimism and a recording of 'O Canada'. A young Vietnamese bride began to cry. A Jamaican matron offered to photograph a Bangladeshi couple. Poon embraced his son. Stanley looked at his watch. The judge wished one and all 'a happy and peaceful life in Canada' as a determined woman holding a child by one hand and her certificate in the other argued with the clerk.

'This paper says I am Yugoslav.' She jabbed a finger at the offending word and forgot her vow of allegiance. 'I am Croatian, not Yugoslav. Yugoslavia does not exist.'

Beagan looked across the proud faces and realised that not one of the newcomers was of western European descent. The only representatives of the founding races in the court were himself and the portrait of the Queen.

It had always been hoped that Canada would mature without nationalism, that the French would live next to the English and Serbs work alongside Croats. In the same way that movies had propagated the American dream, Canada's leaders had created their own myths as a national glue. They had perpetrated the Empire Loyalist fable and the British Empire ideal. They had maintained that a ribbon of steel bound together the Inuit hunter and the Chinese washerwoman, the Newfie fisherman and the cigar-smoking Macedonian used-car salesman. The multi-culturalism myth too was an opportunistic illusion. It had been created by political necessity both to cope with multiracial immigration and to try to obscure Quebec's claims for special status by emphasising unity in diversity. But rather than nurturing that which was shared the policy had drawn attention to the differences. Canada had always welcomed newcomers in the belief that their children would understand the country, but each second generation had been swamped under the successive waves of even newer immigrants. The myths were a poor glue, and no substitute for a philosophy powerful enough to bind together disparate peoples.

As Beagan had seen on Toronto Island and at Caravan, Canadians had retreated into ethnic enclaves rather than assimilate. There was no American melting pot, no continuity to prevent the country from fracturing into competing nationalities, only a common desire for a quiet life with free health care. Less and less cultural knowledge came to be shared. School-age youngsters from Asia could not learn about the voyageurs if they had never seen a canoe. Russian pensioners at the Daily Bread Food Bank did not know that Ukrainian settlers had planted the first prairie wheat. 'I'm a hyphenated-Canadian,' said the owner of the deli where Beagan treated the Reverend to coffee and Black Forest cake. Her divided loyalty reminded him of Gabi Wellfit aboard the *Tadoussac*. 'I'm really German.' Canada had matured into a land of many solitudes.

AFTER THE LOSS of CUAN there was only one direction for me to go. I stepped off the edge of the continent and crossed the Strait of Georgia to a pine-clad archipelago adrift in the sea. On the Gulf Islands with my wife and the boys I made an attempt at retirement but the idleness frustrated me. I soon found myself tracing across the surface of Reverend Hector's globe a thousand fanciful routes across the Pacific, through the Mediterranean, back to Scotland's Western Isles. Over time my enquiries uncovered a bounty of lovely ships that were for sale. Bristol Marine had a barge suitable for fitting out as a verandah-type houseboat, Cantiere Dell'Argentario offered a staunch twin-screw cruiser to explore the Adriatic, and the Paddle Steamer Preservation Society suggested any of a dozen sea-going puffers that lay unloved in Highland lochs. But instead of buying a Norwegian troll, Greek caïque or modified Fifer I decided to build my own ark. After all, I had been designing her in my head for a lifetime, sighting the clean fair lines, and now I imagined her carrying the family away to sea.

Her white-oak keel was laid in a pebble-floored workshop. We planed it by hand and set the moulds across its length. Green spruce ribbands curved around them fore and aft, were balanced by upright braces then replaced with oak ribs. She was planked in cedar, cotton caulked and sanded to a smooth even hull. My two boys crawled around the low-part, as Reverend Hector had three lifetimes before, scrubbing the bottom and picking out shavings from places too small for an adult to reach.

The small trawler yacht with auxiliary sail took form on the shore and when we launched her she rode the waves as I had always imagined she would, as if our hands had hewn her from dreams. She was named *Red Herring* and in the lee of Vancouver Island we ran her from Saltspring to Otter Bay, Boot Cove to Tsawwassen. Through that last summer my family explored the myriad islands and secluded anchorages of the coastal waterways. In the Sansum Narrows curious harbour seals swam alongside us. On August nights too hot for sleep the boys skinny-dipped in the cool Gulf current.

As the season changed and the colour and warmth drained from the land we laid down plans to cruise south-west. We selected our route, stowed supplies and secured spares for the journey. Then one wet September morning I put in to Long Harbour to refuel. The family had gone ashore to buy lunch when an unknown seiner made port. It steered for the pumps. The dock hands boomed me off from the wharf and I turned over the engine. *Red Herring* was powered by a Parsons Pike 56 horse, a fine diesel that could be heard coming forever, but that morning she sounded all wrong. She coughed, wheezed then sighed into silence. Flames leapt up from the engine cowling. In seconds they spread over the hull and into the wheelhouse, licking the mast and scorching the paintwork. The electrics continued to pump fuel into the fire. The attendant had left the glass filter-bulb disconnected. I switched off but it was too late. Charts turned yellow, curled at the edges and burst into flames. The compass crystal cracked. Varnish bubbled on the deck. The fire curled around my legs like an incensed tom-cat then wrapped me in its fury. On the shore the family ran screaming from the restaurant. Beagan dropped his ice cream. At the water's edge they reached out their arms and tried to stretch across the infinite distance of thirty feet. My nostrils filled with the reek of singed hair and blistering skin. I stepped back and fell overboard into the cool embrace of the sea.

I didn't die. The dock hands launched a skiff, rescued me and saved the boat. Their blanket of extinguisher foam transformed her into a water-borne cocoon. The attendant was contrite but our plans were put back. The voyage had to be delayed.

The grafts took well and I soon began to mend. In a month

I was out of hospital. At home I took it easy, walking with a cane, watching the boys flip the canoe and dive underneath to play games in the air pocket. They stayed in the water until their skin turned blue and we warmed them around the great stone fireplace with the old stories.

I read a lot, sorting through reams of family papers and packing them away into the old box trunk. There were sermons and charts, press galleys and the *Kipper*'s hand-stitched Union Jack, Bessie's wedding veil and honeymoon album crammed with photographs of Dad. I found his ridiculous, pom-pommed Tam-o'-shanter, set it on my head and smelt him in its wool. It brought his memory so vividly to mind: red hair, chubby face, his fine folly of ideals, the song to her as he shaved, 'O you tak' the high road and I'll tak' the low road and I'll be in Scotland afore ye.' It made me want to laugh, the love in it all, and I did but it hurt, dear God it hurt. I clutched my chest as I fell crashing against the table, knocking over a bookcase, hardly feeling the bumps against my ribs and thigh. I landed on all fours and cracked my knee on the hardwood floor. The footsteps came running but I heard no breath through my lips and then as if a silver cord had been fastened to me my life was eased like a butterfly up out of its chrysalis. Beneath me lay a body collapsed, lifeless and released from pain. My wife wailed and held me and cried out my name. I tried to touch her, to tell her that it was all right, only the words were muffled, all sound was deadened, until I heard a clear voice call to me. I did not want to turn from the sad scene but a brilliant white light drew me away and I drifted, no flew, up through the roof filled with such joy and a sense of new beginnings that I thought I might die.

CHAPTER XI

———◆———

PARADISE SUBMERGED

THE SILVERY ROPES went slack, the gangway withdrew and the seamless white liner cast off like a shrouded body released from earth's hold. Her parting whistle echoed off the ivory sail-towers of the Cruise Ship Terminal.

'Don't forget us,' cried a voice from the shore.

'Bye Grandma,' shouted a twelve-year-old, 'This Bitch Bites Back' printed across her lycra vest.

The white-haired passengers crowded the decks to wave farewell. Their tears were caught by the flash of a dozen cameras. Florid streamers spilled down the hull and laced strangers together. Retired couples inspected lifeboats that were broader than my grandfather's Peterborough lapstrake had been long. On one ocean-going balcony a pensioner flaunted his complimentary champagne, popped the cork and drank from the bottle. A blue-rinsed widow in an orange lifejacket threw macaroons at the shrieking gulls. They dived towards the swells where seals fed on fish stunned by the propellers' wash. In the harbour the *Regal Princess* turned her bow towards the sea, slipped beneath the Lions Gate Bridge and a boy at my side said, 'She's gone.' Husbands folded weeping daughters into their arms. Families shuffled away down the pier back to emptier lives. But the sense of loss was not in the ship. It was in us. Beyond Prospect Point the liner was no smaller, no less beautiful, no less buoyant than she had been when lashed to the land. At the very moment that she vanished from our eyes someone somewhere watched her sail into view.

'Here she comes,' they cheered.

I, Beagan Gillean, turned away from the ocean terminal too.

It was not yet time for me to travel so far. My destination, as that of those who accompanied me, lay closer to home.

At Horseshoe Bay the Nanaimo ferry glided away from the rocky mainland, past islands enfolded in mist, towards my promised land. Tugs heaved barges of containers up the coast. Seaplanes kicked up rainbows of spray in their dash to northern outposts. In the bow cafeteria the four ghosts seemed to have settled themselves around my table. I imagined Zachary to be displeased; he wanted fresh coffee, not instant, but the maple syrup muffins caught my father's eye. To placate Hector I restrained myself from ordering a beer and drank instead a single mug of tepid tea while listening to two islanders argue with an official from the Loyal Nanaimo Bathtub Society.

'It ain't right. He notched the flywheel,' accused the local man. 'Made his eight-horse go like a ten.'

'We were on Kits Beach, everything was fine,' fumed his friend. 'Now this screws up the whole race.'

Every summer, I told my grandfather, a howling swarm of outboard-powered bathtubs buzzed thirty miles across the Strait of Georgia between Nanaimo and Vancouver. Half the entrants tended to sink before they cleared the harbour. Others ran aground on the Spanish Banks. I wondered aloud if Elsie had raced her tub across the strait before plumbing it into her house.

'I hit a great big mother of a wave,' claimed the local, interrupting my speculation, 'and it just about twisted the motor-mount right off.'

The first tubber to reach the mainland, to stagger up Kitsilano Beach and to ring a bell became the World Champion Bathtubber. The event had been declared 'an epic saga of raw courage and true bathtub seamanship'. Jamie, I decided, would have loved to enter the race.

Departure Bay was the first place-name I encountered that referred to leaving in the land of arrivals. I drove south from the ferry terminal and hopped across the Stuart Channel to the Gulf Islands. Saltspring had changed in the twenty-two years since my father's death. The new waterfront shopping mall was filled with

Japanese tourists, American yachtsmen and deconstructionist poets on sabbatical from eastern universities. Holiday-makers from Hong Kong ordered desserts and sides in 'casual grazing' restaurants. The Everlasting Summer Dried Herb Farm was owned by a band of greying hippies. They had driven their VW campers out from Toronto at the dawning of the Age of Aquarius then cashed in on the property boom and, in a manner of which Zachary would have approved, invested their windfall in health shops and 'natural' souvenir stores. At Flashback Nick-Nacks daytrippers bought 'treasures and icons' and a wilting flower-child named Tina told me, 'I really like your camera. I bought mine in London in the sixties.' When she stopped toying with her beads to finger my lens I felt Hector breathing hell-fire down my neck. Her daughter wore a sheer white cotton dress and giggled behind a copy of *Drying Flowers with Your Microwave*, an island best-seller. 'We have a little row-boat on Vesuvius Bay,' added Tina as if to enflame the Reverend's wrath. 'It's just right for two.'

But down the road nothing had altered at the Quarter Deck Coffee Shop. The familiar screen door swung open blowing in sawdust, boat-builders and the smell of sap. Sloops and smacks, skiffs and salmon seiners were mirrored in the glassy water beyond the window. Oak keels and cold moulded hulls lay in the yard. The coat of arms of the Worshipful Company of Shipwrights still hung behind the hissing, spitting tea urn. A carved dove perched on a bowed hulk set atop a green mound panel. 'Within the Ark Safe for Ever' read the chiselled motto. I took a chair on to the familiar porch and waited for my ride.

After the fire my mother had decided to move us away from the islands. The lawyer had sold our property and we parted with the boat. A chapter had closed and we tried to begin anew. But my father's death had left me both displaced and embittered. As I grew older I seemed to belong to no single place, had called no harbour my own and for years had let the current carry me where it pleased. I had cruised across America, coasted about Europe, run to Australia and in every port cast my need like an anchor in the hope that it might tether me to some town or infatuation or society. It never did and I drifted on without a sail until a storm shipwrecked me on a Scottish island, twenty-one years late and two hundred years later, with the trunk by my side. There, in the dusty pages and wild wet winds, I began to understand that my roots were not in a landscape or even in a country but rather in my memories.

It was the remembrance of things that brought me a sensation of sorrow as *Red Herring* tied up at the Government Wharf. I had traced her new owner through the old boatyard and he had agreed to meet me. Yet even though our cruiser had been refurbished and painted in different colours, I was unprepared for the sight of her haunting lines. They took me back to the cold, mourning dawn in the old house. My brother and I had laid late in bed without joy and eaten breakfast without taste. In the afternoon my mother had taken us to the radio station to sit on stools in an editing booth and watch a producer assemble our father's obituary. Snatches of his voice had echoed through the loudspeaker. Reel after reel had preserved his broadcasts. The producer had cut out words and hesitations, hung whole sentences around his neck and cast the out-takes over his shoulder. The clips of recording tape, the record of our father's thoughts and laughter, had spiralled down on to the floor and been ground underfoot. As the memorial was aired the janitor had swept up the trims and dumped them into the bin. All, that is, but the one that I had slipped into my pocket.

'You heard about the referendum?' asked the new owner as we sailed *Red Herring* out of the harbour and into the islands. 'It was a damn close thing.' The day before Quebec had voted by the narrowest margin to remain part of Canada. The out-going separatist premier had blamed the defeat on the 'ethnic' vote, that is Quebecers not of old French stock. But despite accusations of racism and minority fears that any new state would be founded on chauvinism the Parti Québécois vowed to hold another ballot. Sovereignty remained its fundamental objective. 'They can have their independence for all I care,' said the owner. 'I for one have run out of patience. But I do hate to lose our motto, eh?'

'From Sea to Sea?' I asked as the Parsons Pike diesel putt-putted us around Saltspring. Hector would know the Latin: '*A mari usque ad mare.*'

'Yeah. It won't mean diddley-squat anymore.'

In summers that once seemed to last forever my father had embraced us in this fold of the sea. Beneath the red-barked arbutus tree in a copper-green cove my brother and I had built sandcastles and driftwood rafts. We had disturbed hissing Pisaster sea stars, imagined the fishy breath of passing whales and heard the cough of West Coast trawlers as they dragged their purse-string nets up the Swanson Channel. From *Red Herring*'s bridge I recognised familiar inlets along the broken shore. Behind them I remembered leafy roads that climbed high into the broom. I recalled the alders and cottonwoods and sweet-water streams which ran so clear that they appeared to be pools of vapour, heavier but no less transparent than air. In my mind's eye a red-capped woodpecker tapped at a great cedar and sphagnum beards bristled on shaggy maples. Here and there wisps of mist curled up from valleys dank with the smells of autumn. Yet along the beach were scattered not the solid, moated sandcastles of my childhood but elegant seashell temples and delicate pagodas made of pebbles.

Red Herring navigated around the last promontory, tacked into our old bay and reached the point marked on the chart. The property deed was clutched in my hand. I scanned the channel for my sylvan paradise but saw nothing. I checked the concession numbers and confirmed the co-ordinates. I took another bearing off the headland. We were at the right place yet the cove was empty. There was no island. Then as we drifted on the clear, still waters the tide began to ebb and a swell rippled the surface. A flat black reef broke above the current. The rivulets ran off its surface and the rock revealed itself. A seal would have had trouble finding a dry seat.

'You'd better get a buoy put on that,' suggested *Red Herring*'s owner. 'Otherwise some fool'll run into it and sue you for damages.'

This, then, was my inheritance, my promised island. Paradise was a hazard to navigation. There appeared to be no more new frontiers, no *terra incognita*. The ghosts were silent and in the early evening when the tide turned again the rock vanished below the sea as if it had never existed.

'I can't tell you if the ghosts are really there, if my father's flapping his silver wings and waving a sparkling wand . . .'

'And wearing an earring,' added Elsie Faithful. 'You said he always wanted to wear a gold earring.'

'Probably a crown of curly hair too,' I nodded, glancing over my shoulder. 'Or if their spirit is within, in my mind and genes, sheltering inside my memory.' I took another sip of peppermint tea. 'Whichever it is, I feel they are with me, in everything that I do and see. And that's wonderful. Their presence gives me strength but . . .' I hesitated and looked out of her open windows at the old hills bare as razor-shaved heads. '. . . but some of their views are, well, a little restrictive. It's a bit like still living with your parents when you're thirty-three.' I leaned forward and lowered my voice. 'You see, I can't get to know any women. I can't even have a drink without feeling guilty. It irritates the Reverend.'

It was for the living as much as for the dead that I had travelled the last few hundred miles west from Saltspring to Elsie's clapboard house on the Pacific shore. The narrow waist of Vancouver Island had once contained the greatest weight of living matter per hectare in the world, but that morning, as on many others, the air was thick with chainsaw exhaust fumes. The switchback road wound across the MacKenzie Range, through the scorched glens where fire had followed the loggers' trail of destruction, and I recalled that only three of man's achievements were visible from outer space: the Great Wall of China, the land patterns of Peru's Nazca Indians and the clear-cut forests of British Columbia. An acre of Canadian timber is felled every fifteen seconds.

I had found her small village at the edge of the decimated woodlands, past the 'Forests Forever' signs, beyond Ucluelet's Pioneer Boat Works, and arrived like the fishermen who dropped by to have a shower or phone home, leaving in the sink an armful of salmon as a token of thanks. She had welcomed me as she welcomed them, with tea and fresh bannock bread. There was moose meat in the freezer, bulging stockings of raspberry leaves hanging from the rafters, paintings of sturgeon tacked on to every wall.

'When someone dies and their spirit won't leave the survivors alone we have a last supper for them,' Elsie explained. The taciturn Noah dozed with the Labrador puppy by a broken television behind a thicket of thriving begonias. 'We cook up their favourite food, set them a place at table then send them on their way.'

'But I have four of my forefathers with me.'

'That'll make it a real party. Noah,' she said to her boyfriend, 'go borrow a couple of chairs from next door.'

At the grocery store by the Government Dock I spent a small fortune. It was as if a plague of locust had swept over the shelves and through the freezer. Noah and I lugged half a dozen carrier bags back up the muddy street. The meal that I had chosen would start with finnan haddie, a golden smoked haddock dish, long a family favourite. It would be followed by an entrée of mutton, lamb being too wee a creature for Hector to eat, boiled with carrots and turnips. I would prepare a rich caper sauce to tempt him. We planned to cook stovies and *colcannon* for his sons. They had been partial to potatoes since their earliest, hungry days in Promise, although Zachary preferred his dressed up as *pommes dauphinois*. Elsie even offered to bake a chocolate cake for my father. She had remembered his sweet tooth.

'Ghosts come in three different types,' she explained as I trimmed the gigot. 'First there is the busybody; the curious soul who likes to keep up with things. You know, the long-dead grandmother who appears beside the cot of every new baby born into her family.' She beat the butter to a cream and worked in the sugar. 'Next are the spirits who died with an earthly problem unresolved. They're the Hollywood movies variety who return to the living and redress wrongs.' She whipped the egg whites. 'The third category of ghost sits a little uneasily with Christian beliefs. They're earth-bound spirits who don't know that they're dead and, if confronted, will deny not being alive. "Me dead?" they'll say, "Don't be crazy; I've always lived in this house." They are trapped in an old existence like a long-playing record stuck in a groove.'

I soaked oatmeal then strained it through a fine sieve. The liquid was mixed with Old Mull whisky and heather honey then stirred with a silver spoon to make a potent Athole brose. Even Hector would not refuse a glass. 'So which type are mine?' I asked.

Elsie shrugged. 'Don't know. I guess that's for you to decide.'

As the smells of cooking filled the house I told her about the last days in Vancouver and my watery inheritance. She must have heard the disappointment in my voice for she said, 'You know there are others who found a promised land here and lost it too.' I uncorked a couple of bottles of Bordeaux to let them breathe. 'Have you heard of the Nootka?' I shook my head. 'They were a maritime people who navigated by songline, by snatches of verse.'

'Like the Australian Aborigines did on land?'

'Sure,' said Elsie, laying seven places at the table. 'Their epic poems described every bay and channel and linked together the whole Pacific coast.' There were not seven matching glasses in the cupboard so I collected a mixed batch of tumblers, beakers and toothbrush mugs. Someone would have to drink from a jam-jar. 'Their neighbours were the Squamish, who drew maps that represented water as the positive space, noting sandbars and sea-marks like an Admiralty chart, but left the shore as blank. Then there were the Nanaimos and Kwagewlth, carvers of the finest totem poles, and the Cowichans too, the philosophers of the north-west. They all lived on these waters and followed the runs of salmon along ocean routes so definite that they might be considered the salt-water extensions of rivers. All this was theirs until the white men came.'

Noah had not borrowed enough chairs so we decided to use the trunk as a bench. 'Drake and Cook were looking for the western entrance of the fabled waterway from the Atlantic,' I said, recounting the European version of history. 'And Catherine the Great seized Alaska in a natural extension of Russia's advance across Siberia.' I unearthed Hector's globe, set it at the centre of the table and laid a finger on Mexico. 'Then Carlos III reasserted Spain's title to all the New World's coasts to protect his Central American Empire.'

'The Ahousaht people named all these white sailors *mau mau'l ney*. That means "floating on the water without land". They welcomed George Vancouver and his surveyors and, while their shoreline was plotted, shared salt pork and Salish hospitality.' Elsie laid out the mismatched tin knives, plastic forks and a single silver Haida spoon engraved with a scene of whales and canoes. The spirits would sit between us and a cut wildflower was placed at each setting. Noah fashioned candlesticks from old gin bottles. 'It was the custom of some tribes to give their women to honoured guests. The courtesy spread European diseases through the region and in one year alone a third of the entire Native population on the coast died. Great stretches of Nootka songlines were lost with them.' Outside, the setting sun caught the tops of the last Pacific cedars and arrayed them in cloaks of burnished gold. As dusk gathered around the house Elsie smiled for the first time. 'So your family isn't the first to lose this promised land.'

THE GHOSTS, SMALLER now, floated above Hector's globe on cartographic clouds, looking at this faded panel and that tattered gore, the hemisphere dented by a fall on to *Kipper*'s deck, the frayed edges of Greenland which the Micmac Gogo had blown like a bagpipe's chanter. They eyed the Hebrides and the wide Atlantic, the vast American continent and the Pacific beyond, then ducked their heads as their clouds drifted under the copper bracket. All around them the candles glowed like stars in the night sky.

'It is myself that sees it now as a road to somewhere else,' said Hector, nodding at Canada. 'For the explorers it was an inconvenient obstacle between Europe and Asia, for us a stopping-place between the old world and a promised land.'

'*Une terre conquise, f-f-faute de mieux*,' stuttered Jamie. For want of anything better. 'The voyageurs were after the silk of the Orient, they had to make do with beaver pelts. Homesteaders wanted paradise and settled for Saskatoon.'

'That alone is reason enough for moving on,' laughed Sandy and swallowed the last mouthful of haddock. 'Very good this, but have you seen what's for dessert?'

'Now who would like some mutton?' I asked while carving the roast. The leg was a little tough but the seasoning delicious. 'It seems to me that no other land has had greater hope projected across it than Canada.' I recalled from the diaries that Zachary had a voracious appetite and cut him four thick slices of meat. 'I suppose that after those early dreams were dispelled the country became simply a place of sanctuary, a caring society where the world's oppressed, homeless and fearful could build a new life.'

'At the expense of the Native people,' said Elsie while dishing out vegetables and serving the ghosts. 'Gravy anyone?'

'That's true,' I accepted. 'And it is our responsibility. But for refugees, for the Empire Loyalist, the cleared Highland crofter, Jews who survived the Holocaust and Chinese escaping the Red Guards, it was a place apart from the anger and hatred of the world, a place that wanted no conflicts or arguments.'

'It was a bountiful land,' insisted Zachary, making a point not to speak with his mouth full, 'where any labouring man could make a new start, build a home, raise a family away from the prejudices of the old world.' He tucked into his meal with great gusto. 'And Canada is still all these things; a bridge between west and east, a rich natural resource, a sanctuary . . .'

'But it is no promised land,' said my old man. 'It is not a place that rewards dreams.'

'In the name of Providence, there can not be more?' exclaimed Hector as Elsie set at his place a plate laden with mutton, frozen fiddleheads and stovies. 'I have eaten that fine fish and enough is as good as a feast.'

'Please indulge yourself,' urged Jamie, 'if only for Beagàn's sake.'

'It is a generous portion and I have no need of this food,' Hector said and passed on the plate. 'Although I would not say no to a small glass of that fine refreshment.'

Zachary did not complain about the second serving of mutton, even if he would have preferred fresh Muskoka lamb, and the *pommes dauphinois* went down a treat. Sandy skipped the meat course altogether and went straight for the chocolate cake.

I raised my glass to the minister-mariner, the paddle-wheel publishers and the boat-building broadcaster. They had tried to enlarge the world, to push back the boundaries of ignorance and intolerance, to bring people together with holy water, with radio waves and steamships which delivered newspapers. 'I am proud to be your descendant,' I added and downed the glass.

'It is easier to lose a good name than to gain one,' counselled Hector, draining his toothmug of Athole brose. 'Mischief was always coming over you, Beagan, but for all the quirks and quibbles, your like is not to be found in every peat-bank.'

'Pichon-Longueville,' remarked Zachary in approval. 'And a good year. Surely he didn't find this in this outpost?'

'I seem to recall laying down a f-f-few bottles for him in the trunk,' confessed Jamie.

'Did you now? Did you really.' Zachary took a long gulp and rolled the Bordeaux around his palate. 'A fine vintage, James. I had forgotten what good taste you had in wine.'

'Oh, it was usually on your advice.'

'Well, maybe another wee dram.' Hector passed on the

wine but let Sandy indulge him in a third glass of liquor.

'I'm not sure which is the more ardent spirit, Grand-dad; this malt or you.'

'I recollect one particularly severe winter in Promise,' Hector said after taking a deep draft. The whisky had brought a story to mind. 'You will recall that all my parishioners contributed alms. Aye well, the fortunate were most charitable and the poor who had no money were good enough to give butter instead. The verger, Lachie Dunnachie by name, went out one bitter morning to collect the donations and returned at dusk in very good humour but with only half the names ticked off his list. Well now, I asked why he had failed to call on the other brethren and he replied, "Auch Mr Gillean, them's teetotal."' Hector laughed and took another sip. 'My word, I haven't supped this well since the nineteenth century.'

The good food and plentiful drink had mellowed Zachary too. When Hector and Sandy began talking about boats he leaned towards his brother and whispered, 'I'm sorry, James. . . . Bessie. The child.'

The others fell quiet. Jamie smiled then thanked him and after a moment asked, 'Why did you never marry, Zachary?'

'Why?' He lay down his knife and fork and fussed with his bow tie. 'Because I didn't want to admit my mortality, to accept the finite. You know: birth, marriage, children, death.' He patted the stopped watch in his pocket. 'Nothing frightened me more.'

'We are all mortal too soon,' said Sandy.

'But look you now, *a bhalaich*, it is not finite,' insisted Hector, the old Gaelic curl back in his vowels. He was somewhat in his cups. 'Life has its difficulties, its sorrow, its unfairness, but it does not end. Death is only another stage in our existence.'

'Yes,' Zachary admitted with a terrible sadness in his voice. 'Yes, I see that now.'

'I will put a stone on your cairn, Zachary,' said Hector, then hiccoughed.

'I won't f-f-forget you either,' added his brother.

A man remembered never dies. I thought of Icelandic Opa and his descendants, Ewan Cameron's dogfish snout and Theodore Pike's walk on water. The wine had soothed me as well. 'I used to believe that Canada had killed my father,' I told Elsie as an evening breeze washed the smell of the sea into the room. 'Now I think that his dream might have been betrayed anywhere. His view was simply at odds with the prevailing ethos in the world today: choice without variety, quantity without quality, the dominance of the present at the expense of understanding the past.' I spun the globe without thinking and the ghosts were thrown off, scattered like seeds from a dandelion. 'But his tragedy is more conspicuous here because less is shared. It is cast into relief by the vacuum behind it.'

'So where do the Gilleans go now?' asked Elsie.

'If you're asking me where it ends, I don't know. Here on this coast, where western migration meets eastern expansion, feels like the end of space. I'm not even sure where the journey began.'

'It started with the *Global Trader*'s arrival in Montreal,' stated Zachary, picking himself up from the table. He could not change a literal mind.

'I beg to differ,' stuttered Jamie. 'Surely it began when Beagan f-f-first opened the trunk?' The continuity of words was his comfort and strength.

'Or when the Reverend stepped off the shingle and on to the *Good Intent*,' suggested Sandy, remembering the pain and loss of the hopeful voyage.

'Wait you now my boys, it started when the Celts were driven by the Romans into the sea,' proclaimed Hector, waving his hand west across the face of the globe. He paused to reconsider. 'Forgive me, I mean when Moses led the Israelites out of slavery to search for honeyed Canaan.' He hesitated again. It seemed for a moment that the Old Mull and modern age had conspired to muddle his certainty. But

then he beamed with sudden clarity, '*M' athair, m' anam.*'
My father, my soul. 'You old fool, it began with our own
ark, right enough.'

'IT STARTED WITH the great flood,' said Noah so suddenly that
the puppy barked. His voice was as rough as scree in a riverbed.
'That was when Raven brought back the promise of life, a sprig
of cedar.'

'That's what the Nootka say,' added Elsie.

The candles had burnt low and Noah didn't lift his eyes from
his plate. 'There's a story that they tell about Mah Teg Yelah, the
wife of Thunderbird. She saved herself and the animals by sealing
up a longhouse with pitch so that it floated. When the rains
stopped she sent Raven out in search of land. He found a strip of
sand stretching north from Naikun. It's called Rose Spit today.'

'Raven was a creature of great appetites: hunger, curiosity, lust
and a desire to change things,' Elsie added.

I tried to imagine the hooded eyes, hunched wings and prying
beak probing at the debris which the receding water had left
behind. His spiked claws left crow's foot patterns on the wet
beach.

'He loved playing tricks on the world,' laughed Noah while
cutting himself a second slice of cake. 'So Raven, he hadn't eaten
for forty days and was real busy feeding himself when a flash of
white caught his eye. There, right at his feet, half buried in the
sand he saw this gigantic clam shell. Real, real big. Raven looked
at it and saw that it was full of little creatures, all naked except
for long black hair on their round heads. Luckily he had gorged
himself already so he didn't eat them but they were scared anyway,
man were they scared, by the size of the sea and the height of
the sky and the blackness of the bird.' He licked off a mouthful of
chocolate icing. 'Well he used his tongue, ravens got this smooth
trickster's tongue you know, and he coaxed them out into his
shiny new world.'

'They were the original Haidas, the first humans.'

'So that's where it all began. Up the coast a ways on Rose Spit.'

'As on Mount Ararat,' I said. 'And maybe in the Hebrides.'

'Sure,' replied Noah and fell back into silence.

'The Haidas dominated the coast for almost ten thousand years,' clarified Elsie. 'They built a complex society, filled their long-houses with heraldic carvings, launched great war canoes.' She traced her finger down the western seaboard from the roughly sketched Queen Charlotte Islands to Nootka Sound. 'But it's all gone now. There's only a couple of thousand of them still alive and they've all changed. Most of their villages are abandoned and in ruins. I guess it's a bit like your Highlanders, both in old and New Scotland.' She rubbed her distended stomach then held out a hand. 'Here, give me your shoe.'

'My shoe?' I asked, handing it across the table.

'Native people believe that life is cyclical,' she explained, taking hold of the grubby object. 'The older we grow, the nearer we come to death, the closer we are to the spirits and our rebirth.' She lay the shoe flat on the table and selected a sharp knife. 'That's why children have imaginary friends and senile elders talk to themselves; it's the dead trying to coax them back to the spirit world.'

Elsie raised the knife above her head as I said, 'I don't have a spare pair.' She pierced the sole with a single cut. 'Oh dear,' I sighed.

'A Native child will have a leather wristband or a hole in his shoe,' she continued while enlarging the gash, 'so he can tell the spirit that he cannot travel with him, that he is tied and grounded to the earth.'

She handed back my skewered footwear. A small sturgeon could have swum through the puncture. 'I would have been happy to wear a wristband.'

* * *

No one lives their life disassociated from those who have come before them. That night the noises around me in the dark were my forefathers. I slipped out of bed, opened the trunk and leafed through the rustling papers. As I repacked them my eye fell on a dusty copy of the Apocrypha Old Testament. It opened at the passage when Death is sent by God to Abraham which ends with the words: 'Abraham said, "I understand what you are saying; but I will not follow you." And Death was silent and answered him not a word.'

At dawn I closed the lid. I had planned to wake Noah to help me carry the trunk to the car but that morning it felt surprisingly light. I stowed it and the old globe in the boot and walked west towards the thundering surf. The stiff winds had stunted the spruce into tuckamores. I pushed through their battered stands, disturbed a squabble of terns and felt the wave-scalloped sands under my feet. Crabs scurried out of my path, into salty tidal pools, around bull kelp stems like giant spermatozoa. As I strode down to the shore I remembered the plea of the dispossessed Ozette Chief Tse-Kaw-Wootl, 'I want the sea. That is my country.'

'*An Cuan Sèimh,*' said Hector. The Gaels' Western Sea. 'It is long enough that I have wished to see it.'

'As did the French voyageurs, F-F-Father,' yawned Jamie. He would have preferred an extra hour in bed and his creased shirt-tail hung down over his sporting britches. 'It is their promised *Mer de l'Ouest.*'

'To the Chinese it is the Great Peaceful Ocean,' noted Zachary. He was dressed again in splendid evening dress, and prepared for the journey. 'I may say that the future is there over the horizon; in terms of trade at least.'

'I could look at the sea all day,' said my father Sandy, staring out over the Salish's rich *Shkwen.* 'Not that I can ever see out that far but, well, it's the prospect of those uncharted waters that draws me.'

'And was there ever a better watch to keep?'

The ghosts turned back to look at me, watching them watch the sea. 'Come you now, my boys,' sighed Hector, 'it is no more that he needs us. He has found the love in it.'

'Is it time?' asked Zachary without checking his watch.

'It is, right enough, and for sure we are all a little while from home.' Hector enfolded them in the embrace that was something between mortal laughter and a blending of gases, and I heard them call, '*Slàn leat*, Beagan.' Blessings be with you.

THE PAST WAS like the foam on the crest of a wave, rolling up the beach, stretching over the shingle. I reached to grasp the ephemeral froth but it sighed away whispering half-heard words, slipped through my fingers and out of my palm, away into the sand. There was no longer the need for anger and confusion. Instead I sensed that which everyone feels, that something is eternal: words and water, love and reconciliation, the circle almost circled. On the edge of the Pacific I felt Hector's clothes sea-wet on the shifting *bàta* deck, saw the New World's lamps glow as a constellation of stars, smelt print-shop ink, heard the two-tone whistle echo around Wigwassan Point and remembered my father laugh, laugh as he spoke into the microphone. The tide advanced again, swelled over my shoes, soaked my feet, and I knew that we shared the hope and responsibility of dreams.

ACKNOWLEDGEMENTS

An afterword of thanks to Sir Lachlan and Lady Maclean of Duart for safe harbour on the dark headland and to Allister Campbell for the brimming vessels of Old Mull. May bottletops forever bounce off his Calorgas heater. Rody Gorman of Sabhal Mor Ostaig, Isle of Skye and C. S. Paterson CBE of Caledonian MacBrayne eased the passage through the Hebrides. Angus Macdonald caulked the *Good Intent*'s leaky seams. Tim Sheppard and Ian Matheson of Communications Partnership made possible the Atlantic crossing. Maison du Québec, London, gave warning of navigational hazards along the route to a new world.

In Canada Susan and the late J. G. Crean, Rick Salutin, H. J. P. Schaffter and Bruce Litteljohn helped me trim the sails and set the course. Raymond Johnson of Canada Steamship Lines provided the culinary cruise to the head of the lakes. W. L. and Ruth Boynton, Rita and Peter Kent, Moira Farr, Valorie Crate, Harold Critch, Francine Holowachuk, Chief Simon Baker, the Cree community in Cumberland House, the Ukrainian Cultural Heritage Village, the Reverend Rinson T. K. Lin and the Muskoka, Prince Albert and Nakusp Steamship Historical Societies steered me from Ontario to the Pacific.

JoAnne Robertson's keen eye and handy sextant guided me through particularly treacherous waters; without her the ark would have been lost with all hands. I would have been completely at sea without the support of Rachel Calder, my top-gallant editor Michael Fishwick, Robert Lacey, Annie Robertson and Marina Cianfanelli. The assistance of the Canada Council and the Authors' Foundation is buoyantly acknowledged. But whether on waterways real or imagined, meandering or metaphoric, the blessing for which I am most grateful is the anchor of Katrin and my family.